The Lands of Barbary

GEOFFREY FURLONGE

K.B.E., C.M.G.

JOHN MURRAY

To
ANNE

© GEOFFREY FURLONGE 1966

Printed in Great Britain for
John Murray, Albemarle Street, London
by Cox & Wyman Ltd, London, Fakenham
and Reading

Contents

Illustrations

Photographs not otherwise acknowledged are the author's

Author's Note

I first came to North Africa in 1928, and have served in or visited it at intervals ever since. From the beginning it has had for me a special appeal, deriving I think partly from the sense of antiquity which pervades it but more from the extreme variety which it has to offer – variety of landscape, of climate, and people, above all of colour; and it was this appeal which gradually inspired the desire to write about it.

This book is based mainly on two long journeys (here telescoped into one for clarity) from end to end of it which I undertook in 1960 and 1964. Writing it has proved even more absorbing than I had hoped, for while the country itself provided my backcloth, as I read and researched I found my stage filling up with an almost bewildering diversity of characters, from Roman Emperors to American oil executives, from nomad Bedouin to French wine-kings, from Christian saints and Muslim divines to snake-charmers and Foreign Legionaries. The result does not claim to be either a formal history or a guide-book, still less a treatise for scholars, archaeologists, or economists; but I hope it may give pleasure to those who have been in the Lands of Barbary, or provide a picture of it for those who have not.

Over the transliteration of Arab and Berber names, I have run into the familiar difficulty caused by the differences between our own, the French, and the Italian systems, and have found it impossible to avoid inconsistency. In general, over proper names I have followed middle-of-the-road English practice, without diacritical marks, but over place-names have thought it preferable to adopt the forms shown on the local maps even where these include such horrors as 'Ouezzane' and 'Sciasciara'.

I owe a debt of gratitude to Mrs. Diane Gurney, who prepared the maps; to Mrs. Ann Dearden, who kindly read the manuscript and made many helpful suggestions; to Her

Majesty's Representatives in the four countries, and their staffs, for much hospitality and help; to Mr. R. P. Goodchild, Director of Antiquities in Cyrenaica, Mr. G. H. Brenchley, of the Agricultural Advisory Service, and the library of the Royal Geographical Society for valuable information; to the National Tourist Offices of Morocco and Tunisia, for several photographs; and, last but far from least, to my wife for constant encouragement – and toleration. I must also acknowledge my indebtedness to Mr. Nevill Barbour, whose Chatham House publication *A Survey of North-West Africa* is the only comprehensive work in the English language on the area; to Mr. D. E. L. Haynes, author of *The Archaeology of Tripolitania*; to Mr. Edward Behr, author of *The Algerian Problem*; and to the French writers MM. C.-A. Julien and E. F. Gautier; for all information which I have obtained from their works.

Any opinions expressed are, of course, entirely my own and do not necessarily reflect the views of the British Government, from whose service I retired over five years ago.

LONDON,
August 1965

CHAPTER I

The other Marble Arch

I parked the car by the roadside near the Marble Arch and went to sleep.

I was awakened, not by the throb of traffic along the Bayswater Road, but by the braying of a donkey; and as I came to, the Marble Arch before my eyes was surrounded, not by Victorian terraces and speakers on soap-boxes, but by brown expanses of desert, shimmering with heat-haze and stippled with camel-thorn, across which in both directions a black ribbon of bitumen stretched to the horizon. Nothing moved except the little whirlwinds which they call 'sand-devils', a crow or two, a flock of the pied wagtails which haunted the road (the previous night I had picked a dead one out of my radiator), and the little party whose donkey's voice had jerked me back to consciousness.

For this was Libya, and the object rising incongruously from the waste before me was not George IV's monstrosity, but the concrete monument which the swelling bullfrog Mussolini had erected on the borderline between his provinces of Cyrenaica and Tripolitania – presumably in the hope that by thus imitating Roman Emperors he might be thought to resemble one – and which a homesick Eighth Army had dubbed with the familiar name.

I was in no hurry, and comfortable, for the light breeze which was driving the sand-devils was also keeping away the flies and tempering the November heat, so I lay back in my seat and began for the first time to think about the land into which I had come when, a fortnight previously, I had crossed the frontier out of Egypt; the land which was known in the 17th century as 'The Barbary States' but which the Arabs call 'Jezirat al Maghrib', or 'The Island of the Sunset'.

This Arabic name (which in its shortened form of 'Maghrib' I shall use in future) is not only imaginative but apt; for the Maghrib is in effect a piece of land surrounded by seas – a 3,000-mile strip of cultivation, pasture, and mountain bounded on the north by the Mediterranean, on the west by the Atlantic, and on the south and east by the sand-seas of the Sahara and the 'Western Desert' of Egypt respectively. Each of the four independent States between which this land is shared, Libya, Tunisia, Algeria, and Morocco, also includes a piece of the Sahara which, with the discovery of oil, is actually or potentially of greater economic importance than all the non-desert areas.

The 'island' is shaped roughly like a bill-hook. Its broad handle is the Jebel Akhdar region of Cyrenaica; its 'tang', the narrow Jefara plain and the Jebel Nafusa plateau of Tripolitania; its blade, the mountains, plains, and plateaux of Tunisia, Algeria, and Morocco; and its cutting edge the triple chain of the Atlas Mountains, which run from the Atlantic in the southwest to the Mediterranean in the north-east. The flaw in the simile is that the handle has a gap in it: for in the Gulf of Sirte, where I now was, the Sahara comes right down to the sea and makes four hundred miles of hopeless waste, with the result that Cyrenaica, with much the same sort of people as the rest of the Maghrib, has a rather different history.

Through the centuries invaders from outside have flooded over this island like tides over a reef. Palaeolithic man came, we have no idea whence, anything up to half a million years ago, and left his traces here and there. Neolithic man left more traces, some perhaps as early as the fourth millennium B.C.; because there was no indigenous metal industry, his culture may have survived well into historical times. By the third millennium B.C. the first people of whom we have knowledge, derived from ancient Egyptian records and Roman histories, were already established in the Maghrib: these were the people whom the Egyptians called 'Libyans' and the Romans 'Barbari' – whence our words Berber and Barbary – and they form one component of the population of today. About 1100 B.C. the Phoenicians from the Levant began to set up stations along the coast, from the greatest of which, Carthage, an empire developed. In 631 B.C. Greeks began to colonize Cyrenaica; and from 146

B.C. the Romans, having destroyed the Carthaginian Empire, assimilated both the Carthaginians and the Cyrenaican Greeks into a colony which lasted for 600 years and comprised all the Maghrib except southern Morocco. When their power decayed, the Vandals came over from Spain and for about a century dominated the coastal belt without ruling much of the interior. They were followed by the Byzantines, who re-created the Roman presence on a smaller scale and also ruled for about a century.

In the seventh century A.D. came a veritable tidal wave, which was destined not merely to flow over, but to submerge, the Maghrib: this was the Arabs, who in that remarkable spiritual explosion which resulted from the apotheosis of Muhammad and his foundation of the Islamic religion, broke out from their desert homelands and swept first through the Middle East and then across the whole breadth of North Africa, where they replaced the Byzantines and, having converted the Berbers to Islam, settled down and interbred with them, so that they form the second main component of the population. Another Arab invasion followed four centuries later.

Between the twelfth and thirteenth centuries various points along the coast were temporarily occupied by Normans, Portuguese, or Spaniards; and in the eighteenth century the Algerians, like sheep appealing to wolves to protect them from foxes, called in the Turks to help them to eject the Spaniards, only to find that the Turks, having done so, would not leave but on the contrary occupied and ruled not only Algeria but Tunisia and Libya as well (though not Morocco, and without much intermingling). In the nineteenth century Europe came again, when the French in 1830 invaded, and subsequently annexed, Algeria, and in 1881 established a protectorate over Tunisia; in 1911 Italy annexed Libya; and in 1912 the French and Spaniards between them established a protectorate over Morocco.

Since the end of the Second World War the colonizing tide has receded. The Italians were expelled by the Eighth Army from Libya, which achieved independence in 1951; the French relinquished control of Morocco and Tunisia, which also became independent, in 1956, and were forced out of Algeria by

1962; and now these four countries, each with its own characteristics, outlook, and problems, face the future on their own.

From the road behind me came a rattle of small hooves and
guttural objurgations in a language which was not Arabic. The
donkey which had awakened me was approaching, together
with four companions loaded with sacks of grain and a group of
humans in dingy white robes and untidy turbans who were
shuffling along in the heel-less slippers worn throughout the
Maghrib.

Seen from close to, the men were tall, long-headed, and
under their weathering, fair; and most had blue eyes. They
were 'unmixed' Berbers, of one of three main types found in the
country. Another type, also long-headed but shorter, darker,
and with black hair and hooked noses, was familiar to me from
expeditions into the Atlas Mountains thirty years before; a
third, broad-headed and of medium height and brown colour-
ing, is found in the Sahara; and there are numerous variations
of these strains.

It is tantalizing to think how little we know of these aborigines.
France administered many of them for over a hundred years,
yet the many French savants who have studied them give the
impression of throwing up their hands in despair over the
questions of who they are and when and whence they came;
and no one else seems any more positive. The names under
which their race goes provide no clue: the Roman appellation
'Barbari', meaning 'uncultured', was obviously a term of con-
tempt; they themselves go to the opposite extreme by calling
themselves '*Imazighen*', which signifies 'of noble origin'; and the
Egyptian name for them, '*Libou*', whence comes 'Libya', tells
us no more.* Ethnologists seem generally to agree that they are
of Hamitic rather than Semitic origin, and philologists hesitantly

---

* The word 'Moor', the definition of which is 'an inhabitant of North West
Africa' and which I shall occasionally use in that sense, comes from an alternative
Roman name for the Berbers, 'Mauri', which at first applied only to the northern
Moroccans but was later extended to cover the Algerians also; it was probably de-
rived from a Greek word meaning 'dark-skinned.'

place their language in the Hamitic group and detect resemblances between it and ancient Egyptian.

One of many theories is that the three main types referred to above result from a basic race, long-headed, dark-haired, and brown-skinned, which by the end of the Palaeolithic era, say 10,000 B.C., had established itself throughout the Mediterranean basin, having superimposed on it two successive waves of immigrants, one fair-haired, blond, and blue-eyed, the other negroid. The theory assumes that these last came from the South, possibly because the Sahara in which they formerly roamed had begun to dry up, but leaves unanswered the question which I personally find the most intriguing, namely who were the blond invaders and whence did they come. In any case, the supporting evidence is thin.

Nor can we say with any certainty what proportions of the present population of the Maghrib are pure Berber, pure Arab, or hybrid. The Arabs endowed the Berbers with the Islamic religion which they all profess, and with the Arabic language which a high proportion of them speak. But the Arab invaders were relatively few in numbers – perhaps not more than 150,000 in the seventh century invasion, and 50,000 in the eleventh century one – by comparison with the indigenous Berbers, and the Arab strain must therefore be much diluted. The question is further confused by the persistence with which tribesmen of obvious Berber, or at least mixed, blood, describe themselves as 'Arabs', apparently for motives of snobbery: the Arabs have a saying that 'If you ask a mule his parentage, he will reply that his father was a horse'. The most we can say is that the Arab strain is strongest in the most heavily settled areas, e.g. Tunisia, the centres of Algeria and of Morocco, and the Jebel Akhdar of Cyrenaica, and weakest in the mountainous areas.

This is borne out by the distribution of the Berber language. At one time this appears to have been a good deal more widely used than today (even as far as the Canary Islands, where it was known as Guanche), and to have been written, whereas it is now only spoken and has therefore developed wide differences between its various local dialects.

Statistically the Berber-speakers, many of whom also speak

Arabic, are said to form 35 per cent, 30 per cent and 25 per cent of the populations of Morocco, Algeria, and Libya respectively, but only 1 per cent of that of Tunisia. The vast majority of them are found in the Atlas and Rif massifs of Morocco, the Aures and Kabylie massifs of Algeria, and the Jebel Nafusa of Libya.

In themselves the Berbers are tough, happy-go-lucky individualists, owning loyalty primarily to family or tribal groups, capable of fierce resistance to attempts to dominate them but also of adaptation to such dominance once established. Their healthiness was a byword in antiquity; and although a high proportion of them are still very backward the race does not lack either intelligence or ability, so that in Morocco in particular men of unquestioned Berber stock are well represented in the Government and in the higher ranks of the Civil Service and the professions. The Arab strain which they absorbed between the seventh and the eleventh centuries brought a keener intelligence, but also a more intense emotionalism and instability. These characteristics, combined with the individualism and combativeness of the Berber, perhaps explain why the race never became a nation; why the history of the Central Maghrib, from the time of the fusion of the Arabs and Berbers until the Turks took it over, should have been a welter of conflicts between rival dynasties based on different tribes; why only one of these dynasties (the Almohads in the thirteenth century) succeeded in extending their rule over the whole Maghrib, and that but briefly; and why Morocco, left in nominal independence until the twentieth century, fell into utter confusion. It remained to be seen whether the European tutelage which had preceded the acquisition of independence by the component parts of the Maghrib since the last war, and which had brought them education and material progress, had also inculcated in their peoples the qualities which they needed to make a success of that independence.

This was one of the questions to which I wanted to know the answer. I had already penetrated well into the Maghrib, and was now in the 'gap in the handle'; and before crossing the

Mediterranean on my way home I intended to traverse the country from north to south as well as from east to west, and to learn what I could of what it had been, what it was, and in what direction its peoples were heading.

CHAPTER 2

The Green Mountain

I must now go back a few days, to the time when I crossed from
Egypt into the Maghrib. My entry at Sollum was inglorious.
The Libyan Passport Control authorities, apprised of my
coming, were merely amused at the absence from my passport
of the entry permit which it should have borne, and remedied
the omission, but my car-papers were a more serious matter.
Production of my International Carnet resulted in a spate of
Libyan Arabic of which I gradually gathered the drift: apparently a few months previously a Central European had brought
in a car on such a document, had flogged it in Tripoli, and had
decamped over the frontier with the proceeds, leaving the
Libyan Customs deprived of their duty; and the Libyan Government, their application to the Federation for reimbursement
having been rejected, took revenge by declaring all such car-
nets invalid for Libya. (The matter has been settled since.) Moreover the frontier Customs post was in charge of a corporal whose
officer had gone to Tobruk for the day, leaving him with cate-
goric instructions to admit no car arriving with such a carnet
and with no discretion to vary them. He was embarrassed but
helpless, and could do nothing but make vain attempts to raise
his officer on an archaic telephone. After forty-five minutes of
this the friendly passport officials proposed a solution which he
felt able to accept: I might go on to Tobruk and find the officer
myself, provided that I took a soldier with me. I looked ruefully
at the packed interior of my vehicle and began to heave luggage
about to make room for the hulking young Berber who was to be
my custodian, when the officer suddenly came on the line and
gave permission for me to come to Tobruk alone on condition
that I came to see him at once on arrival. (When I did find him
he was charming, but felt obliged to instruct me to report to
Higher Authority in Benghazi, by whom I was subsequently

dealt with firmly and compelled to furnish a banker's guarantee for the duty.)

So I drove on towards the west. I was still in the desert, and on either side browns, yellows, and buffs shaded imperceptibly into each other, with hardly a feature to catch the eye; so that the appearance of a rusty heap of metal was an event worthy of attention.

It was the remains of a tank, and was one of the few relics of the Desert War still to be seen near the road, for the tribesman is as efficient a scavenger of metal as his goat of all else, so that of all the mountains of material which must have been left even after Disposals had finished their operations hardly a trace remains except an occasional object which, like this, is at once too heavy and too battered to be worth removing. Inland, away from the road, it is a different story; oil companies' maps still show ugly green blotches representing uncleared minefields.

One of the few relics, I said; yet to one of my generation the whole of the route which I had followed from Alexandria to this point had been one long reminder of the campaign, as was to be the coastal road for many hundreds of miles onwards. Every successive place-name – Mersa Matruh, Sollum, Halfiya, Bardia, Derna, Tobruk, Benghazi – lit up like a flash of lightning the memory of those dreary days of 1941 and 1942 when we hung on the radio craving for success to offset the disasters elsewhere, the rationing, and the daily dose of bombs. Later our appetite for victory, whetted by Alamein, was fed by the ultimate triumph in Tunisia; and although since the war the flood of conflicting memoirs, and the outpourings of amateur strategists, have done their best to persuade us that our desert victories were won in spite of our generals, for my generation those generals – first Wavell, then Alex and Monty – remain heroes. Whatever the truth about the commanders, at least no one has dared to smear the image of the rank-and-file, the tea-drinking Rats who, once given the tools and the leadership, so superbly finished the job. No one who knows anything about deserts could underestimate what they endured in that long struggle, not only with Rommel, but with heat and flies and dirt.

But place-names and scrap-iron are not the only memorials to them in this land of their endeavour. When, two hours later, I approached Tobruk, I first turned aside to visit one of the most enduring of all, the War Cemetery. It was of the standard pattern of those maintained on all our former battlefields by that dedicated body, the Commonwealth War Graves Commission: rows of slim headstones, each with its name, description, regimental badge, and relatives' message, identical in shape except where a broader one indicates that the crew of a burnt-out aircraft or tank could not be separated in death; the Cross of Sacrifice, and the Stone of Remembrance inscribed with 'Their Name Liveth for Evermore'; around and between them such trees and bushes and flowers as skill and care could raise despite water shortage and unfriendly soil.

In the course of my journey through the Maghrib I was to see many more of these cemeteries, but none approached that at Alamein. I had visited it a few days before in the company of the Commission's regional representative, a New Zealander whose life for years past had clearly been devoted to its creation and who was sad that age had caught him up and compelled his retirement at the moment of achievement. Without his guidance I might have passed it by, for here British understatement, allied to taste and craftsmanship, has been carried to the point of genius. The Commission's aim was to construct a monument which should blend harmoniously with the terrain in which the desert campaign had been fought, the great plains with their rocky outcrops and sparse vegetation. Hence the motive is horizontal: a ninety-yard cloister, inscribed on its inner walls with the names of the 11,945 who fell in the desert or the Middle East or who, as airmen, died even farther afield, during the Second World War; behind it the cemetery proper, with 7,354 dead, the Cross, and the Stone. Here there can be no rich lawns or resplendent flower-beds, as in gentler sites; but there are terraces of hardy grass, and tea-roses and geraniums and verbena, and bougainvillaea and flowering shrubs, and acacias to give some shade. The Germans and Italians both have their own memorials at Alamein, solid structures erected on the tops of neighbouring hills; and their self-assertiveness only throws into relief the dignity of this place where the Commonwealth honours its dead.

In Tobruk, after dealing with the Customs officer, I made my way to a quay overlooking an inlet, where I lunched with my feet dangling over clear water and my crumbs were disputed by shoals of minnows. Very quiet it looked that day, the little port, with hardly a trace of the destruction and death which had reigned there from 1941 to 1943 during the long agony of its capture and siege and recapture, when the hulks of bombed ships littered its shores and life was one long grey ordeal for the garrison and for the Navy who kept it supplied; and very quiet the little town, where gaps in every street bore witness to the severity of the bombardments which it had had to suffer. But soon, I learnt, its tranquillity will be shattered once more and this time for as long as the world needs oil, for Tobruk is destined to become the terminal of a pipeline bringing crude from British Petroleum's strike in the Sand Sea inland, and the oilmen will see to it that this Oriental town becomes a scene of European efficiency and bustle.

It was a peaceful interlude, and I went on refreshed to spend the night at the Eighth Army's next capture, Derna. This is an unpretentious little town with a tree-shaded central square, on which I found a bed in an exceedingly simple inn. (I complained when dinner was not served at the specified hour, and the Sudanese waiter responded with the perfectly reasonable question 'Do you have to travel or are you just hungry?')

Derna, as Darnis, emerges into history at the end of the third century A.D., when the Emperor Diocletian, in the course of a general overhaul of the Roman administrative system which involved splitting most of the existing provinces into two, made it the capital of 'Lower Libya', a new subdivision which stretched along the coast as far as Alexandria. It shared the ruin which befell all the towns of Cyrenaica after the second Arab invasion in the eleventh century, but in 1493 was revived by the arrival of a number of Muslim families expelled from Spain when the Arab Kingdom of Granada was conquered by

the Spaniards, and in 1735 Muhammad Bey Karamanli, the
head of the Turkish family who had established themselves as
hereditary Governors of Libya, is credited with providing it
with a water supply by diverting the waters of the Derna Valley
and also with endowing it with its Great Mosque, a notable
building with forty-two domes. But the most curious episode in
its history occurred in 1805, when it became the scene of a re-
course to 'gunboat diplomacy' by that democratic power the
United States. It came about thus.

In the seventeenth century Algeria and Tunisia, as well as
Libya, were ruled, nominally on behalf of the Sublime Porte
but in practice independently, by Turkish Governors who, like
the rulers of independent Morocco, derived a rich revenue from
corsair operations in the Mediterranean. Great Britain had
come to terms with these potentates for the free passage of
her shipping, and under the umbrella of this agreement the
American colonies had built up a lucrative trade with the
Levant. When they became independent, they were notified by
the Turks that their shipping was no longer immune from
attack and invited to negotiate new agreements, naturally involving money payments, The Americans, having tried and
failed to induce other European powers to assume protection
for their shipping, were constrained to form a committee (composed of John Adams, Benjamin Jackson, and Thomas Jeffer-
son) to undertake the negotiations, and to provide it with
$80,000 as arguments. With Morocco agreement was soon
reached and $10,000 paid over as a *douceur*, but with the three
Turkish provinces negotiations were delayed by changes of
personnel and before they were concluded Algerian corsairs had
captured several American ships and held their crews to ran-
som. After ten years treaties were finally signed with all three,
at a cost of over $600,000 in ransoms, and American Consuls
appointed to the three capitals, Algiers, Tunis, and Tripoli.
William Eaton at Tripoli seems from the first to have adopted
what can only be described as an imperialistic view of the
Turkish authorities, with whom his relations soon became so
strained that he sought means of coercing them. His chance
soon came: in 1801 Yusuf Karamanli, the Governor (who had

incidentally been helpful to Napoleon during his Egyptian campaign), attempted to extort more 'protection money' from the Americans and when they refused cut down the flag over their Consulate. This meant war; it dragged on for four years, until in 1805, Eaton, in a desperate attempt to end it by deposing Yusuf and replacing him by a friendly successor, set out from Alexandria at the head of a mixed force which included some United States Marines and marched along the coast until they reached the Gulf of Bomba, between Tobruk and Derna. By this time they were at their last gasp from fatigue and privations, but were rescued by three American naval vessels which providentially arrived, and with their aid captured Derna. They were besieged there, but a month later peace was concluded. The march inspired the line 'From the halls of Montezuma to the shore of Tripoli' in the Ballad of the Marine Corps, Derna being taken by poetic licence to be part of the territory of far-distant Tripoli.

From Derna onwards the terrain completely changes. Instead of the gravel plains running down to sandy beaches across which I had travelled ever since Alexandria, two-thousand-foot mountains rise abruptly from a rocky foreshore, with olive and fruit trees on their flanks and forest intermingled with grain-fields and pasture on the plateau behind. This is the Jebel Akhdar, the 'Green Mountain' of Cyrenaica, and it looks so much like southern Europe that it must have appeared positively homelike to the Greeks who first braved the two-hundred-mile sea-passage across from the Cyclades and landed on its coast.

These Greeks, according to legend (there is more legend than history about pre-Roman North Africa, with a consequent gain in picturesqueness at the probable expense of accuracy), were Dorians from Santorin under a certain Battus, who had consulted the Delphic Oracle about his stammer and had been advised, no doubt to his astonishment, to go forth and found a colony in Africa. Accordingly in 631 B.C. he and his followers landed on an island off the Cyrenaican coast, where he was given immediate proof of the infallibility of the oracle, for on setting foot on shore he was attacked by a lion, shouted in terror, and never stammered again. The island turned out to be barren and disappointing, and so did a site on the mainland to which the colonists migrated after a second application to the oracle, but six years later they were led to a third site by friendly Berbers, who told them that there was 'a hole in the heavens' above it; and here at last they found the abundant water and the pasture which the oracle had promised them, and founded settlements which eventually became the cities of Cyrene and its port Apollonia.

I came to the ruins of these cities next day. Of Apollonia not much remains, for the sea-level has risen and its harbour basin and quays are now under water offshore, visible only from the air; and its Greekness has been overlain by later, chiefly Byzantine, construction. But it has for me a supreme virtue, quiet; I found no one in the ruins down there by a placid sea and could wander, or sit, undisturbed amongst walls and columns. I spent most time in the so-called 'Eastern Church' (Eastern in orientation, Byzantine in faith), where columns of lovely pink *cipollino* marble stand out against the azure Mediterranean.

Cyrene, on the plateau a dozen miles inland, was very different. For one thing, the site is vast, though so much cut up by bluffs and hillocks that only gradually does its size become apparent. For another, I found the ruins occupied by Arab families picnicking with the aid of the transistor radios which have become part of the Way of Life in the Maghrib. My examination of the Greek amphitheatre and of the complex of Greek tombs and ruins which surround the original *raison d'être* of the city, the stream gushing out of the hillside which is called the Fountain of Apollo, was therefore summary. I made my way instead to the farther end, where stand the fine Roman forum and the market-place, and parked under acacia trees. Here a small boy tried to sell me a wounded fluttering finch and was indignant at being forced to release it; to my relief, it flew away.

Much of Cyrene is a confusion of superimposed construction, mainly Byzantine, under which the lines of the original Greek city have been almost entirely erased. Its history, and that of the other Greek settlements in Cyrenaica between their foundation and their final ruin seventeen hundred years later, is equally confused and its general lines equally difficult to trace. For the first two hundred years after their foundation, Cyrene and Apollonia were ruled by eight kings of the original dynasty of Battus, all of whom, as the Delphic Oracle had predicted or perhaps ordained, bore either his name or that of his son Arcesilaus. It was a disturbed period, for the colonies were bedevilled by both dynastic quarrels and revolts of the Berbers, whose original friendliness, as more and more immigrants arrived, turned to fear that their lands would be taken from them – much as the Arabs in Palestine revolted against Zionist immigration in the 1930's. One palace feud led to a breakaway section of the Battaid dynasty founding a new city, Barca, on the lower plateau, only to have it sacked a few years later, about 515 B.C., by a Persian army sent in by Cambyses at the invitation of one of the contending functions who wished to take revenge on the other. Two other cities were founded later; one, Tauchira, served as a port for Barca, while the other, Euhesperides, was apparently intended solely for overseas trade as its hinterland had strictly limited production.

We know little of what goods the colonists exported, but one item which certainly bulked large was silphium, a plant said to have grown wild along the coast between Derna and Benghazi and to have been collected by the Berbers and sold to the Greek colonists, who shipped it to Greece; a famous Greek vase of the sixth century B.C. in the Louvre depicts one of the Kings Arcesilaus supervising the weighing of the crop, which was evidently a Royal monopoly. It eventually became extinct, Pliny says through being eaten by sheep, and botanical opinion is apparently divided as to what it was and what its properties were. One suggestion is that it was *ferula tingitana*, a type of asafoetida which, as the name implies, grew in the region of Tingi (Tangier), another that it was *thapsia silphion*, an umbelliferous plant which an Italian traveller claims to have found in the hills near Cyrene as late as 1819; and its properties have been variously claimed as antiseptic, anti-spasmodic, deobstruent, diuretic, or those of an elixir of life. At any rate, its fame was such that a representation, too unclear to serve as identification, appears on Cyrenaican coins as the national emblem of the colony. When it became extinct, this was replaced by an image of the nymph Kurana, from whom Cyrene derived its name: she was a Greek with exceptionally beautiful arms and an engaging habit of strangling wild beasts with them, wherefore she is usually represented as thus disposing of a lion.

About 440 B.C. the eighth king of Cyrene was assassinated in Euhesperides and a republic proclaimed in Cyrene, which achieved primacy over the other cities. During this period the frontier between Cyrenaica and Tripolitania seems to have been laid down by means of an agreement* between the Greeks and the dominant power farther along the coast, Carthage. A century later, in 322 B.C., the Greek colonies for the first time lost their independence, by committing the classic error of appealing to a strong power to help them to oust an interloper and then finding themselves unable to oust their ally. In Cyrene a Spartan adventurer named Thibron had managed to seize power and the colonists applied for help to Ptolemy, a former General of Alexander the Great, who had possessed himself of Egypt and founded there the dynasty which ended with Cleopatra. Ptolemy sent in one of his generals, Ophellas, to restore order, and once Thibron had been overcome and hanged he installed Ophellas as Governor of the colonies in his name.

In 300 B.C. a successor Governor, Magas, who was Ptolemy's stepson, began to reign independently. In 283 he proclaimed himself King of the colonies – which thus in a sense recovered independence – and in 274 went so far as to attempt an invasion of Egypt, but was forced to turn back by an occurrence which is repeated like a theme song through the history of the Maghrib a revolt of Berbers, along his lines of communication. His death, in 250 B.C., produced a Racine-like drama of mother-daughter conflict: his widow tried to sever the dynastic connection with the Ptolemies by breaking the engagement of her daughter Berenice to the heir to the Ptolemaic throne and marrying her off to another Greek, Demetrius, but spoilt it all by falling in love with Demetrius herself; whereupon Berenice, with more spirit than filial devotion, had her mother assassinated and married the Ptolemaic heir-apparent, on whose

* See pages 33-4.

accession in 246 Cyrenaica was automatically restored to the Ptolemaic fold.

Under the new régime, the cities took on a different form, which they were to retain for the rest of their active existence: Euhesperides, which had silted up, was replaced by a new city named Berenice after the Queen, near the site of the present Benghazi; Barca was renamed Ptolemais and planned anew; and Tauchira was renamed Arsinoe, after another scion of the Ptolemaic line. These three cities, together with Cyrene and Apollonia, became known as the 'Pentapolis'.

Then came Rome, which by the middle of the second century B.C. was the rising Mediterranean power. By 163 B.C. she had already made her presence felt in Egypt by arbitrating another Ptolemaic dynastic – in this case fraternal – feud, as a result of which the brother who was awarded the Governorship of Cyrenaica showed his gratitude by willing it to Rome if he should die without an heir. He did not, but his son carried out his wishes, and by 96 B.C. Rome, which had conquered Carthage just fifty years before and thus established itself in the centre of the Maghrib, was also formally invested with sovereignty over Cyrenaica. The Romans at this time were not at all keen to extend their commitments to yet another dominion, and it was another fifty years before they could bring themselves to accept the responsibilities of administering it, but once they did so they set to work with their usual thoroughness, and the next two centuries saw the Cyrenaican cities rebuilt and embellished and the countryside developed to an unprecedented pitch of prosperity.

In A.D. 115 there was a setback, when the Jewish community of Cyrenaica erupted in a revolt which spread all over the Middle East and was only suppressed after immense loss of life and destruction, especially in Cyrene, which some say never fully recovered. This Jewish community, incidentally, had originally been formed of Jews fleeing from Palestine in the course of the diaspora, but its numbers had been swelled by Berbers proselytized by the immigrants. The suppression of the revolt resulted in many of them moving on again, some south-westward until they scattered across West Africa, others westward to the southern confines of Algeria and Morocco. In the struggle of the Berbers against the Arab invaders in the seventh century, two tribes particularly mentioned by the Arab historian Ibn Khaldun, the Jerawa of the Aures mountains and the Nafusa of Tripolitania, are both described by him as being Jewish, and the chieftainess of the former was named Kohina, which suggests an affinity with the huge family of Cohen.

Nevertheless Cyrene was to revive under the Antonines, especially under the rule of that attractive character Septimius Severus (of whom we shall hear much presently), and seems to have remained the chief of the Pentapolis cities for another 150 years. During the reign of Claudius II it was renamed Claudiopolis, but after his death resumed its original name (rather as Varna, in Bulgaria, became 'Stalin' for a brief period in the 1950's which ended abruptly with his death). In A.D. 297 however, Cyrene suffered demotion when Diocletian in the course of his reorganization created the new provinces of Lower Libya and Upper Libya: for while, as we have seen, Derna became the capital of the former, Ptolemais and not Cyrene became the capital of the latter, which comprised the Pentapolis and the Jebel Akhdar.

Constantine's foundation of the 'New Rome' at Byzantium in the fourth century had little direct effect on Cyrenaica, which in this respect differed from the rest of the Maghrib: for whereas the region to the west of the 'gap' was dominated first by the western Romans, then by the Vandals who expelled them, and then by the Byzantines who expelled the Vandals, Cyrenaica to the east merely remained in the power of Rome, with an almost imperceptible transition from western to eastern Roman authority. But Constantine's adoption of Christianity ensured that this should, sooner or later, become the major religion of the subject province.

We do not know how or when Christianity actually entered it. 'Simon of Cyrene' is mentioned in three of the four Gospels as carrying the Cross through the Via Dolorosa, and 'men of . . . Cyrene' are mentioned in the Acts as preaching Christianity in Antioch, but there is no record of a Bishop from Cyrenaica before the third century, and even in the fourth, when there were

Bishops in the Pentapolis cities, Cyrene itself seems to have still been a centre of pagan cults. In 365, however, the city was largely destroyed by an earthquake, and archaeological excavations have revealed traces of its pagan temples having been thereafter desecrated, perhaps as an act of expiation after this obvious sign of Divine displeasure, so that from then onwards Christianity would seem to have had the upper hand in Cyrene also. By the fifth century Bishops had been established in most towns of the province. The Church of Cyrenaica seems to have looked eastward to Alexandria rather than westward to Carthage, where another Church had grown up; another example of the divisive effect of the 'gap'.

In the next fifty years after the earthquake Cyrene was largely rebuilt, but from then onwards began the decline of the Pentapolis, with the power of Rome weakening and the Berber tribes from the outside beginning to seep through on to the remnants of Roman civilization like water through a breached dyke. Under Justinian, the Pentapolis had a brief revival and there was some rebuilding, but more and more the countryside between the cities passed under the control of a local tribe called the Luata, who according to some authorities were Berbers with an admixture of both Greek and Roman blood. In 608 the last act of the drama of Byzantine Cyrenaica was played out, when Heraclius, Prefect of Africa, revolted against the Emperor and, with the aid of his troops and some Luata auxiliaries, conquered first Egypt and then Constantinople. But soon afterwards the Persians invaded Egypt, and whilst Heraclius was expending his strength in resisting them the Arabs began their invasion of the Maghrib, on which they were soon to impose their rule and their religion; and before this new menace the remaining presence of Byzantium melted away.

Under the Arabs, the Pentapolis came under the domination of successive Caliphates, first the Omayyads of Damascus and then the Abbasids of Baghdad. In the eleventh century came disaster, when Cyrenaica was invaded, in circumstances which I will describe later, by two nomad Arab tribes, the Beni Hilal and the Beni Sulaim, who reduced its cities to ruins and its interior to grazing for their flocks. Thereafter it lay under the long-range domination of the rulers of Egypt, the Fatimids and their successors the Ayyubids, until in 1640 the Turkish Governor of Tripoli installed a representative in Benghazi. From then on Cyrenaica nominally formed part of the Ottoman dominions, but whilst its ports retained some vitality the interior seems to have remained in a state of chaos, until in 1911 it was annexed by the Italians and as from the 1920's began a new life as a development area of the Italian Colonial Empire.

CHAPTER 3

Sanusis and Oil

When I left Cyrene it was blowing a full *ghibli*, that hot, dusty wind off the Sahara which in Egypt is called the *khamsin* (Arabic for 'fifty', the number of days for which it is reputed to blow at a stretch) and which, after crossing the Mediterranean and picking up a load of humidity on the way, reappears as the *mistral* in the south of France, the *sirocco* in Italy, and the *föhn* in Switzerland. It was unbearably stuffy, and I took refuge in Baida, a small town on the plateau where a new palace and a rash of not unattractive public buildings bear witness to the unexpected, and perhaps temporary, status as one of the federal capitals of Libya which it has acquired because of King Idris's preference for the uplands where the sect of which he is the head first found a home.

This sect, the Sanusi (or Senussi), has for over a century counted amongst its adherents almost the whole population of Cyrenaica, as well as many in the eastern part of Tripolitania. It was the unquenchable resistance of its members to the Italians, and the help which they gave to the Eighth Army during the Desert War, which staked a first claim to the independence which all Libya now enjoys.

Its founder, who bore the impressive name of Muhammad bin Ali bin as-Sanusi al Khattabi al Hasani al Idrisi al Muhajiri, was born at Mostaganem, in Algeria, about the beginning of the nineteenth century (the date is as uncertain as most Oriental dates in those registerless days), and claimed descent from Fatima, daughter of the Prophet. By the time that he was thirty he had developed reformist views on the Islamic religion and began to travel round Algeria and the Sahara, and later Tunisia and Tripolitania, preaching a return to its pristine purity and spirituality. He went on to Cairo, where he fell foul of the learned doctors of the University of Al-Azhar for his unorthodoxy, and then to Mecca, near which he founded a *zawiya*, Abu Qubais (a *zawiya* is not a monastery, for celibacy has no place in it, but rather a stronghold of the Faith which serves as both a school and a retreat). Whilst in Arabia he made contact with the Wahhabis, the fanatical desert sect at the head of which Ibn Saud established his kingdom in the 1920's, and this contact embroiled him with the orthodox of Mecca, who had probably already heard unfavourable reports of him from Cairo. By 1843 he was forced to leave the Hejaz and came to Derna, whence he founded another *zawiya*, known as 'Al-Baida' (the White), at the place now bearing that name, and made it the headquarters of what became known as the Sanusi movement. But once again his uncompromising unorthodoxy brought him into conflict, this time with the Turkish overlords of Cyrenaica, so that he was forced to move on. He took refuge with the people of the oasis of Jaghbub, in the south; and there, in 1859, he died.

He was succeeded by his second son As-Sanusi Al-Mahdi, whom he had chosen in preference to his elder son after a test of faith which involved jumping from the top of a palm-tree and landing without injury. The son actively propagated his father's movement and founded new *zawiyas* in Fez, Damascus, Istanbul and as far afield as India, besides consolidating the hold which it already had over the tribes of the eastern Sahara and the central Sudan and extending it to the people of the Libyan oases and along the coast of Tripolitania. By 1894 the hostility of the Turks had become so strong that he was forced, like his father, to withdraw southwards; he made his headquarters in the oasis of Jauf, near Kufra. There he came out in opposition to a forward movement which the French were at that time beginning in Wadai, in Equatorial Africa, and tried to prevent their forces from occupying Kanem, in Chad, but he failed and in 1902 died.

His nephew Ahmed ash-Sharif, who succeeded him, continued his policy of opposition to the French and fought them intermittently from 1904 to 1911, but ended by losing all Wadai and retired to Jauf. Having become imbued with pan-Islamic ideas, he came out in support of the Muslim Turks, although they had always oppressed his family, when the Italians invaded Libya in 1911, and from then until 1915 Sanusi bands constantly harassed the ports which were all that the Italians had managed to occupy. He also allowed himself to be induced by German bribery to extend his hostility to the British in Egypt, and in 1915 rejected their offers of conciliation conveyed to him by his cousin Seyyid Muhammad Idris (the son of As-Sanusi al-Mahdi, and the present ruler of Libya), with whom the British had become friendly, and sent his forces into Egypt. His ill-organized attack was, however, easily repulsed by the British forces and he retired to Jaghbub, where he was assailed by French forces pushing forward from Kanem. As his powers waned, his cousin's influence increased; and in 1917 the latter, having reached agreement with both British and Italians, was recognized by all the principal Sanusi chieftains as Grand Sheikh of the Order. The following year the discredited Ahmed was evacuated in a German submarine via Italy to Turkey; and in 1919 Seyyid Idris sent his brother Rida to Rome to make formal acknowledgement of Italian sovereignty on his behalf, whereupon he was recognized by the Italians as the hereditary Amir of the oases of Kufra, Jaghbub, Augila, and Ajedabia, i.e. of the area extending southwards from the Gulf of Sirte in which his sect was paramount.

But his honeymoon with the Italians did not last long. In 1922 he was offered by the Arab leaders of Tripolitania the Amirate, or Governorship, of that province also, and accepted it. By now, however, Mussolini and the Fascist régime were in power and were no longer prepared to see the Italian position in Libya limited in effect to squatters' rights along the coast. They there-fore opposed this extension of Seyyid Idris's functions, and their attitude towards him became so unfavourable that he prudently withdrew to Egypt and remained there for the next twenty years, during which time the Egyptian Government refused an Italian request for his extradition on grounds of 'subversion'. The Sanusi, under the general direction of his brother Rida, continued guerrilla activities against the Italians until, in 1927, Rida surrendered to them and was exiled to Sicily. Seyyid Idris bided his time, keeping in close touch with his people.

His opportunity came in 1940, when Italy declared war on Great Britain and the Western Desert was evidently going to

c

become a theatre of military operations. He lost no time in offering the services of his people to the British, and a Sanusi force was raised in Egypt for service with the British forces. He hoped to induce the British Government in return to give a definite undertaking that they would support the independence of Cyrenaica, perhaps under their protection, after the war, but they were not prepared to go further than the public declaration of Mr. Eden (as he then was) that the Sanusi people should never again fall under Italian domination, and with this Seyyid Idris, though some of his followers murmured, professed to be content. In 1944, after the expulsion of the Axis forces from Libya, he was able to revisit his country, but declined to live in it until it should become self-governing.

He finally returned in 1947. By that time the future of the three provinces of Libya, Tripolitania, Cyrenaica and the Fezzan, was in considerable doubt, for the Great Powers who had the disposal of them were in total disagreement. All felt that, in view of the dearth of trained administrators, technicians, and natural resources, the whole country ought to be put under some form of tutelage; but whereas the United States favoured a trusteeship administered by the United Nations Organization (which was hardly equipped for the task) and the Russians, to the general surprise, put forward a claim for the trusteeship over Tripolitania, the French supported a claim by the Italians to be granted the trusteeship over the whole of Libya, which the British, bound by their pledge to the Sanusi, felt obliged to oppose. The best agreement that could be reached was that the decision should be postponed until after ratification of the Peace Treaties and that a Four Power Commission should then be sent to Libya to find out what its people wanted.

This Commission finally went out in 1948, but its members could only agree on one point, the unfitness of the Libyans to govern themselves, and sent in separate reports to their Governments. The United Nations Political Committee tackled the problem in April 1949, and its principal members were at once at odds. Agreement might have been reached on Cyrenaica, where the Sanusi clearly demonstrated that they wanted independence under Seyyid Idris and were willing to accept British trusteeship for the time being, and also on the Fezzan, the inland province bordering on Algeria, which France was anxious to control in order to safeguard the Algerian frontier and the inhabitants of which had expressed no clear views. But Tripolitania was a stumbling-block. The Russians had passed from the stage of wanting its trusteeship themselves, through support for its return to Italy under trusteeship, to support for the American proposal for United Nations trusteeship; the French, supported by some South American countries, still favoured Italian trusteeship, which was vehemently opposed by the Arab States and by the Tripolitanians themselves; and the British, in a last effort to secure a solution, reached private agreement with the Italians on a compromise under which Great Britain would hold the trusteeship over Tripolitania for three years and Italy for the next seven, after which it would become independent. This proposal came to the General Assembly and by one vote failed to obtain the necessary two-thirds majority, a verdict which produced such violent rejoicings in Tripolitania as to suggest that it could never have worked. Six months later, by which time all the Powers concerned had withdrawn their claims to the trusteeship, the Political Committee agreed that Libya should become an independent and united State 'as soon as possible' and that a United Nations High Commissioner should be sent out to help the Libyans to determine the form of their future Constitution.

Dr. Pelt arrived in 1950 and a Constituent Assembly was set up, but for many months could reach no conclusions on account of differences of view between the provinces: for while the peoples of Cyrenaica and the Fezzan from the first demanded a monarchy under Seyyid Idris, and the Tripolitanians came to agree that this was the only solution that everyone could accept, the two former pressed for a federal form of Constitution in order to guard against the possibility of their provinces being dominated by the more sophisticated Tripolitanians, whereas the latter wanted a unitary State. The Amir Idris, whose wisdom was generally respected, threw his weight on the side of federation, and the Assembly succeeded within the appointed time in reaching agreement that Libya should be a Federal Kingdom under him.

Thus it was that on January 1st 1952 King Idris I ascended the newly-created throne of the United Kingdom of Libya. For most of the Cyrenaicans, and of the sparse population of the Fezzan, he was a venerated religious leader as well as a temporal one; for the Tripolitanians, on the other hand, he was simply an acknowledged chieftain who for thirty years had been a symbol of resistance to Italian domination. To drive such disparate subjects in double harness was a delicate task, made no easier by the country's extreme poverty, for this forced it into a dependence on foreign aid which its emerging Nationalists found distasteful. But the King's prestige was maintained, and was perhaps almost enhanced by his age, his frequent illnesses, and his remoteness: for he never found the atmosphere of Tripoli congenial, and with advancing years tended to withdraw more and more into seclusion, first at Tobruk and latterly at Baida, and to hold aloof from political manoeuvrings, tribal disputes, and inter-provincial friction. But his advice, wise and objective, was always available and at moments of crisis usually decisive. He became in fact something of a legend in his lifetime.

From Baida I left the Jebel Akhdar, with its broad acres of cultivation and its scrub-oak forests. I came through Barce, a small town which in 1963 was completely wrecked by an earthquake but is now, as I heard later, to be the object of the most ambitious reconstruction plan which the Libyan Government have so far produced, and came down to the seacoast. I passed briefly through the ruins of two more of the Pentapolis cities, Tauchira (later Arsinoe), now called Tocra, at which excavations are still in their early stages and there is little to see, and Barca (later Ptolemais), now called Tolmeitha, which was a huge place and although unrestored is still impressive, with its Byzantine gateway and church, its theatres (including a tiny one which I believe has recently been used for amateur productions), and its lovely mosaic floors with their representations of North African fauna.

In the evening I came to Benghazi, once, as Euhesperides and later Berenice, the fifth city of the Pentapolis, although modern building has blotted out almost every trace of that past. Its present name is derived from Sidi Ghazi, one of the numerous Muslim holy men whose names are commemorated in the Maghrib, who died in A.D. 1450 and was buried near the site of the present lighthouse. The city seems to have shared in the ruin which afflicted the rest of Cyrenaica after the second Arab invasion in the eleventh century, but later to have been re-settled by immigrants and to have reacquired some sea-trade. In the seventeenth, and again in the eighteenth, centuries it fell into the hands of semi-independent Turkish Governors of Tripoli, but in the nineteenth century the last of these was expelled by the Turkish Government, under whose direct administration it became a provincial capital; and it retained this status under the Italians when they annexed Libya. During the Desert War it suffered severely, being three times captured by the Eighth Army and twice recaptured by the Germans, with bombings and demolitions on each occasion, but reconstruction began after the war and, having been made a Federal Capital of Libya when independence came, it has now begun to profit from the vicinity of the oil-strikes in the hinterland and the new oil-ports in the 'gap'.

I made two journeys into the desert to see the sites of these oil developments. The first was to a producing field about a hundred miles inland from the Gulf of Sirte, and I flew to it in a little oil-company plane, for most of the way following the road which the company had built with oil by-products to connect the site with the coast as soon as the strike was sure. Like a black pencil-line this road stretched ahead, across dunes and *wadis* and rocky outcrops, and when a change of engine-note signified that we were about to land I could still see nothing but the eternally repeated features of the desert. But then a collection of machinery, incongruous in that waste, came into view, and near it a space marked by whitewashed stones, with a windsock; and as the plane came to rest a truck emerged from behind a dune and drove to meet us. Ten minutes' bumping over gravel brought us to the signs of human handiwork: some huts and sheds, a clutch of fat cylinders, rows of pipes, some high light-standards, some boards of gauges. Across it all drifted black smoke from two fires raging spectacularly in the desert near by, where surplus gas was being burnt off until such time as arrangements could be made for it to be piped to the coast for use. I looked round for operatives, but could see only a handful; an oil-field in production, it appears, is so largely automatic that little manpower is needed except to check that all is functioning normally, and its produce pours to the sea and the refineries by itself.

We flew back to the coast, landing at a spot which I must have driven past five years before. There had been nothing there then, but there was plenty now. A cluster of enormous storage tanks had arisen on a knoll, and a power-plant and a small refinery were in operation beside the sea. Metal constructions serving as offices and messes stood near by, and inland a village of bungalows was being erected, in which staff who at present commuted from Benghazi would be housed, with air-conditioning and all the amenities which were once luxuries but which oil companies provide as a matter of course. Offshore was an object looking like a huge half-submerged practice golf-ball, which was explained to me as a new type of mooring, 143 feet high, to which tankers could be attached by the bow only and allowed to swing with wind or tide, what time the pipes from the storage-tanks attached to it continued to discharge into their holds. A tanker was loading at it now, and three others were loading on other, standard-type, moorings. Here there was no lack of operatives; everywhere men were busy, and even when construction was complete and the builders had gone the operation of the refinery and of the discharge of the crude would require a substantial staff, so that the oil-town of Mersa Brega, the first human agglomeration of any size in the 'gap', will be a permanent feature, to be followed by others as more companies strike oil and more pipelines are laid to this convenient coast.

My next journey, by a similar plane, took me more to the east and a good deal farther inland, until the gravel expanses and the rocks were left behind and below lay the sort of country so often photographed (in Nevada) to represent the Middle East in films, so seldom seen in the Middle East itself: line upon line of dunes, their sharp crests looking like a child's scribbles on a piece of dull yellow paper. This was the Sand Sea, that challenge to movement which the Long Range Desert Group so triumphantly mastered during the campaign, and it seemed as though nothing human could survive in it. But here again, after half an hour across it, black objects appeared which looked even more out of place on that smoothly stippled surface and which resolved themselves as we descended into a cluster of prefabricated huts and caravans, a laager of transport, and the tall spike of a drilling-rig : for this was a different kind of field, one in which oil had been struck but drilling was still going on to determine its extent, and to which a pipeline had not yet been laid.

We landed on a space which had somehow been contrived between dunes, and were collected by a Land-Rover, which took us up the side of a dune, over a col, and down the other, as though on beige snow, and repeated the process several times until the camp came into view. It was a group of caravans put together in a regular pattern; and within these air-conditioned monsters, one of which was a mess with *Vie Parisienne* illustrations on its walls and a bar dispensing Pernod and grenadine, a team of French drillers was off duty. Their leader, a young Breton who had drilled wells all over the world, accepted the fact that oil is usually found in deserts and regarded this place as a normal assignment, unpleasant in high summer but perfectly tolerable, to be got through, after which he and his team would go elsewhere; in any case, frequent changes in scene – a fortnight on and a fortnight in France – avoided any risk of the *cafard*, the black depression which was the scourge of the Foreign Legion. On a different site, some miles away, another drilling team, this time Texans, was operating, and here I realized that the main hardship of oil-searching is the oil itself, for these men in their dungarees had to endure being soaked in oil for all of every working day as the great drill came up from its downward plunges and they had to check with minute care what it brought with it for indications of what it was passing through.

In the tiny office set up in a pair of caravans I was shown a map of the sites where oil had, or had not, been struck, and of the sites in this particular concession earmarked for future drilling. There seemed little logic in the pattern of the productive wells, a line of which would be interrupted by dry holes and would then continue, but the team seemed quietly confident: this field was good and had proved so, and they had only to go on drilling to find more sooner or later. During my visit a different kind of technician arrived, sand-coloured, in a sand-coloured vehicle: he was a pipeline specialist engaged in surveying the course which the future pipeline to this field should follow, the main problem being whether it could be run through the Sand Sea or must be curved round its outside.

As we returned to Benghazi, I was thinking of a story which I had been told over lunch in the mess, of an American Liberator bomber which the surveyors had found near by a few weeks before. Its log had shown that it had been returning from a raid on Italy in 1942 and had lost its way so completely that the captain had ordered the crew to bale out under the impression that they were near the sea and would soon be picked up along the coastal road. The plane had then landed itself *with its radio set intact,* so that had the crew stayed with it all would have been rescued; as it was, none was ever heard of again. It was one more example of the unbreakable desert rule: if in trouble, stick to your transport; it can be seen for miles when a man cannot, so that you stand at least a fair chance of being found if searched for, whereas the number of men who have walked to safety is infinitesimal.

Back in Benghazi, I looked into the facts of Libya's oil. They were impressive. Apart from the companies already producing, all of which were still seeking more, a dozen others, American, British, Italian, Japanese, French, were boring the surface of the desert like woodpeckers on a dead tree, and in process of time some would almost certainly strike too. In 1963 the Libyan Treasury, which before 1960 had drawn virtually nothing from oil, had received £22.5 million in royalties and in 1964 £45 million; and the indications were that the figures would rise in arithmetical, if not geometrical, progression. (It is ironic that the Italians, having snatched Libya, should have remained in ignorance of the wealth within their grasp and should have continued to refer contemptuously to their possession as *'una scatalone di sabbia'* – a heap of sand; but they were not alone in their ignorance, for the French who divided up the desert in the south of their three North African possessions also failed to realize that these areas might one day be more important to the countries concerned than all their fertility.)

Fantastic figures these, for a country formerly so poor; but so much wealth carries dangers too, for it is a heady wine for a people not accustomed to it. The King had set an admirable example of frugality and good sense, and the Libyan Government were genuinely anxious to use as much of their revenue as possible for development which would provide work for their unemployed – which the oil industry does not. But they were finding, as other undeveloped countries had already found, that great wealth is not always easy to spend usefully when water and natural resources are lacking, and that the essential preliminaries of planning, surveying, costing, and contracting take so long that the majority who do not benefit directly from the revenues begin to murmur at the absence of visible progress, and uncomfortable pressures build up.

CHAPTER 4

Romans and Italians

We are back where I began this book, by the Marble Arch, on the boundary between Cyrenaica and Tripolitania. I had left Benghazi early that day, and all morning had driven along the coastal road, the Via Mussolini as it was called in the days when Italian colonization took itself seriously and the Duce came out in his special Bugatti and drove himself the 650 miles between Benghazi and Tripoli at an alleged average speed of 91 m.p.h. I had seen nothing off the road except two oil ports, an occasional group of Bedouin tents, herds of grazing camels; little on it, except lorries, a private car or two, oil companies' caravans, strings of donkeys, and every few miles a little collection of tin-roofed shanties or mud huts with a petrol-pump and a pull-in café for drivers. All around me had been the scrub-tufted waste, with an occasional glimpse of the sea away to my right, and the wind blowing dust on to my windscreen.

Now I had left behind all traces of Greece, and ahead of me was a different country in which, before the Romans came, the dominant power had been Carthage, that great city of antiquity on the coast near the modern Tunis, another thousand miles to the west from where I now was. By the time of the foundation of the first Greek colonies in Cyrenaica this city was already an established power with ambitions towards the economic domination of the western Mediterranean, in which however its trade was being seriously challenged by that of the European Greeks. The Carthaginians might therefore have been expected to react violently when these outposts of Greece came into being on the shore of the Maghrib; they did in fact so react when in 520 B.C. a different sort of Greek, Spartans under their King Dorieus, attempted to settle in Tripolitania, and with the aid of local Berbers expelled the intruders. But to understand why, instead of attacking the Pentapolis, they first tolerated the Greeks and then agreed upon a division of Libya with them, I had only to look round at the desolation in which I sat: to get at them, the Carthaginians would have been faced with two unpalatable alternatives, either to mount an expensive and hazardous seaborne expedition, or to face the logistical problems of crossing 400 barren miles with, I believe, only three water-points, without the aid of camels, which seem to have been unknown in the Maghrib until the Romans introduced them in about the third century A.D.

In the pre-camel era, in fact, only one army seems even to have attempted the crossing; for Cambyses the Persian, when his troops occupied Cyrenaica about 515 B.C. and sacked Barca, planned to attack Carthage but, significantly, chose the sea-route (and had to give up the project because the Phoenicians who provided most of his fleet would not sail against their kinsfolk); and Alexander the Great, who in 322 B.C. got as far as Siwa in the Western Desert, soon afterwards went back to the Middle East without ever attempting to push farther westwards. The one commander who had the temerity to tackle the 'gap' was Ophellas, the Macedonian who was Ptolemy I's first Governor of Cyrenaica: in 310 B.C. he set out in response to an appeal for support from a Sicilian Greek named Agathocles, with whom he had made an alliance and who had landed on the Tunisian coast to attack Carthage, but his Army, composed of Greek soldiery, Libyan mercenaries, and so many camp-followers that it was described as 'a people on the march', found the summer heat in the 'gap' so demoralizing that it largely disintegrated *en route;* and although Ophellas himself reached Agathocles' camp it was only to be murdered by Agathocles, who had in the meantime been defeated by the Carthaginians and presumably wanted to take it out on somebody.

The legend purporting to explain how the Carthaginians and the Greeks reached agreement on a boundary-line between their respective territories, and also why this line divides the 'gap' unequally, runs as follows. Once the Greeks were settled in Cyrenaica and had begun to trade, they came into conflict with the Carthaginians, already settled in Tripolitania, and over a long period skirmishes took place without definite result, until each side came to recognize the impossibility of overcoming the other. They therefore agreed on a device to delimit their respective spheres: this was for each to dispatch a mission to run towards the other, the boundary to run from the point where the two missions met. Carthage was represented by two brothers named Philaeni, who ran so much faster than their adversaries that they met them about two-thirds of the way across the 'gap', whereupon the Greeks, using a technique familiar in our times, refused to accept the result on the grounds that the Philaeni must have started too soon. The Carthaginians shamed them by offering to re-run the contest, but the Greeks countered with two alternative offers: that the Carthaginians should either allow their mission to be buried on the spot, or should retreat to some point farther back, where the Greek mission, following up, would allow themselves to be buried. The Philaeni, rather than yield a foot of ground, chose self-immolation, and funerary mounds called the Arae Philaenorum were erected over their graves. Such is the legend; it sounds more heroic than authentic, and the names of the Philaeni more Greek than Punic, but it is a matter of historical fact that a frontier between Carthage and the Pentapolis had been laid down by the fourth century B.C., and a Roman monument has been found near the foot of the Jebel al-Ala, a two-humped hillock on the present provincial boundary which is about the only prominent feature in the featureless landscape of that region and must have been familiar to mariners and landsmen alike, which suggests that this line may be of considerable antiquity.

My surroundings when I awoke next morning were very different. The previous day had been the hardest of the tour, to date; for, having left the Marble Arch in early afternoon and driven for many more hours, I had found accommodation on even the lowest scale unobtainable and had been forced to drive even farther in the twilight. It had been a nightmare journey, for somewhere that day there had been a market, and the road was thronged with animals and donkey-carts, with never a tail-light between them, which loomed up abruptly from outside the range of my headlights. But after another three hours these headlights no longer spent themselves in space on either side of the road, but began fitfully to illumine prickly-pear hedges, and olive-trees, and now and then the wall of a whitewashed villa; and I knew that I had crossed the 'gap' and was in the 'tang of the billhook', the cultivated coastal belt of Tripolitania which is called the Jefara and which leads to the Gulf of Gabes and Tunisia. In Misurata, another unpretentious little town, I found a humble Italian hotel which made up in willingness what it lacked in amenities, and there I could rest.

I drove out in clear crisp morning air through the main street, where Arab shopkeepers were taking down the shutters from their tiny boxes, and came within the hour to a low wall beyond which, at the end of an avenue of gum-trees, I could see columns and blocks of stone. I had been here before, and had looked forward to this return more keenly than, perhaps, anything else in my journey; for this was Lepcis Magna, one of the three cities which give Tripolitania its name and which in Roman times were known collectively as the 'Emporia', as witness to the importance of their entrepot trade; and to my mind it is the loveliest ruin in the Maghrib.

Lepcis, like the other two Emporia cities, was almost certainly founded by Phoenicians (Sallust says by refugees from Sidon), but we do not know when. Excavations have uncovered Phoenician tombs, but have brought up nothing dating earlier that about 500 B.C.; and Herodotus' account of the landing and expulsion of Dorieus and his Spartans in 520 B.C. does not mention any participation by the people of Lepcis, near the site of which the landing took place, which suggests that it was still not in existence at that time. But once founded it must have grown rapidly, for by the time that it came within the purview of the Latin historians, which was about 160 B.C., it was already the leading city of the region. At this time the cities of the Emporia were being harassed by a Berber chieftain named Massinissa, who was in league with the Romans and had been recognized by them as the King of an independent Numidia (corresponding to most of central and southern Algeria). The Emporia were nominally subject to Carthage; but Carthage, having by now fought two exhausting wars with Rome, had become too weak to defend them and could do no better than appeal to Rome for assistance in containing Massinissa. This was a disastrous move, for Rome was already thinking in terms of expansion in North Africa, and the Senate seem to have decided that an expensive and possibly indecisive military assault on Carthage might be avoided if its people and the Numidians could be set against one another. They accordingly awarded the Emporia to Massinissa and ordered Carthage to pay him an indemnity for 'wrongful detention' – language which Hitler might have used. Massinissa's success whetted his ambition to rule a Libyan State which would comprise the whole Maghrib and would have Carthage as its capital, and in the year 150 he picked a quarrel with Carthage and defeated her forces. But to Roman fears of Carthage were now added fears that Massinissa in control of Carthage might prove an even greater menace, and the Senate came to the conclusion that Carthage must be not only conquered but destroyed. They therefore brought about the Third Punic War, during which Massinissa died but as a result of which Carthage was duly razed.

The Emporia thereafter became nominally subject to Massinissa's successor Micipsa, but he had less ambition, so that they were able to retain their individuality and some autonomy; in 106, for example, Lepcis made a 'Treaty of Friendship and Alliance' with Rome, in order to avoid becoming embroiled in a conflict between Rome and Massinissa's great-nephew Jugurtha. But fifty years later it apparently lost its autonomy rather unluckily by becoming involved in the Caesar-Pompey War: it was seized by another Berber King of Numidia, Juba I, who was allied with Pompey against Caesar, and when Caesar won and abolished the Kingdom of Numidia he imposed an annual 'stipendium' or tribute of 3 million pounds of olive-oil annually on either Lepcis individually or the Emporia collectively (we do not know which) and thus reduced it, or them, to the status of subjects.

But although the Emporia never regained their freedom, the Roman occupation brought them an expansion and a pros-

perity of which they could never have dreamt, by creating conditions in which their trade could flourish. Thanks to the Pax
Romana which subdued the Berbers, they could develop the
extremely profitable trade-route which goes via Mirzuk down
through Chad to Kano in northern Nigeria, along which came
gold, and ivory, and precious stones, and ostrich-feathers, and
perhaps some slaves, for Roman homes, and certainly wild
beasts for the insatiable Roman arenas. Even more profitable
were the exports of local produce from the hinterland, which
the Phoenicians had first begun to cultivate and which the
Romans developed enormously: grain, and fruit, and above all
olive-oil, which was considered too coarse for eating but was
prized for cooking and lighting. There was profit, too, in the
import and distribution of Roman manufactured goods like
lamps and pottery.

Under Septimius Severus Lepcis enjoyed its greatest building
boom, as was natural: for this first of the African Emperors,
who spoke Latin with a strong African accent, liked African
food, chose his Phoenician wife Julia because her horoscope was
propitious (it may have been, but not for him, for a more
adulterous virago he could hardly have picked upon), and died in
York in 211, was himself a son of Lepcis, having been born there
in A.D. 164, and was particularly concerned with its welfare.
The defences which he constructed, of which I shall be speaking
later, kept the Emporia reasonably intact for another century;
but by the middle of the fourth century A.D. the Roman decline had set in, and Lepcis was a chief sufferer. In 363 came the
first of three invasions by a tribe called the Austerians, whose
origin is uncertain but whose destructiveness is not, for they
laid waste all the country round the Emporia, whilst Roman
Proconsuls and Commanders intrigued futilely against each
other; and the loss of its olive-groves and surrounding agriculture dealt Lepcis a blow from which it never really recovered.
A century later the Vandals, who had come in from Spain on
the heels of a receding Roman power, destroyed the walls, on
the pretext that they might protect rebels, thus leaving the city
defenceless against both raiding Berbers and encroaching sand-
dunes. The Byzantines who succeeded the Vandals a century

later found Lepcis largely buried, dug it out, and fortified a much
reduced perimeter, and under their rule the city had a slight
revival, but its active existence flickered out after the coming of
the Arabs in the seventh century and it degenerated into a ruin,
which was used as a quarry by people who should have known
better : over 600 of its columns are said to have been incorporated
in Versailles by Louis XIV, and several more were sent home
by a British Consul as a present to the Prince Regent and used
in George IV's 'folly' at Virginia Water. What remained was
gradually covered anew by the sand, until the Italians began to
dig it out between the two world wars.

I should advise anyone visiting Lepcis for the first time to go
through Septimius Severus's triumphal arch, which is immediately inside the entrance, to follow the main axial street, the
Cardo, for about 600 yards, and then to turn left along a side
street which leads to the theatre. Here, from the back of the
gallery, you can see the whole expanse of the ruins and realize
not only how large an extent they cover, but also how many
sand- and scrub-covered mounds, obviously concealing ruins,
still await the excavator. To the north, perhaps a quarter of a
mile away, lies the sea, the breezes from which must have come
pleasingly to audiences on summer evenings; on its edge, the remains of a lighthouse, and beyond it the dried-up port with its
quays and mooring-blocks and the foundations of colonnaded
warehouses; in a half-circle round the foreground the market,
the Severan Basilica with its superb incised decoration on the
columns, the Forum, the baths with their elaborate hot-water
system and communal public latrines, and the Palaestra, the
post-bagnum exercise ground. Around stand less completely
restored remains of temples, law-courts, and more baths, the
whole linked by paved streets on which chariot-wheel marks are
clear.

My own preference is for the market, which has kiosks and
porticoes, and counters on which are carved representations of
the wares sold on them (fish on the fishmongers, for example)
and on one of which are the standard measures of length and
holes of standard volume; but everywhere the construction, of
locally quarried limestone (or sandstone for backing) and of

The market at Lepcis Magna, Libya
The temple of Liber Pater at Sabratha, Libya

Market-day under the palms

marble imported half-finished from the eastern Mediterranean and worked up locally by Greek craftsmen, is of a high order and reflects the image of a solid community possessed of a high civic sense and money to spend. One must be grateful for the sand which preserved it through the ages, for the Italians who brought so much of it to the light, and for the British and Libyan archaeologists who have carried on the work since the war and are still doing so.

A small man in a European suit, wearing a fez of the floppy type which still survives in the Maghrib, attached himself to me as I went through the ruins. He spoke only Arabic, and his knowledge was not profound, but his enthusiasm was manifest, and a credit to the Antiquities Department to which he apparently belonged; I had already noticed in Cyrenaica the keenness of this Department, which augurs well for the future of Libya's unique heritage of ruins. In his company I spent a long day tramping, scrambling, gazing, and photographing, with a delectable hour at noon stretched on stone slabs down by the sea on which the Romans, too, could well have done their sunbathing.

Reluctantly, almost sadly, I left this giant among ruins and drove on towards Tripoli. The road was now bordered with eucalyptus trees – the Italian anti-malaria panacea – and on either side of it cultivation and habitations multiplied, until I found myself in suburban streets, and came out at length on the Lungomare, the parade beside the harbour which leads to the medieval Castello, now a museum, the focal point of Tripoli.

Under the name of Oea, Tripoli was, like Lepcis, founded by Phoenicians and was the second city of the Emporia, but unlike Lepcis it has few Roman remains, other than a fine four-sided arch of Marcus Aurelius by the sea, which has an octagonal dome on a rectangular plan and is, I believe, a notable architectural feat. Oea had much the same history as Lepcis until the departure of the Byzantines and the coming of the Arabs, but then, instead of falling into decay as Lepcis did, it continued in being as an active port. It came first under the Omayyad Caliphate of Damascus and then under the Abbasid Caliphate of

D

Baghdad, but in A.D. 758 was captured by a Berber sect, the Ibadites, and for the next four centuries was held in succession by the Berber dynasties which became pre-eminent in turn in the central Maghrib and whose stories come later. In 1140 it was taken and held for fourteen years by that remarkable Norman Roger II of Sicily, who, having ousted the Byzantines from that island, was ruling there in Oriental splendour and now wanted to carve out a fief for himself along the North African shore; but it was retaken by the Almohads, one of the greatest of the Berber dynasties, and later passed to their successors the Hafsids. In 1510 it fell to a Spaniard, Pedro Navarro, in the course of a Spanish 'crusade' in the Maghrib of which we shall hear much farther along the coast. In 1530 Charles V handed it over to the Knights of Malta, who hung on to it precariously until, in 1551, it was captured by a Turkish corsair, Dragut, and became nominally incorporated in the Ottoman Empire. For two centuries thereafter it and its province were ruled by a series of adventurers who paid only the sketchiest allegiance to the Porte, and in the seventeenth century one of these, Yusuf Karamanli, established himself as a hereditary and virtually independent ruler, also installing a representative in Benghazi and, as we have seen, indulging in piracy which brought him into conflict with, *inter alia*, the Americans. In 1835 the internal squabbles of the Karamanli family became such that the Porte was moved to intervene and replace them by its own nominees, whose successors ruled until in 1911 the Italians invaded and captured the territory. Since then Tripoli has evolved from an Arab village into at least the façade of a European town, with a brave front of clean and well-built streets of shops and offices, and quarters of villas and blocks of modern flats, and churches and filling-stations; but behind lies the *suq*, the narrow twisting streets of tiny Arab shops, with mosques and laden donkeys, dirt and noise and colour.

I had spent the summer of 1938 here, in charge of the British Consulate, and had thus had ample opportunity to see how Italian colonization worked. The Governor-General was Balbo, a wiry little man who had been a famous aviator and told me in atrocious French of his plans for the further development of the

colony. He seemed friendly and decent; but his Fascist hench-
men were not. In my experience, they were a gang of petty
racketeers, who were making money as fast as possible by any
and every means. A favourite device was to give a monopoly of a
profitable trade to a 'Società Fascista' to which only Party
members could belong, thus squeezing out the local inhabitants
and long-established foreign colonies like our respectable Maltese.
A more unpleasant manifestation of Fascist ambition was the
vast military parades held on all possible occasions, in which
desert equipment, suitable for the invasion of British-held
Egypt, figured prominently; we were not to know, until
Wavell's forces exposed it, how much braggadocio and how
little fighting spirit lay behind this paraphernalia.

But not all aspects of Italian colonization were bad. Italy's
original acquisition of Libya in 1911 had, of course, been a bla-
tant grab, inspired by France's expansion in the rest of the
Maghrib and designed to forestall the Kaiser's ambitions in that
direction; even Daniel Varè, that silver-tongued apologist for
the Fascists, could say only that it was 'not openly opposed' by
any other Power and that such disapproval as was expressed was
inspired by (unspecified) 'vested interests'.The conquest took a
long time to complete, for the Italians, having brushed aside
feeble Turkish resistance and caused the Sultan of Turkey to
accept defeat by the curious device of announcing that he had
granted the Libyans 'full autonomy', were for many years
pinned down in the coastal belt by the far tougher resistance of
the local population, and in 1919, as already described, went so
far as to recognize the main resistance leader, Seyyid Idris, as
Amir of an autonomous region of Cyrenaica. But Mussolini and
the Fascists, once settled in, had different ideas and set about im-
posing their authority throughout the country, partly because
they regarded the possession of colonies as a status symbol which
they hoped would put them on an equal footing with Great
Britain and France, partly perhaps through a wistful desire to
recreate something of the glories of Rome, later because they
also thought that Libya might solve the problem, at that time
apparently intractable by other means, of over-population in
Italy.

I myself witnessed the arrival of one of several convoys bringing immigrants from Piedmont, who had been seen off at
Genoa with brass bands, ships dressed overall, and speeches
adulating their civilizing mission in Africa; they were met with
similar panoply in Tripoli, and at once conveyed in waiting
fleets of lorries to appointed sites in the Tripolitanian steppe,
where they found whitewashed cabins, each containing a year's
supply of provisions topped by an Italian flag and the framed
text of one of Mussolini's *obiter dicta*, farm animals in the stalls, a
well already dug, and fields already sown. In eighteen months,
they were told, they must be self-supporting; in twenty years
they would by annual contributions have bought their farms if
they did not weaken. Most did not; so well, in fact, did these
hardy and hard-working peasants take to colonial life, and so
much did they become identified with the land into which they
had been pitchforked, that some even chose to remain, and were
permitted by the Libyan Government to remain, after Libyan
independence. (In Cyrenaica it was a different story; the Sanusi
were a harder people than the Tripolitanians and had suffered
more, so that once the British occupying forces were withdrawn
no Italian was safe, and the farms which I had seen on the Jebel
Akhdar were entirely locally-occupied – the malicious alleged by
the animals, whilst the farmers camped in their tents outside.)

The settlers' contribution to the agrarian economy of Tripolitania was there for all to see. In other respects, too, the Italian
occupation brought tangible benefits. Medical and veterinary
services were inaugurated in a land which had known them
not; a road-system was laid down, despite great difficulties of
terrain; and a beginning was made on the control of that arch-
enemy of Libya, the Saharan sand, by the planting of imported
Australian eucalyptus-trees and special grasses to stabilize the
dunes which threatened – and still threaten – to advance and
swallow up more of the exiguous cultivable land.

On the debit side was the Italian treatment of the indigenous
population. The stories, widely believed at the time, that dissident leaders were liquidated by being dropped from aeroplanes
were, I believe, wholly apocryphal – I met someone who claimed
to know their inventor – but there is no doubt that the Libyans

were starved of education, that their interests were ruthlessly
subordinated to those of the Italians, and that they were treated
as, and made to feel, second-class citizens. This was brought
home to me on my first evening in Tripoli, in 1938, when I was
walking home along the Lungomare amongst a mainly Muslim
throng. As the sun set, a gun was fired from the Castello, at that
time the Governorate, and on the instant I found myself the
only person in the street both moving and facing eastward, for
everyone else had stopped in his tracks (those in cars or cabs leap-
ing out of them), had turned west to face the Castello, and was
doing the Fascist salute. I was never again in the street at that
hour.

This time I saw more of Italian colonization in the course of
several journeys round and inland from Tripoli; for the coastal
belt abounds in trees, gardens, vineyards, and olive-groves,
many of them still owned and operated by Italians. But only a
few miles inland the picture begins to change. Sand becomes
visible between the cultivation, and indeed in the soil itself, so
that it is easy to see how much the Italians must have done during their comparatively brief tenure to consolidate and fertilize
the land – and also how soon it could revert to desert if left un-
tended. Within thirty miles of the coast are increasingly frequent patches of pure sand, and then you reach the edge of the
Jefara, whence a steep escarpment leads up on to the Jebel
Nafusa, a hill-region on which are tidy little ex-Italian towns
like Tarhuna and Garian (where a colony of Jews still lives in
caves scooped out of the bottom of deep pits and seems entirely
comfortable there), each surrounded by its trees and gardens.
As the land slopes southwards, there is ever less cultivation and
more grazing or useless country, until the edge of the steppe is
reached and the desert begins: this is the Fezzan, the third
province of Libya, which consists merely of a string of oases in
desert and holds only 5 per cent of the total population, but
could well become of great importance if big oil-strikes were
made in it.

The coastal belt has undergone many vicissitudes. So far as
we know, it was almost uncultivated until the coming of the
Phoenicians; but they, as anyone can see who is familiar with

their homeland, the Levant littoral, had great knowledge of
agriculture. They are believed to have introduced the vine,
fruit-trees, and above all the olive, for which conditions are
particularly suitable as it can withstand the burning heat of the
ghibli and the sparseness of the rainfall; and the remains of a
dam found in the Wadi Caam show that they made at least a
beginning with water-conservation. But it was when the Romans
took over, bringing security, better communications, and the
water-conservation methods for which they were famous where-
ever they went, that agriculture in the Jefara really began
to flourish. Comparatively few Romans seem to have become
settlers, the pattern of development being rather of Roman
capital and enterprise operating from the cities of the Emporia
by the use of cheap local labour; but records indicate a tenfold
increase of production between Caesar's time and Nero's, less
than a century later, and all over the Jebel Nafusa inland, and
especially at its eastern end, are the ruins of farms and olive-
presses showing that what today is at best seasonal pasturage
was in Roman times a region of intense olive production.

It has been suggested that the Romans could only undertake
agriculture on this scale because the climate of Libya in their
day was less harsh than now. Probably they did enjoy a slightly
greater rainfall because the country was more wooded: since
their time it has been successively denuded by the improvidence
of Berbers and Arabs and the appetites of their goats and camels.
But the constant mentions of water shortage in Latin historians'
accounts of Roman campaigns in Libya suggest that there can
have been no drastic change of climate, such as occurred in the
Sahara in palaeolithic times and caused the disappearance of
the hippopotami and other tropical fauna depicted in the cave-
paintings of the Tassili and Wadi Djerat. Many wild animals
shown in mosaics from Roman villas have long been extinct in
the Maghrib, but their extinction was almost certainly due to the
same cause as is operating in East Africa today – the incompati-
bility between their survival and the needs of an increasing
agricultural population. The production achieved by the
Romans was, in fact, primarily due to their admirable use of the
water resources available to them, while the desiccation and

erosion which set in later resulted from the destruction, by wanton act or neglect, of the extensive network of barrages, cisterns, and aqueducts on which their agriculture was based.

Their development of the Jefara must have begun soon after they took over the Emporia cities about 45 B.C., but its extension to the Jebel was only made possible by the entry on the scene, twenty years later, of the 'Legio III Augusta', the force which for the next 260 years was to embody the might of Rome in the Maghrib. Its advent was due to Augustus, who had just annexed the formerly independent Berber Kingdom of Numidia and incorporated it in the Senatorial Province of 'Africa', and realized that the Proconsul of the new province, which included Tripolitania and most of what are now Tunisia and eastern Algeria, would have a long land-frontier to defend against the perennial danger of Berber raiders from the south. Within five years of its being placed at the Proconsul's disposal the Legion was in action in Tripolitania against the Garamantes, a formidable tribe inhabiting what is now the Fezzan, who used four-horsed chariots and dominated the main Saharan trade-routes; they had participated in a revolt against Roman authority which had spread from the west and were duly chastised by the Legion, their capital Garama (now Germa) and Cydames (Ghadames) being captured. Five years later they revolted again and this time it took the Legion twenty years to master them. In 14 A.D. a deserter from the Legion of Berber origin, Tacfarinas, raised a revolt in the Aures mountains of southern Algeria, and although the Garamantes, who had promised him support, seem merely to have done a little raiding, he kept the Romans at bay for another seven years, and forced them to bring in another Legion, the IX Hispana from Pannonia (Austro-Hungary) as a reinforcement, before being killed. In A.D. 68 the Garamantes broke out again; they had been called in by Oea to help in a local dispute with Lepcis and took joyful advantage of the invitation to devastate the surrounding countryside, until Festus, the commander of the Legion, drove them out and pursued them back to their native Fezzan. Festus seems to have subdued them so thoroughly that about thirty years later the Romans were able to use their territory as a base for two long and remarkable expeditions into the Sahara : one of these was military and involved a three-months' march southwards, presumably into the Sudan, while the other, led by one Julius Maternus of Lepcis accompanied by the King of the Garamantes, and apparently commercial, reached 'an Aethiopian country called Agysimba where rhinocerus congregate', which has been variously identified as Chad, Air, and the Tibesti massif. At about the same time another turbulent tribe, the Nasimones, who lived in eastern Tripolitania within the Roman aegis, revolted against excessive Roman taxation and were likewise punished.

There followed a century of relative peace, until around A.D. 200 one or other of these tribes began again to menace the cultivated area. At this point the Emperor Septimius Severus revisited his native land and, having crushed the invaders, set in train a complete reorganization of the defence system. Hitherto the Legion had operated a defence in depth, garrisoning the coastal areas and striking southwards when necessary, but this was now replaced by a system of static defence, consisting of three parallel zones known as the *limes*. The outer zone was composed of three main forts, at places now known as Bu Ngem, El-Gharia el Gharbia, and Ghadames, each of which lay on a main line of communication between the coast and the interior. The middle zone consisted of a series of settlements occupied by *limitanei*, discharged legionaries who were granted tax-free plots of land on condition that they undertook to defend them against Berber incursions. The ruins of some of these settlements are still visible today, the largest being at Ghirza, about 100 miles in from the Gulf of Sirte; here are at least six fortified farms, many buildings and conservation works, and some elaborate mausolea. The innermost zone was a road running along the top of the Jebel escarpment from Lepcis (where an inscription records its construction) to Tacape, the modern Gabes, in Tunisia; this was not a fortified line, but merely a means of lateral communication.

The system remained almost unchanged for as long as Rome remained strong. But in 238 the Legio III Augusta was disbanded, and thereafter the defence of the *limes* was entrusted to local levies and authority decentralized so that each section of the *limes* was responsible for its own protection; and the diminishing effectiveness of the defence from this time onwards in dealing with the periodical tribal aggressions from outside suggests that the levies often found it more expedient to make common cause with the assailants than to oppose them. By 429, when the Vandals under Genseric crossed from Spain and occupied the Maghrib coast as far as the 'gap', the *limes* were no longer a real defence, and although the Byzantines, when they had expelled the Vandals, made some attempt to reconstitute them, they found the greatest difficulty in coping with the Garamantes, the Nasimones, and the Luata* and barely succeeded in maintaining themselves until, in the middle of the seventh century, the Arabs came and swept them away.

On leaving Tripoli on my way out of Libya, I turned aside to visit Sabratha, the third of the Emporia, which lies only about forty miles to the west. It had much the same origin and history as Lepcis Magna, and shared the same fate after the Arab conquest; but because its hinterland was less fertile, including as it did much salt-marsh, and was chronically short of water, its exportable surplus of local produce must have been relatively small and the city therefore more dependent on the trans-Saharan trade for its prosperity. Significantly, its emblem was an elephant, and in Ostia, the former port of Rome, a 'Sabratha Agency' inscribed with this emblem has, I understand, been found. Such a city would decay quickly once Roman authority had so much weakened that the tribes of the interior could lay intolerable tolls on the caravans.

Its ruins are less extensive than those of Lepcis. It has more excavated temples, and more villas, mosaics and frescoes from which have enriched the Tripoli Museum, but the baths are less elaborate – perhaps on account of the water-shortage – and there is nothing to compare with the market at Lepcis. The *pièce de resistance* is the theatre, which has a particularly massive three-storeyed stage building, but it has been over-restored for

* See page 19.

my taste and looks glaring and artificial. In 1938 I had watched
a performance of a Greek play staged in it in honour of King
Victor Emmanuel, who had come over on a State tour of his
dominion. It was magnificently done, with a torchlight proces-
sion to usher in the Royal party and every modern lighting-
device to enhance the setting; I recall particularly the final scene,
when all the spotlights were trained on the golden helmet of the
goddess on the topmost storey; but also the obvious exhaustion
and frailty of the King, which made me wonder how much
longer he would continue to jump through the hoops which
Mussolini continued to hold up for him. Today I preferred the
Temple of Liber Patcr, down there by the sea, with its columns
of stuccoed sandstone glowing golden against their deep blue
background.

I drove on towards the Tunisian frontier. The north-west wind
which had been blowing incessantly was heaping red sand across
the road; for I had left behind the gardens and vineyards and
olive-groves and prickly-pear hedges, and the bareness of the
flat country on either side of the road was unrelieved by any
verdure other than tufts of grass on the salt-flats and aloes, those
symbols of aridity. There was little traffic, other than the usual
strings of donkeys driven by Berber women in black cloaks over
red embroidered dresses and men in their striped hooded cloaks
and yellow slippers.

As I drove, I was thinking of the country I was leaving, and of
its people. I had admired the great spaces, the coastline, and the
glorious monuments of the one, and the toughness, the courtesy,
and the cheerfulness of the other; and I wondered what the future held in store for them. Their economic future should be
assured, for the liquid wealth flowing through the pipelines,
even if at present dammed by difficulties of development, must
eventually seep down through the layers of population and
provide means of ameliorating their present poverty. But they
seemed to me to be facing three main problems.

The first, to which I have already referred, was to prevent the
impact of so much wealth from dislocating and corrupting their
social structure, as had happened elsewhere; I had already heard

of a tendency to abandon the rigours of agriculture or pasturage in favour of job-seeking on the fringes of the oil-companies or in the towns, and in other similar countries a weakening of tribal authority so caused had led to unrest and a lowering of standards. On this, one could only trust to the good sense of the people and the example set by their rulers. The second problem, that of maintaining their independence against predatory neighbours, should be soluble provided that they could keep their internal cohesion; and this was the third problem, for the ascetic Sanusi of Cyrenaica differ fundamentally from the more sophisticated Tripolitanians, and their differences are intensified by the divisive effect of the 'gap' between their respective provinces. At present the throne provided the essential link, but could this be preserved once its venerable occupant had quitted the scene? Only the future could answer; and the feeling which dominated me as I left Libya was uncertainty.

CHAPTER 5

Lotus-Eaters and Arabs

It took me two hours to extricate myself from two sets of frontier officials who were inquisitive, painstaking, and slow: no Arabic country has yet thought of easing formalities for the traveller. Once through, I was on a smooth and empty road leading to the west, after forty miles of which – done in forty minutes – I turned northwards along a secondary road between two of the dreary salt-flats known locally as *sebkhas*. This brought me to the oasis of Zarzis, a heavily watered area which with its palms and olives and vines is in sharp contrast to the miles of desolation surrounding it; and here, while refuelling, I broke a rule and accepted a hitch-hiker, a little man in the rusty dark suit which marks the minor French-trained official, because he claimed to be a native of the Island of Jerba, whither I was bound, and I hoped that he would tell me about it on the way. A dozen miles farther on the road came out on to the seacoast and continued across a narrow causeway, at the end of which lay the long, low, green shape of the island itself.

I had long wanted to visit Jerba, not only because it is the legendary home of the Lotus-Eaters who seduced Ulysses' companions (I have also seen it identified with Ogygia, where Calypso held Ulysses himself in bondage, but it can hardly be both and the former seems the more likely), but also because its history, which begins in neolithic times (nothing earlier has, I understand, been found on it) is an epitome of that of the Maghrib. Its people are almost entirely 'unmixed' Berbers, whose ancestors evidently occupied the island when their race spread across the Maghrib, but the Jerba community seems always to have been isolated and through centuries of in-breeding has evolved a distinctive type, long-headed like the majority of Berbers but shorter than the average and sallow rather than dark or blond. Around 1000 B.C. the Phoenicians, having already founded Utica but not yet Carthage, evidently picked on the channel between the island and the mainland as another suitable haven for their ships and founded a station called Meninx on the landward side of the island. Next came the Romans, who during their occupation built the original causeway across the channel; it was subsequently deliberately breached by isolationist islanders and only restored, by the French, in 1953. In the first century A.D., after the fall of Jerusalem, a contingent of Jewish refugees settled on Jerba in two villages, Hara Kebira and Hara Srira, their community being later swelled by the Berbers whom they proselytized and also by refugees from Spain. In the seventh century A.D. the Arabs, having occupied the mainland, also occupied Jerba and converted its non-Jewish inhabitants to Islam, but a century later, when the great schismatic movement of Kharijism* swept the Maghrib, the islanders embraced its creed and were enabled by their isolation to preserve it even when its other adherents were expelled from the Maghrib proper to the confines of the Sahara. Their religious separation in turn enhanced their isolation, and is probably the main reason why a good third of them speak the Berber language, as against only about 1 per cent of the other Tunisians.

Then came Europe. In 1134 Roger II of Sicily, whose ambitions in the Maghrib we noted at Tripoli, briefly occupied Jerba, and in 1284 it fell to Roger de Loria, an Aragonese, followed by Raymond Montaner, a Catalan; but in 1335 it was retaken by a Berber dynasty from Morocco, the Merinids, in alliance with another dynasty at that time ruling in Tunis, the Hafsids. Early in the sixteenth century it became a base for the Turkish corsairs Barbarossa; it was then captured and briefly garrisoned by the Spaniards when they attempted to lay hands on the central Maghrib, but in 1560 a Papal fleet headed by the Viceroy of Naples and the Knights of Malta was caught and destroyed in the Jerba channel by another Turkish corsair, Dragut, who massacred the garrison and in effect put an end to Spanish ambitions in the Maghrib. Thereafter, while the Turks gradually conquered the mainland, Jerba seems to have been left largely to itself until 1650, when it was incorporated in the

* See Chapter 10.

Turkish 'Pashalik', or Governorate, of Tunis and from then onwards followed the fate of the rest of the country.

In the last two centuries the Kharijite creed on the island has
lost ground to orthodox Islam (of the Malikite rite, the most austere of the four main divisions of Islam, which predominates in
the Maghrib, and can now count barely half the population
amongst its members; while the Jewish community has since
1949 been decimated by emigration to Israel. These, however,
are the only significant changes in a way of life which in essence
remains what it has been for many centuries.

I drove across the causeway, which is seven kilometres long.
The greenness of the water bore witness to the shallowness of
the channel, which alone made the building of the causeway
feasible for the Romans, even with their forced labour; Jerba is,
in fact, merely a splinter off the mainland mounted on a shelf,
and the fishermen benefit accordingly.

The island when I reached it looked like one great oasis, for
there seemed to be a palm, an olive- or fruit-tree, or a vine on
every square yard and a well or a cistern every few hundred
yards. My passenger said that in fact it contained two thousand
wells and three thousand cisterns, but that these barely sufficed
for its half million palms, rather more vines, and many thousands of olive- and fruit-trees, as there were no rivers, and too
much boring merely led to salination; also the soil was not
good. On the other hand, he said, the 60,000 islanders were by
no means all dependent on agriculture; something like a sixth
of the men were on the mainland, mostly as grocers – in Tunis
and other towns 'Jerbi' is used as a synonym for grocer, so complete is the hold of the islanders on this trade – while others who
had remained on the island were engaged in handicrafts or in
fishing, especially for sponges, which rival those of the Greek
Islands.

My road led through Mahboubine, a village in the centre
where a charming little mosque called the 'Jami' al-Katib', or
'The Mosque of the Scribe', is a credit to its Turkish builders;
and then through the two Jewish villages, which I was told
have since their depopulation given up the gold and silver
filigree work for which they were once famous. In Hara Srira

the synagogue, which has some fine silver work, especially the casket in which the Torah is kept, is called 'Al-Ghariba', or 'The Stranger', after a legendary girl who arrived from nowhere and for her supernatural powers was revered as a saint, but died without ever revealing who she was. My journey ended at Houmt Souk, on the north coast, the only town of any size on the island, where I put up at a small hotel by the little port and, that evening, went exploring. The *suqs* were unremarkable, except for the wide-brimmed straw hats which all the cheerful little brown-skinned men in the streets were wearing: for these were of a type which I had not seen elsewhere and, I am told, resemble the *petasus* or slave-hat of Roman times. In a back street I found an old, old man with a primitive loom made of olive-branches, on which he was weaving a blanket-rug of traditional striped Berber pattern, and later I came upon the 'artisanat', originally founded by the French, in which the products of this cottage industry are sold to tourists or else exported to the mainland. Then I went down to the sea, where stands the crumbling shell of the Bordj el Kebir, the fort built by the Vice-Regent of Naples in 1560 before his troops were massacred by Dragut, and near it on the sands is a sign commemorating a macabre relic of that massacre, the pyramid of skulls which Dragut erected and which remained until, in 1848, the Bey of Tunis demolished it and gave its components decent burial.

That tragedy of the past seemed very remote that evening. The port held only a pair of those graceful coasting schooners called *mahonnes* and a tangle of the smaller lateen-rigged vessels called *qaribs*, which are used for the sponge-fishing; in the shallows a few women were idly delving for shellfish; there was no sound, and the air felt heavy and languorous, so that Tennyson's 'a land in which it seemed always afternoon' came unbidden to the mind; and, whether by association or chance, that night I slept as I had not slept for years.

Next day I drove round the island. East of Houmt Souk I came to the first and only signs of modernity I was to find, a pair of luxury hotels on the edge of the sea, and then to a shrine of that latter-day cult of sun-worship, a village of the Club

Mediterranée, where devotees from across the ocean were performing their tanning rites under straw shelters. On the south
coast I found Guellala, a tumbledown village entirely consecra-
ted to the making of pottery: a thousand families live in this
neighbourhood and have no other occupation. Their dried-mud
huts adjoined the kilns, from which I saw a day's production
extracted and loaded on to camels for transport to the landing-
stages, whence it is shipped to the mainland; it was unremarkable, but the water-jars of unglazed clay were of a design which
could well have derived its inspiration from ancient Greece. I
passed Adjim, a tiny port whence a ferry goes to the mainland,
and came up the west coast, past another ruined Turkish fort,
the Bordj Djillidj, and so back to Houmt Souk. All day I had
had the sea on my left, green and translucent, offering to the
bather the choice of a thousand sandy coves; and all day I had
seen no one except the potters and the sun-worshippers, nor
passed another vehicle.

I left Houmt Souk in the morning and returned to Adjim,
where the ferry had just sailed, but courteously came back for
me. I was in two minds whether to entrust my car to a con-
traption consisting only of a small launch with a platform of
planks lashed across it, which already held a van and a motor-
cycle; but, as usual in these countries, it worked, and in
twenty minutes a little chug-chug engine brought it to the mainland port of Djorf, where I disembarked with some thankful-
ness.

From Djorf the road passes close by the ruins of Gighti, once
a Roman town of some importance, but there is not much to be
seen there now. Thence it is only a short way inland, through
the same bare and salt-encrusted plains, to Medenine, a much
photographed little town, the central *place* of which is surrounded by domed cells of dried mud and rubble, used for storage
or residence, many of them ranged in layers so that the effect
is that of a giant pigeon-cote. Round here Montgomery concentrated his forces in 1943 for the attack on the Mareth Line;
and a few miles farther on the coast road crosses the Wadi
Zigzaou, a deep watercourse with steep rocky sides (where a
barrage is now being built) which formed the core of the

Old Tripoli, Libya

A Jew at the synagogue of 'Al-Ghariba' on Jerba Island, Tunisia

Mareth Line itself. It was easy to see, when I came to it, why this position, originally constructed by the French as a defence against the Italians in Libya but on that occasion being manned by Germans and Italians against Commonwealth and Free French, had resisted direct assault and had had to be turned by a brilliant flanking movement through a defile in the escarpment to the south.

From this point onwards, the coast bends abruptly towards the north-west and the Jefara plain across which I had been travelling ever since Lepcis narrows to a point as the escarpment which cuts it off from the plateau inside it bends northwards to meet the coast; and beyond this point the Sahara thrusts to the coast from the west in a series of huge salt depressions which must at one time have been under the waters of the Mediterranean.

In this stretch lies Gabes, the first sizeable town I had come to in Tunisia. Under the name of Tacapae it was a main link in the Roman communication system, as it lay at the end of two important roads, the lateral one from Lepcis along the top of the escarpment which I have mentioned as forming the inner zone of the *limes*, and another, said to have been 270 kilometres in length, which connected it with the original headquarters of the Legio III Augusta at Haidra, near the Algerian frontier. Gabes has never attained the same importance since, and was badly damaged in the Mareth Line operation of 1943, but has always kept going by virtue of the fishing in its shallow gulf and the commerce in dates from the immense palmgrove surrounding it.

I walked that evening on its shore, where two teams of fishermen were engaged in that seemingly interminable task of hauling in a seine net; one team actually brought theirs ashore as I watched and the water came alive with the white flashes of jumping fish, mostly the sardines which swarm off this coast. A small boy accosted me, having divined my nationality and being anxious to improve the English which he was being taught, apparently by a Frenchman and not too badly, in the local school; I answered him and found that to talk to a small boy on a Maghrib beach is like throwing a stick for a dog and

E

collecting every dog in sight, for within minutes I was the centre
of an all-male group (masculine predominance still reigns, and
two sisters who had the temerity to join in were chased away)
who hung on my words. When I left I was solemnly escorted to
my car and bidden a formal, almost ceremonious, farewell.
Then I went into the palm-grove, where hardly a soul was
visible except a man up a tree, his feet in a sling round its
trunk, engaged in cutting off its crest, and the only sounds were
the dry rustle of fronds and occasional voices from the dried-mud
huts hidden in the greenery. I entered one of the gardens between the trunks, and a man emerged and greeted me with grave
politeness, while children peeped over the low mud walls; and
in that evening hour the tumult of civilization seemed very far
away.

After Gabes the main road forks, one branch going up the
coast towards Tunis, the other inland between the 'Tell', the
great plateau which fills the interior of Tunisia and Algeria, and
the line of the salt depressions which run westwards from the
Gulf of Gabes. I took the latter, and drove across hot dry steppe
country, its bareness relieved from time to time by olive-groves,
to Gafsa, a small town in a palm-grove which in 106 B.C., as
Capsa, was burnt by the Roman General Marius during his
campaign against the Berber leader Jugurtha, in A.D. 1556
was captured by the Turkish corsair Dragut (of Jerba fame)
from the ruling head of the Hafsid dynasty, and in 1943
changed hands three times between Axis and Allies before being
finally taken by the Americans. It is surrounded by deposits of
phosphates, which are an important asset to Tunisia, but its
own chief asset is the possession of the only abundant spring-
water in a so far arid countryside, which has enabled it to produce vegetables and fruit, as well as dates, and hence to become
a supply centre for the region and for the nomads who migrate
across it. I was told, however, that the position was likely to
change in the future, because well-boring experiments in the
vicinity had given promising results and the Tunisian Government, in co-operation with F.A.O., had embarked on a long-

term scheme designed to transform the region immediately to the south of Gafsa into a producer of fruit, and thus to anchor the population which hitherto had tended to migrate seasonally to the north in search of work and had by so doing been creating problems.

About sixty miles farther to the south lies the biggest of the salt depressions, the Shott el Jerid, and around it are a string of oases so rich in date-palms that the ever-poetic Arabs liken them to 'a pearl necklace'. The largest of them, Nefta and Tozeur, are on the west, and Tozeur is rather improbably linked with Gafsa by a railway coming through from Sfax, a port to the north of Gabes, but I found them quite accessible by road. Both are beautiful; the only local building material is brick made from the sand and quartz of the vicinity, but with this the builders have erected walls decorated with intricate geometrical patterns and surmounted with battlements, and houses surmounted with domes. Nefta is the more impressive of the two, for above its palm-grove rises a sharp ridge crowned with the remains of a Roman fort (the place was called Nefte by the Romans); and from this viewpoint you can look to the west across sand-dunes towards Algeria, to the east across the alternate sandy hillocks and salt-pans of the Jerid towards the sea, and to the south across the Jerid towards the country of the Nefzawa.

This latter is the most remote region of all Tunisia. The Nefzawa are a Berber tribe with a long history which has un-doubtedly received much Arab blood through interbreeding with Arab tribes periodically migrating through its area, and must now be very mixed. It is also very poor; some of its sections are nomadic, others cultivate the smaller palm-groves to the east of the Jerid. Farther to the south Tunisia tapers to a point in the Sahara.

From Nefta I returned to Gafsa, and went through it to the north-east into the foothills of the Tell, which showed greener the farther I advanced, until just beyond a small and mean village I saw in a field a Roman triumphal arch with three adjacent temples behind it and other less identifiable ruins scattered around them. This was Sbeitla, the former Sufetula, a place which seems to have been destined to serve as the site of decisive battles: for it was here that in A.D. 647 the Byzantine General Gregory, who was ruling most of the Maghrib independently of Constantinople, was defeated by the Arab invaders in an engagement which spelt the end of the Roman presence in the Maghrib, and here that in 1943 the Axis forces were defeated by the Guards' Brigade in an engagement which spelt the end of the Axis presence there. But today no more gracious spot could be found, with the golden limestone of the ruins lit by a gentle sun and sheep pasturing round the bases of the columns.

From Sbeitla I struck eastwards from the cool heights of the Tell down to the steppe country below, and came, half-way to the coast, to a town which was very different from the imitation-French of Gabes; it was a town of low whitewashed houses and narrow *suqs*, in the embrace of a high rampart, which clearly owed little to European influence but rather flaunted its Oriental origin. This was Kairouan; and here we meet the people who form the second main component of the Maghrib population, who gave the Maghrib a common language and its religion, and whose domination ensured that it should adopt an Oriental type of civilization and an Oriental direction in its political outlook – the Arabs.

There were two Arab invasions of the Maghrib, in different centuries, of different composition, and with different aims. The first, which began in A.D. 643, and took the best part of seventy years to complete, was composed of several successive waves; for the warrior-missionaries of the Faith, having defeated the Byzantines and swept through the country, encountered – as the French, Spaniards, and Italians were later to encounter – the exceptional toughness and resilience of the Berbers, who after being conquered and converted to Islam repeatedly (Arab historians say twelve times) renounced their conversion and recoiled on their conquerors, three times driving them right back into Libya. It was in fact fifty years from their first arrival before the Arabs were able to occupy and destroy Carthage, from which the remnants of the Byzantines were evacuated, and another twenty years before they felt secure enough in the Maghrib to use it as a base, and its people as mercenaries, for a further advance across the Straits of Gibraltar into Spain. These successive waves of Arabs seem to have been unaccompanied by their families, so that once their occupation was stable they naturally intermarried with the Berbers and thus produced the mixed race to which a high proportion of the people outside the mountain massifs belong.

The second Arab invasion was entirely different. It took place in the middle of the eleventh century, and was made up of two Arab tribes, the Beni Hilal and the Beni Sulaim, who came originally from northern Arabia but had been banished to Upper Egypt by the Fatimid Caliph of Cairo for persistent disturbance of the peace, particularly the pillaging of pilgrim caravans on the way to Mecca. In 1048 the Caliph's representative in the Maghrib, the Governor of Kairouan, transferred his allegiance to a rival Caliph in Baghdad, and the Fatimid Caliph, partly to take revenge on him but probably also to rid Egypt of some unusually turbulent elements, incited the banished tribes to invade the Maghrib. They came *en masse*, unlike their predecessors bringing their families with them, and instead of settling down amongst the existing population they remained nomads and predators, pillaging the cultivation and the villages until they had transformed the face of the land by converting much of its agriculture, which had survived from Roman times unharmed by the first Arab invasion, into pasturage for their herds. Only the coastal strips seem to have escaped their ravages; Libya, and the centre of Tunisia and Algeria, suffered particularly badly. It seems to have been the better part of three centuries before they were fully incorporated into the Maghrib population, and Arabists claim to be able to distinguish their descendants from those of the original, more sedentary, invaders by the type of Arabic they speak.

Kairouan itself was founded in A.D. 670 by Oqba ibn Nafi, a swashbuckling character who had led the third wave of the first Arab invasion of the Maghrib (Berber resistance having thrown back the first two) and who is famous for his histrionic gesture, when he came to the seacoast, of riding his horse into the sea and calling upon Allah to witness that he could bring the Faith no further. He seems to have been a sound military strategist, for his avowed object was to create an 'Armoury of the Faith' (Kairouan means 'armoury') which would serve as a base for future Arab military expansion, and the site which he chose, in the very middle of the sort of plain in which his tribal levies would feel at home, was also shrewdly designed to command the coast, the road from Egypt, and the Tell from which either Byzantine or Berber opposition might be expected to come. During the first thirty years of its existence Kairouan was closely involved in the Berber counter-assaults against the Arabs: in 682-3 it was captured and sacked by the first of two legendary Berber heroes, one Kusaila, who with his tribe, the Aureba, had just caused the death of Oqba in a battle near Biskra, in south Algeria; and although Kusaila was in turn killed four years later by a new Arab commander, Zuhair, in a battle near Kairouan, Zuhair seems to have been forced to retreat to Libya, where he himself was killed, and Kairouan was again captured by the Berbers. But the Arabs came again, and by the early part of the eighth century their domination of the Maghrib was firm.

It was from then onwards that Kairouan enjoyed its greatest period, for it became the seat of the Governor through whom the Caliph of Islam, at that time an Omayyad established in Damascus, ruled not only the whole of the western Maghrib, but Spain as well. Later in the same century, however, the Abbasid Caliphs of Baghdad, who had replaced the Omayyads, began to delegate their powers, and their Governor of Kairouan found himself shorn successively of authority until he held sway only over Ifriqiya (the Arabicized form of the Roman 'Africa', and denoting the same area, namely north-eastern Algeria, northern Tunisia, and Tripolitania).

During the second half of the eighth century Kairouan suffered severely in the long-drawn-out revolt of the schismatic Kharijites and in 758 was sacked by them with great slaughter. In 800 the Caliph Harun ar-Rashid of Baghdad, of Arabian Nights fame, instituted in Kairouan an Arab dynasty entitled the Aghlabids, to whom he gave a large measure of autonomy on condition that they paid formal homage, and tribute, to Baghdad; and it was during the period of this dynasty, which lasted until 909, that Kairouan acquired a reputation as a centre of Islamic learning and culture, and its Great Mosque, which Oqba had founded, was completely rebuilt by the Aghlabid Ziyadat Allah. Being at the same time masters of the east coast of Tunisia with its shallow waters and its long tradition of maritime trade and fishing, the Aghlabids also developed a fleet and in 827 conquered Sicily. Towards the end of that century, however, they transferred their capital to Tunis, so that Kairouan lost some of its importance; it was diminished still more when a new dynasty, the Fatimids, who had succeeded the Aghlabids, created their own capital at the neighbouring port of Mahdiya; and in 1052 it received a blow from which it never really recovered when it was sacked by the Beni Hilal during the second Arab invasion, described above. It has, however, retained some of its academic reputation even to this day.

It hardly looked like the capital of an empire when I reached its centre and took a room in a tiny hotel by its municipal garden. From my balcony I could look down on the rows of apparently unemployed who had found the garden walls a heaven-sent perch; on the full cafés, the occupants of which alternated between frenzied argument and moody brooding, but missed nothing of what went on around them; on the sparse traffic of bicycles, battered old cars, and donkeys; on the sweetmeat-sellers and rows of horse-cabs, all somnolent in the noontide heat. When it grew cooler I went out and drove round the walls until I found the prescribed gate from which I could penetrate the labyrinth of twisting streets behind and arrive at the Great Mosque, at that hour almost deserted apart from a languid official who took my pass, instructed me to remove my shoes, and encouraged me to climb to the top of the broad minaret. Inside the great hall of prayer was cool and silent; there is no attempt at unity of design, but it has some fine woodcarving on the pulpit, said to be from Iraq, and amongst its innumerable columns, most of them looted from Roman or Byzantine ruins at Hadrumetum or Carthage, are two of particularly ornamental porphyry. From the minaret I could look over the flat roofs of the old town and the gardens which flank it on one side. Very shut-in it looked, like many towns with a long history of piety and bigotry (Damascus and Fez, for example); and its inhabitants, whose 'scowls and averted looks' were noted by an English traveller a hundred years ago, seemed, if not actually hostile, aloof and withdrawn into themselves, with little interest in the infidel stranger except as a possible source of revenue.

From Kairouan my next objective was its supplanter Mahdiya, and I therefore continued eastwards until I crossed the road which runs up the east coast of Tunisia and by a winding by-road reached the seashore by a little fishing-port. Beyond this a narrow peninsula jutted out into the shallow waters of the Mediterranean, with a village athwart its neck and the crumbling ruin of a castle visible behind it.

Mahdiya is an example – there are many in the Maghrib – of a ruler who had established a dynasty by force of arms deciding to express his personality by founding his own capital. This happened early in the tenth century as a result of a revolt against the Aghlabids stirred up by a religious propagandist called Abu Abdullah, a missionary sent out by the Ismaili sect (this is one of the subdivisions of the Shi'a division of Islam and holds that Ismail, the seventh of the Caliphs who followed Muhammad, was the last legitimate one and all who came after were usurpers; it had its centre in Salamiya, a village in eastern Syria, and its head is the Aga Khan). Arrived in the Maghrib, Abu Abdullah found the Kutama, a tribe belonging to the Sanhaja* division of the Berbers settled in the Kabylie Mountains of Eastern Algeria, receptive to his teaching, and having organized them for war he succeeded between 902 and 909 in capturing step by step all the territory of the Aghlabids; he ended by occupying Kairouan and Raqqada, an administrative centre which the Aghlabids had founded near by. Meanwhile, so the picturesque story goes, Obaidallah, a divine of unknown origin who was recognized by the Ismailis as their Mahdi, or leader, had heard of Abu Abdullah's success with the Kutama and had set out from Syria to join them, but had had to run the gauntlet

* See Note 1.

of opposition along the route stirred up by the Abbasid Caliphate, by whom he was regarded as a dangerous heretic, and
had finally (though it is not clear why) taken refuge in
Sijilmassa, a stronghold south of the Atlas Mountains of Morocco.
There in 909 Abu Abdullah came to offer him an empire, and
brought him back in triumph to Raqqada, where he founded a
new Caliphate, called Fatimid after the Prophet's daughter, and
took over the realm of the Aghlabids and the system of administration which they had elaborated in it. He won over their
former subjects, who had suffered from their over-taxation and
oppression, by promising to redress their grievances, and soon
showed himself to be a masterful and ruthless leader, executing
Abu Abdullah for trying to interfere with his plans and merci-
lessly crushing revolts of the Kutama caused by his refusal to
allow them to pillage the towns and villages of Ifriqiya, as well
as other revolts in Tripolitania and Sicily. Once having consolidated his authority, he began a series of attempts to extend
his rule to Egypt, but twice, in 915 and 920, was beaten back by
Abbasid troops. Meanwhile he had decided that Raqqada,
situated as it was in the middle of a flat plain, was entirely un-
suited to his mountaineer followers, and had sought around for
a site for a new capital which would be more easily defensible
against the opposition which he no doubt anticipated from
orthodox Islam. The peninsula now before me, the only one of
its type on the coast of Ifriqiya, on which both Phoenicians and
Romans had had small settlements, appeared to him well
placed both for defence and for the seaborne expeditions which,
having seized the Aghlabid fleet, he already had in view, and
accordingly in 912 he founded there a stronghold and called it
after the title of Mahdi which he assumed from that time.

From this base, after his failures in Egypt, he embarked on
the conquest of the rest of the Maghrib, presumably with the
idea of providing himself with a more solid backing for future
ventures, and he soon put an end to a kingdom which the schismatic Kharijites had established at Tiaret, in western Algeria;
but he then died, and his son and successor was soon faced with
a grave challenge from an extreme branch of the Kharijites, led
by another of those politico-religious figures of whom so many

appear in the history of the Maghrib, a certain Abu Yazid, known as 'The Man with the Donkey' on account of the poverty which he embraced. This man succeeded without difficulty in stirring up opposition to the Fatimid régime, which could not only be represented as heretical but had by this time shown itself to be as tyrannical as its predecessors, and his followers, aided by the local population, sacked Kairouan, but with such excesses as to arouse a reaction; so that when they besieged Mahdiya but failed to take it, Obaidallah's grandson was able to rally opposition and to recapture Kairouan, before which Abu Yazid was defeated and driven to his death from wounds in the Hodna hills of eastern Algeria. Thereafter the Fatimid fortunes varied: they lost the western Maghrib and with difficulty retained Sicily, but in 969, in the reign of the Caliph El-Moizz, a Fatimid army achieved the ambition of the founder of the dynasty by conquering Egypt, where El-Moizz founded Cairo and transferred his capital to it; so that, instead of the Maghrib being ruled by Middle Easterners, the Middle East was ruled by Berbers from the Maghrib.

A century later, a Fatimid Caliph in Cairo* brought about the second Arab invasion which caused such devastation in the Maghrib. Mahdiya was amongst the places ravaged by these 'locusts', as a contemporary writer called the Bedouin invaders, but seems to have preserved some kind of an existence for the next three hundred years, for in the twelfth century it was occupied by Roger II of Sicily in the course of his Maghrib adventure, was recaptured by another Berber dynasty, the Almohads, and in the fifteenth century became the headquarters of the Turkish corsair Dragut. In 1550, however, the Spaniards took it after a long siege, dismantled its fortifications, and evacuated it, since when it has declined to its present humble situation.

I went through the ruined castle, apparently the remains of Obaidallah's original foundation which had been refurbished by the Turks before being wrecked by the Spaniards, but although the Tunisian Department of Antiquity is expensively reconstructing it I found little of interest. I then drove to the

* See page 59.

extreme tip of the peninsula, where I sat on a rock, in a steamy haze, and looked out over the shimmering green of the sea. It was here that, in 1907, divers found the hulk of a galley which had evidently been chartered by a Roman Governor to bring home the Greek and Oriental treasures which he had collected during his period of service overseas, no doubt for the embellishment of the villa in which he proposed to spend his retirement, and the trove brought up from it fills four complete rooms of the Bardo Museum in Tunis.

I returned to the coast road and drove northwards. From here on I was in the 'Sahil', a narrow strip of fertile land lying along the coast, down to which run the valleys from the higher ground inland. This is one of the great olive-growing regions of the Maghrib, and up to 1964 much of it was farmed by Europeans, as was evident from the neatness and regularity of the plantations and from the red-roofed European villas along the roads, reminiscent rather of Provence than of North Africa. It is in fact Arab (or Berber) country with a strong French accent. I found this to be literally true when I asked the way of a man on a bicycle, for he looked blank when I tried him in French, reacted joyfully when I switched to Arabic, and answered me in what he obviously thought was Arabic – but half his words were French.

This experience illustrated one of the main differences between French and Italian methods of colonization. Libya was an Italian colony for forty years; Tunisia a French Protectorate for seventy-five. The Italians regarded Libya as a prestige symbol and a dumping-ground for surplus Piedmontese, and its indigenous population as an inferior race to be looked after, given just enough education to increase their usefulness, and then used, but always kept under; while the French, who seemed in practice to make little difference in their policy towards colonies and protectorates, tended until the last moment to regard all their North African territories as inalienable parts of France and their populations as the raw material of Frenchmen, to be taught to think and speak as much like French, and to adopt as French a way of life, as possible. Hence Tunisia (and Algeria, and Morocco) is far more French in appearance than Libya is

Italian; and whereas the Libyans show few signs of their former
Italian subjection, the peoples of the other three countries,
down to a surprisingly low level, speak intelligible French and,
in the towns at least, wear a veneer of Gallicism.

It was perhaps their very success in inculcating their culture
which caused the French, in the years following the Second
World War, so badly to miscalculate the attitude of their
North African populations towards them. Right up until 1955,
when Moroccan resistance reached a point where independence
could no longer be withheld and Tunisia was more peacefully
reaching the same position, most French officials and residents
seem genuinely to have believed that the Nationalists in the
three territories were a handful of hotheads and criminals who
commanded no real support and that the bulk of the populations
desired only to remain in perpetuity under the rule of the
French who had conferred so many benefits on them. In
Algeria, as we shall see, this attitude persisted longer and led to
stark tragedy. In Tunisia tragedy was averted, thanks to a
Nationalist who was also a statesman and who manoeuvred his
country a step at a time in independence.

I went northwards through a green countryside. The young corn
was springing in the fields between the olive-groves, and although the season was still too early for the wild flowers which
later bedeck the roadsides, there were yellow daisies everywhere,
and almond-blossom in the villages. It was hot at midday, and
I spent the noontide break under olive-trees in which cicadas
shrilled and tiny warblers were restless and vocal. An old man
driving a donkey approached, his shoes carried on his head; he
returned my salutation gravely, tied his beast to a trunk, and
without fuss lay down on his *jellaba* for his siesta.

Just north of Mahdiya, on another little promontory off the
road, lies Thapsus, where Caesar gained his decisive victory over
Pompey's General Cato, in alliance with Juba I of Numidia, in
46 B.C. To reach this battlefield Cato had performed the feat of
marching an army of fifteen cohorts across the 'gap' from
Cyrenaica, but he had wintered at Lepcis Magna *en route*. Both

he and Juba committed suicide after their defeat, which cost Numidia its independence.

I passed through Hamamet, formerly a small seaside resort with a fifteenth-century fort on the shore and a fishing-port of much charm, which is now being intensively developed as both a tourist and an artistic centre: new hotels are sprouting, and a theatre with every modern appurtenance opened with an inaugural performance of 'Othello' in Arabic in 1964. Then I cut across the base of the Cap Bon peninsula, and came through the outskirts of Tunis down to the coast, where on a cliff lies the little village of Sidi Bou Said. There, in a white hotel with a garden full of bougainvillaea and oleanders, the smell of mimosa in the air and the varied blues of the Gulf of Tunis and the open sea beyond showing through the cypresses, I could fancy myself on the Riviera – were it not that, at the foot of the steep village street, a signpost pointed to 'Carthage'.

CHAPTER 6

Carthage and Tunis

'Delenda est Carthago!' Through the centuries you can feel the menace of Cato's fulmination before the Roman Senate, which resulted not only in the end of a nation, but in the extinction of a whole way of life : for within a few years of its first utterance the story of the Carthaginians was finished. It seems, too, as though by it a curse was laid on the site; for although the Romans themselves rebuilt the razed city, and it served for another 800 years as a capital for them and for their successors the Vandals and the Byzantines, its destiny, destruction by the Arabs and relegation to the status of a quarry for building-stone, was the more tragic. Today the vast area on the hill overlooking the wonderful Gulf of Tunis, with its half-excavated but unrestored ruins of baths and theatres and villas and churches, looks derelict and forlorn. An Arab rides by on his donkey, and the wind stirs the thistles, but nothing else moves on what was once the capital of half the known world.

The year 814 B.C., or thereabouts, is the date given by the classical writers for the foundation of Carthage; but there are no real historical records of the first six centuries of its existence, and the completeness of its destruction has confounded the archaeologists. The story of its foundation is itself a legend, sufficiently familiar : of Dido, widow of a rich King of Tyre whom her brother had murdered, escaping with his treasure and a few followers and sailing the Mediterranean until she reached the Maghrib shore; of her request to the local Berbers for 'as much land as could be enclosed in a bull's hide'; of her woman's wit, when the request was unsuspectingly granted, in cutting a hide into thin strips which, tied together, could enclose a sizeable parcel of land; of her founding on this a citadel which she called 'Byrsa', meaning 'a hide'; of the arrival of Aeneas and his followers, fugitives from an (anachronistic) fall of Troy in search of a new kingdom; of Dido's surrender to his charms during a lengthy dalliance; and of her self-immolation when, in the manner of gay adventurers, he sailed away to pursue his destiny. Dido's trick with the hide might be paralleled today in the land of her descendants the Lebanese, and a hill in the middle of the site of Carthage is called Byrsa; but this Punic word also, I understand, means 'fortress', and the origin of Carthage was almost certainly more mundane: it was in fact one of a series of stations founded by the Phoenicians along the coast of the Maghrib for the purpose of servicing their Mediterranean trade-routes, which achieved paramountcy over the others because it was the best sited for defence.

The Phoenicians were as enterprising and skilled traders as the world has ever seen; to this the Old Testament, Homer, Herodotus, and Latin literature all bear witness. In every port of Greece and Egypt and Asia Minor these Levantine bagmen were familiar, and they seem to have been generally tolerated, if despised, because they were useful. But the eastern Mediterranean and its hinterlands to the north, south, and east proved quite inadequate as a field of operations for such intrepid mariners as they became, and from the second millennium B.C. their cockle-shells ranged far and wide not only in the Middle Sea itself but beyond the Straits of Gibraltar. They found that silver was being mined at Tartessus in Andalusia, and tin along the Iberian coast and in Cornwall, by miners who were ignorant of the scarcity-values which these minerals could command in the Middle East, so that it was possible to buy them cheaply and transport them to the Levant for sale at vast profit in the interior. As this, and other, trade grew, the Phoenicians began to feel the need for places along the routes where their ships could provision, water, shelter, and if necessary winter. If we are to believe Pliny, they established the first of their stations in 1101 B.C. at Utica, on what was then the west coast of the Gulf of Tunis (the site is now well inland, owing to silt brought down by the Madjarda, the main river of Tunisia), and about the same time founded another at Gades, which is now Cadiz.

Others followed along the Maghrib coast and in Sicily, Malta, and later Sardinia; the argosies multiplied; and Phoenicia, already enjoying a near-monopoly of the supply of manufactured goods to the eastern Mediterranean countries, prospered all the more. Gradually, too, trade began to develop with the Maghrib hinterland and the stations became also depots for import and export goods.

From the seventh century B.C. onwards, the position seems to have changed to the detriment of Phoenicia in two ways, one economic, one military. Greek industry suddenly improved so much that Greek manufactured goods began first to rival and then to supersede Phoenician in the markets of the eastern Mediterranean. Worse than this, Phoenicia itself was menaced by the rising power of the Assyrians from Mesopotamia, who under their Kings Sargon, Sennacherib, and Esarhaddon pressed ever more closely on Tyre, its chief city, and thus made it ever harder for the Phoenicians to support their overseas stations. Other races began to profit from their weakness. Their monopoly of trade in the western Mediterranean began to be challenged, first by the Etruscans, from Italy, and then by the Greeks; and the latter spread all along the south coast of Europe, mopping up the Phoenicians *en route*, until they were threatening to take over Tartessus and its silver; it was incidentally at about this time that the Greeks began to colonize Cyrenaica. If the Phoenicians were to preserve their trade-routes along the North African coast, which had suddenly become of vital importance since those along the European coasts might be denied to them, naval protection had to be provided for any convoy menaced by Greek corsairs; and it was in Carthage that they gradually concentrated all their naval resources outside the homeland, because, standing on a peninsula cut off from the mainland by hills and well supplied with water and good soil, it offered unique advantages for defence on a coast where natural strongholds are rare. Today one side of the peninsula has, like Utica, been silted up by the Madjarda, but from the air the strength of the position is manifest.

By 574 B.C., when Tyre was captured by Nebuchednezzar and lost its independence, the concentration was complete.

Berbers and ornamental brickwork at Tozeur, Tunisia

The Arch of Diocletian at Sufetula, Tunisia

From then on the protection of the Phoenician colonies devolved on Carthage, and the Carthaginians, although they long remained symbolically tributaries of Tyre, became a power in their own right. With their new freedom of action they began to prosper. They came to terms with the Etruscans and concluded with them an anti-Greek alliance, by virtue of which they strengthened their hold on the western Mediterranean to the point where the Greeks were totally excluded from it. It was at about this time (520 B.C.) that they expelled Dorieus and his Spartans when they tried to settle in Tripolitania. What was perhaps more important for the future was that they began to look with different eyes on the country in which they lived. Carthage hitherto had been likened to 'a ship anchored off the coast of Africa', since its purpose had been to protect the seaborne trade, rather like Gibraltar on the route to India in the nineteenth century, and any trade which it developed with the interior had been incidental. Now, however, the Carthaginians began to use their native skills to plant olives and fruit-trees in the Sahil of Tunisia and the Jefara of Tripolitania, and also to develop the trans-Saharan trade which was so greatly to benefit the Emporia in the future. They reaped the benefit of these new enterprises in the following century, when an anti-Athenian alliance which they had made with the Persians ended in disaster at Salamis and they found themselves excluded from the eastern Mediterranean as they had excluded the Greeks from the western, and they extended their occupation of the Maghrib to include most of what is now Tunisia. This, however, remained the extent of their territorial acquisitions in the Maghrib; and once an attempt which they made in 409 B.C. to conquer Sicily failed they never again held any territory in Europe. It was on the contrary Europe which became a danger to them. In 310 B.C. they fought off the invasion of Agathocles the Sicilian; but within fifty years came the far greater threat of the rising power of Rome.

Commercial rivalry was at the root of the Punic Wars which began in 262 B.C. and ended in 146 B.C. with the utter destruction of Carthage, for once Rome was consolidated and had begun to expand there was no room for two powers in the western

F

Mediterranean. The wars have been exhaustively documented and I will refer to them only in so far as they directly impinged on the Maghrib. The First, which was almost entirely fought at sea, did not, except that it was followed in the Maghrib by the mutiny of Carthaginian mercenaries which forms the subject of Flaubert's 'Salammbo'. But the Second, already colourful through the participation of Hannibal and his Moroccan elephants, ended with a Roman victory on the soil of the Maghrib, at Zama in the Madjarda Valley, in which Massinissa, the Berber King of Numidia, fought with the Romans. The Third, after Hannibal's exile and death, was brought about by an unscrupulous piece of power-politics by Rome, but is memorable for the military prowess of Scipio Aemilianus, for his engineering feat in building the mole across the gulf which completed the investment of Carthage and made possible the final assault, and for his refinement of destruction in ploughing the site with salt.

But the disappearance of the Carthaginians as a nation did not mean that they ceased to exist and influence the life of the Maghrib, and before they fade from our scene it is worth while to consider for a moment what sort of people they were and what kind of a heritage they could have left, beaing always in mind that they themselves left few records and that we are therefore dependent on the reporting, and the judgements, of their Roman enemies.

According to one of these, they were a 'hard and gloomy' people, capable of extreme cowardice when frightened and of extreme cruelty when angry, obstinate, austere, and caring little for amusements or the arts; an estimate which is no doubt distorted, but perhaps not entirely false. For the Carthaginians were certainly traders rather than warriors, and fought their wars so far as they could with Berber mercenaries – much the same troops as the Goums who under French leadership gave so good an account of themselves in the Italian campaign of the Second World War. The charge of cruelty is supported by accounts of mass human sacrifices in which they seem to have indulged, and especially the sacrifice of children to Moloch to which the numerous children's coffins in the Carthage cemetery bear witness. Their literature seems to have been negligible, and such architecture and *objets d'art* of their workmanship as have survived show no high level of achievement.

Their legacy to posterity was thus limited. But their language seems to have continued in use for many centuries after the destruction of Carthage: in the third century A.D. Septimius Severus, the African-born Emperor, had to send his sister away from Rome to her native Lepcis because she only spoke Punic and was laughed at in Roman society; and in the fifth century St. Augustine, writing to the Pope about a vacant Bishopric in the Maghrib, insisted that only candidates with a knowledge of Punic should be considered. A more fundamental legacy of theirs has been deduced from the observed fact that after the Arab conquest of the western Mediterranean their language and culture struck quicker and deeper roots in those regions where the Carthaginians had been paramount, namely Ifriqiya, Andalusia, and Sicily, than elsewhere: it is argued that this was because the Punic language is closely related to Arabic and Carthaginian culture was Oriental, so that the people of these regions were, so to speak, conditioned in advance to becoming an Arab society. So perhaps Carthage did not so much disappear as become absorbed into the society of her former empire.

It was 117 years before the Romans began to resettle and rebuild Carthage. In the meantime they were gradually extending their hegemony in the Maghrib. They had at once annexed the districts which the Carthaginians had directly administered, and had made of them a province which they called 'Africa', from a Punic root meaning 'cut off'; this presumably referred to the fact that Carthage had been 'cut off' from its motherland of Phoenicia, and the word was eventually extended to cover the whole of the continent. At first they left intact the neighbouring Berber Kingdom of Numidia (which corresponded to the rest of northern Tunisia and eastern Algeria) because its King Massinissa had helped them against Carthage, but from 107 to 104 B.C. they were compelled to wage war against Massinissa's

grandson Jugurtha, who was finally defeated and strangled
in Rome, and in 46 B.C. Caesar, after his defeat of Pompey's
forces at Thapsus, annexed Numidia because its then King
Juba I had been allied with Pompey; he called it 'Africa
Nova', the former 'Africa' becoming 'Africa Vetus'. About
30 B.C. Octavius, after his victory over Anthony at Actium, re-
constituted Numidia and placed Juba's son Juba II, who was
married to Anthony's daughter by Cleopatra, on its throne, but in
25 B.C. he transferred Juba II to Mauretania, the next territory
to the west, and incorporated Numidia and 'Africa Vetus', control of which he had in the meantime relinquished to the Senate, in a new Senatorial province called 'Africa', which included
Tripolitania (Cyrenaica was linked with Crete in another
Senatorial province); it was at this point that the Legio III
Augusta entered the scene. Carthage, the rebuilding of which
had been completed in the first century, became the capital of
'Africa'.

In A.D. 37 Caligula virtually amputated Numidia from
'Africa' by giving its military commander administrative
powers, and this step was regularized by Septimius Severus a
century and a half later; while at the end of the third century
A.D. Diocletian, in his great administrative reorganization, cut
'Africa' in two, the northern part being called Zeugitana and the
southern Byzacena. Carthage became the capital of Zeugitana;
and it also became the centre of a Christian Church which
spread through the settled parts of the Maghrib.*

In 439 it was captured by Genseric the Vandal King when he
drove out the Romans, and became his capital, but in 534 it
passed to the Byzantines and again became the capital of
Zeugitana. Its story ends in 698 with its destruction by the
Arab Commander Hassan ibn Numan.

From my base in Sidi Bou Said I ranged widely in Tunisia,
sometimes off but more often on the superb roads which are a
legacy from the French. I traversed the Tell, an undulating
region of lush pasture-land and cereal cultivation, as far as the

* See Chapter 7.

Algerian frontier, and there dreamed away a week-end in a little French hotel in a great forest of cork-oaks. I visited Bizerta, once the Phoenician station of Hippo Diarrythus, where Agathocles landed in 310 B.C. for his abortive assault on Carthage and which, rebuilt in the Middle Ages, became a special refuge for Muslims expelled from Spain; it is now the second port of Tunisia, and until 1963 was also a French naval base and a bone of Franco-Tunisian contention, but the base has been handed over and the town is the poorer. Near it, in the new industrial centre of 'Menzel Bourguiba', a British firm was erecting Tunisia's first steel-plant. I went to Beja, once the Roman colony of Vaga and the centre of so rich a grain-growing area that in the fourteenth century 'a thousand camels a day were needed to carry away the crop'; along the north coast, a region of vines and olives and citrus; and round the Cap Bon Peninsula, where in 1943 Alexander's tanks cut off the fleeing Axis forces and brought about their final capitulation, and where the quarries which supplied the stone for Carthage are still visible, with little farms of great antiquity between its rocky headlands. In the Sahil I found Sousse, the former Hadrumetum, which under Trajan was denoted the 'Colonia Ulpia Trajana Augusta Frugifera Hadrumeta' – a convincing tribute to the fertility of this strip of coastland – and which, under Diocletian's reorganization, became the capital of the southern portion of the divided Province of Africa; and Sfax, which has a charming fishing port but which for me was spoilt by the stench of a factory to windward where the phosphates from Gafsa were being turned into superphosphates.

Everywhere I found Roman remains: Bulla Regia with its subterranean villas; Thuburba Major and Maktar; Dougga, which has a theatre, some exquisite temples, and one of the few notable Phoenician remains in the country; perhaps most impressive of all, the aqueduct, I believe originally sixty miles long, which brought water to Roman Carthage and which, when I first saw its arches stretching across the plain and flushed pink in the rays of the setting sun, was a thing of beauty. The very number of these remains shows how densely the Roman Province of Africa must have been colonized; but the

most striking evidence of this is provided by the Colosseum at
Edj-Djem, the former Thysdrus, on the road from Tunis to Gabes,
which I had by-passed on my inward journey but went back to
see: excellently restored, it towers over a small mean flat-roofed
village which clings to its skirts in the middle of a bare plain,
and at its prime held 60,000 spectators, whereas you would be
hard to put it to find 600 in the vicinity today.

Tunis I found meretricious, neither Maghribi nor French. It
contains some excellent things: the thirteenth-century 'Mosque
of the Olives'; the Alaoui Museum in the Bardo, with its
glorious mosaics transferred from Roman villas, its curious
Phoenician statuettes, and the contents of the Mahdiya galley;
and the *suqs* with their store of Berber rugs, such as I had seen
made in Jerba, and its cheerful bustling crowds. But much of
the residential and business areas are bad imitations of a
French provincial town; and the beggars were a plague.

Nevertheless it is from Tunis that Tunisia must be studied: for
this country has always been dominated by cities, first Carthage,
then Kairouan and Mahdiya, and now Tunis itself. It was
founded in A.D. 698 at a critical time in the history of the
first Arab invasion of the Maghrib. In 695 the Arabs, after their
expulsion by the Berbers under Kusaila, had returned under a
new commander, Hassan ibn Numan. His beginning was in-
auspicious, for he came up against the second of the legendary
Berber figures, the Jewess known as 'El-Kohina'. This Berber
Boadicea had acquired a reputation as a sorceress amongst her
tribe, the Jerawa of the Aures Mountains of southern Algeria,
and succeeded in rallying the Berbers to such good purpose
that, with the aid of what remained of Byzantine power, they
threw Hassan back into Tripolitania. He returned in 698, eliminated the Byzantines by capturing Carthage, which he destroyed finally, and having secured the mastery of the seas by
dispersing the Byzantine fleet he founded Tunis as his new naval
base at the protected end of the gulf on which it stands. He then
turned on the Berbers, and according to Arab historians found
useful allies not only amongst individual Byzantines but also
amongst the sedentary Berbers, because El-Kohina's followers
were mostly nomads and had been making themselves un-

popular throughout the country by pillaging the farmers: this kind of nomad-sedentary friction recurs constantly in the history of the Maghrib. He conquered, and El-Kohina was killed, having first instructed her sons to take service with her conqueror – a gesture regarded as normal in a people for whom the family is of such paramount importance that its survival must be assured at any cost – and enjoined on her followers a 'scorched-earth' policy; to the latter is attributed the bareness of the country round Thysdrus (Edj-Djem), where she had her headquarters.

Then followed the period, already described, when first Kairouan and then Mahdiya were the chief towns of Ifriqiya; but then came the second Arab invasion, in which both these towns were ruined and which resulted in a century of chaos, with the interior of the country dominated by the Beni Hilal, the main constituent of the invasion, but the ports held first by a dynasty called the Zirids and later by Roger II of Sicily.

In 1159, however, the Almohads, a Berber dynasty from Morocco, who had spread across the Maghrib and mastered the Beni Hilal in the interior, put an end to the Norman hold on the coast and proceeded to govern the whole country from Marrakesh, in southern Morocco. They found, however, that from this distance they could not effectively deal with the troubles which repeatedly broke out in Ifriqiya, and in 1207 instituted in Tunis an autonomous régime which took its name, the Hafsids, from the first Governor, Abu Muhammad ibn Abu-Hafs. This dynasty was paramount in Ifriqiya for the best part of three centuries, and in 1270 managed to come to terms with a French invasion, ostensibly intended to convert the country to Christianity but with obvious commercial undertones, when its leader, the French King St. Louis, died at Carthage (an ugly neo-Byzantine cathedral dedicated to him overlooks its site today).

In the fourteenth century the Hafsids were weakened by internal dissensions and twice lost Tunis to another Berber dynasty from Morocco, the Merinids (who had succeeded the Almohads there), and although at the end of the fourteenth and beginning of the fifteenth centuries strong rulers restored the authority of the Hafsids and even extended it into Tripolitania, by the end of the fifteenth century the dynasty had decayed, the interior was again given over to the nomads, and the ports along the north coast had become lairs of pirates who preyed on Mediterranean shipping. This led to the next major episodes in the history of the Maghrib, which I shall be describing later: an incursion of the Spaniards, who put an end to the Hafsids, and then the coming of the Turks who expelled the Spaniards and assumed control.

By the end of the sixteenth century the Turks were masters of all the Maghrib except Morocco. Their authority was first vested in 'Beylerbeys' resident in Algiers, but in 1587, when the holder of that title died, they divided their possessions into the 'Regencies' of Libya, Tunisia, and Algeria, the boundaries of which have become the national frontiers of today, and installed a Pasha in each. Thereafter the Regencies developed differently.

In Tunisia the Pasha had under him an Ojaq, or militia, commanded by an Agha and divided into forty sections each commanded by a Dey, and also troops used for collecting taxes and controlling the nomads, commanded by Beys. In 1590, after a local mutiny, the Deys chose one of their number to command the militia in collaboration with the Agha, and the third such Dey relegated the Pasha to the role of a figurehead. In the next fifty years the Deys were in their turn gradually ousted by the Beys, and in 1671 the Bey Mourad secured a quasi-hereditary status for his office, the control of the Porte becoming increasingly remote and his successors becoming more and more completely identified with the country. Meanwhile Tunisia, while it stagnated like all Ottoman dominions, became fairly prosperous; piracy from its shores, though never attaining the proportions of that practised from Algiers, nevertheless became a major source of profit, as did the skills of craftsmanship or horticulture brought in during the seventeenth century by Muslim refugees from Spain, expelled under the Edict of 1609, or Jews from Leghorn.

In 1705 Husain ibn Ali, who commanded the Spahis or mounted troops, became Bey, suppressed the title of Dey, and instituted a dynasty, a step in which the Porte acquiesced by appointing him Pasha and Regent of the Province of Tunisia, with virtually absolute internal autonomy, subject only to the payment of a nominal tribute and to limitations in respect of external affairs. Despite internal troubles in the eighteenth and nineteenth centuries, Husain's descendants succeeded in remaining in power up to and through the French Protectorate, and the last of them was only deposed in 1957, after Tunisia had achieved its independence.

The French Protectorate came about in 1881, when the French, by that time heavily committed in Algeria and anxious that no other Power should establish itself in a neighbouring territory, made an incursion of Tunisian brigands into Algeria a pretext for invading Tunisia, which was occupied without resistance; and by 1883 the ruling Bey had signed conventions regularizing total French management of the country. This forward move on the part of the French had been made with the encouragement of Bismarck, who hoped by sending 'the fiery steed of French ambition caracoling in the sands of Tunis', as he put it, to divert that same ambition from any ideas of reconquering Alsace and Lorraine; but it cost France the friendship of the newly-established Italian State, which thought of Tunisia as its own preserve because of the large number of Italians, mostly Sicilians, already settled there.

Under the French wing, many more settlers, French, Spanish, and Maltese as well as Italian, bought estates in the Tell and the Sahil and their efforts enormously improved the country's economy. But as time went by the French tended more and more to treat it as a colony, and Nationalism became vocal as early as 1907. Between the two world wars it was alternately suppressed and tolerated according to the complexion of French politics at the time. During the Second World War the fighting in Tunisia prevented evolution, but directly after it French repression was resumed, and the principal Tunisian Nationalist, Habib Bourguiba, who had worked tirelessly for Tunisian autonomy and had been in and out of French prisons for years (but had rejected Italian offers of support for future Tunisian independence in return for Tunisian help for the

Axis), was constrained to carry on the struggle from Cairo. French intransigence, fostered by the French settler lobby in Paris, in fact produced a dangerous deadlock.

In 1954, however, this was broken by a show of reasonableness on the part of the Mèndés-France Government: Bourguiba was permitted to return to Tunisia, and long negotiations in Paris resulted in 1955 in a Convention providing for Tunisian autonomy. But by then this had already been outstripped by events, for almost immediately afterwards France granted Morocco, her other North African Protectorate, full independence, and Bourguiba was able to convince the French Government that Tunisia could be given no less. A new Convention providing for independence was signed in 1956, and the following year the country was declared a Republic with Bourguiba as its first President.

On my journey round the country I talked to many Tunisians, whom I found in the main intelligent, approachable (except at Kairouan), and keenly concerned with the present and the future of their country. From what they told me, and from what I learnt otherwise, a picture built up of how Tunisia had evolved since independence, and of what it was trying to do now.

Being a small and compact country, with a long tradition of settled existence and a relatively homogeneous population, and possessing in Bourguiba a leader of unrivalled shrewdness and experience, Tunisia's problems were at first economic rather than political: for it had no oil (a little has been found since), nor much in the way of minerals apart from phosphates, and its chief exportable assets were olive-oil, wine, and touristic attractions, to develop which required as much assistance as could be obtained, including credits and marketing facilities abroad. The French, who wished to retain a 'special position', and who from the first spread themselves in the matter of cultural and educational assistance, might have given economic assistance too, but in the event failed to offer more than preferential treatment for Tunisian produce in France, owing to a series of clashes in which they were involved with Tunisian Nationalism, first over Tunisian assistance to the Algerian freedom move-

ment; then over the Tunisian demand for the handing-over of
the French naval base at Bizerta, which led to actual fighting
before the United Nations ruled in Tunisia's favour and the
French found it politic to yield; and in 1964 over the expropriation of foreign agricultural land, most of it French, which
Nationalist pressures impelled Bourguiba to pronounce.

The United States, however, provided substantial aid, with
which a three-year development plan was completed, to be
followed by a five-year plan in which the Gafsa region* will
figure prominently; and the economic outlook seemed not un-
promising, the more so as tourism was showing clear signs of
rapid growth.

In the world at large Tunisia was taking an honourable
place. Her representatives had from the first proved themselves
active and capable in the United Nations and had played a
prominent role in the Organization of African States and similar bodies. Only in the Arab League, where Bourguiba was
apt to react against President Nasser's authoritarianism and to
take a line on the Palestine issue which was too moderate for
Middle Eastern tastes, was there friction; but Tunisia contrived
to keep on reasonably good terms with its North African neighbours, and no threat to its existence was perceptible. The test
of its cohesion would come when its leader had to quit the
scene; but by and large its prospects seemed to me bright –
brighter, as I was to find, than those of any other Maghribi
State.

* See page 57.

CHAPTER 7

The Legion and the Church

The road by which I left Tunisia, running south-westwards into Algeria, soon drew me back from the country's present into its past.

Not that that past was obvious in the first place to which I came, Medjez el Bab; at first sight this village looked like dozens of others on the Tell. But its roofs were of tiles instead of the usual dried mud, and this betrayed its fifteenth-century origin: for its founders had been Muslim refugees from Andalusia, who had brought their building techniques with them. As for the next place along the road, El Kef, this, with its tin-roofed stores, lorries, and petrol-pumps within its girdle of eucalyptus trees, looked even more contemporary; but it is in fact far older, for it was here that the Carthaginians after the First Punic War garrisoned the mercenaries with whom they had fought it and kept them waiting so long for their pay that they mutinied (the 'Salammbo' story) and all but overthrew Carthage before being suppressed. It was here, too, that after the Roman occupation Octavius founded the colony of Sicca Veneria (so called because on the site was a temple dedicated to some local goddess whom the Romans identified with Venus), which became of some strategic importance because it lay athwart the communications with Numidia to the west, and later became the centre of a confederation of colonies known as Cirta Nova. Just beyond it a signpost pointed to 'Sakhiet', and this recalled history of a different era, for in 1958 this small village on the Algerian frontier was heavily bombed by the French Air Force for having allegedly helped the Algerian rebels (as they were still called then), an incident which poisoned Franco-Tunisian relations for many months and provided the Algerians with invaluable propaganda material for use in the United Nations.

The road wound on through the hills of the Tell; and then I came to another village which, by contrast, wore its history on its sleeve, for it lay beside a very obvious complex of ruins. This was Haidra, and here – and for the next three days – I was in the ambit of the Legio III Augusta; for the ruins were those of Ammadaea, where in 25 B.C. the Proconsul of the Province of Africa established the first winter-quarters of the Legion after it had been placed at his disposition by Augustus. Ammadaea became a nodal point in the Roman system of strategic communications, where the *decumanus*, or east–west road, from Gabes, already mentioned, met a *cardo*, or north-south road, coming down from Carthage and going through to the next camp, Theveste. Here, too, at the end of the second century A.D., Septimius Severus founded a colony of veterans (*limitanei*), so that the most prominent of the ruins is a triumphal arch dedicated to him; but Ammadaea still had some military importance in the Byzantine epoch, and the best-preserved of its other ruins – a capitol, a theatre, and many others – are Byzantine.

About A.D. 75 Vespasian transferred the headquarters of the Legion from Ammadaea to Theveste, and this was my next objective. To reach it I had to cross the frontier into Algeria, which I accomplished after one and a half hours of delay and frustration; my car was the only one on the road, but lack of traffic seemed merely to have convinced both sets of officials that anyone travelling that way must *ipso facto* be an undesirable character. But once clear, my way took me through leagues of meadows which the wild mallow had transformed into sheets of mauve; and I came soon to a fair-sized town which looked as if it was bursting out of the massive Byzantine ramparts encircling it on two sides. This was Tebessa, as Theveste is now called, and here, from an alleged hotel which set a new low standard for the journey, I went out to see what remained of the former stronghold.

Theveste was important not only as a headquarters of the Legion, which in fact it seems to have been for only a few years, before someone, probably Trajan, decided to move it to Lambaesis: in addition it was for nearly two centuries an integral part of the *limes*, which until Septimius Severus moved them farther south came up from Capsa (Gafsa) in the south-east and went on westwards; it lay on a main trunk-road from Carthage through Ammadaea (the road along which I had just come); from it other roads went westwards to Thamugadi and Lambaesis and north-westwards to hit the coast between Bône and Phillippeville; and under Trajan another veterans' colony was founded here. Later it was sacked, but not destroyed, by the Vandals; and in A.D. 535, after the Byzantine take-over, a famous General, Soloman, rebuilt its fortifications and endowed it with the great rampart which is still so prominent.

Incidentally the achievement of the Byzantines in the Maghrib was very great. In Cyrene, Lepcis Magna, here in Theveste, and in many other places they have left solid constructions which had often made imaginative use of existing resources and which demonstrated their determination to rule. It is sad that their ardour should have been so soon dissipated, so that they lost their empire to a harder, tougher, but also far less civilized race from the desert.

In Theveste, however, it was not so much their ramparts which impressed me, nor even a fine arch dedicated to Septimius Severus's son Caracalla which forms the gateway to where the citadel once was, as a fourth-century Christian basilica which I found half a mile outside the town within a locked enclosure. When I arrived and shook the gate, a silent Arab materialized out of space, admitted me, and locked me in, so that for the next hour I was alone in this enchanting place. Its white stone walls rose from a floor of grass, strewn with blocks, and the close surrounding it was a carpet of mallow, edged with flame marigolds, golden hawkweed, crimson vetch, and flowers of a dozen other colours. At one end was a formal garden, and everywhere were beds and sarcophagi full of purple and white irises. I found chancel and transepts and side chapels, monks' cells and galleries, and in one corner fifty stalls and mangers of the same period, where the devout could feed their animals during services. Beyond the walls of the close were fields in which cattle grazed; and the only sound was the song of multitudinous birds.

I have spoken of Christianity in Cyrenaica. The quite separate form which flourished between Tripolitania and the Atlantic until well after the Arab conquest, to which the intriguing name of 'The Lost Church of Carthage' has been given, seems to have been introduced through the ports some time in the first century, and took root in Carthage, which was always its centre. Its liturgy must initially have been Greek, but its preachers and writers seem by the late second century to have turned over to Latin, and as some of them were of high quality their contribution to the spread of Christianity, by making its teachings available in the world-language of the day, must have been considerable. It suffered much persecution: Septimius Severus is alleged to have proscribed both Jewish proselytism and Christian propaganda, and there are heroic stories of Christians suffering martyrdom either for refusing on pacifist principle to perform military service or, like St. Perpetua, a housewife of Tebessa itself who with her family and slaves was thrown to the lions in the Carthage amphitheatre in 203, for refusing to deny their faith. But it also produced some renowned figures, like Tertullian, the theologian and propagandist, who was a Berber born in Carthage in the second century, and Cyprian, also Carthage-born, who was mainly responsible for organizing the Church on firm foundations but was executed by the Proconsul in 258, in pursuance of another persecution ordered by the Emperor Valerian, and subsequently canonized.

Early in the third century the first African Ecclesiastical Council, attended by seventy-one Bishops from the Provinces of Africa and Numidia, was held in Carthage, but fifty years later yet another persecution, this time ordered by Diocletian, caused a serious schism, that of the Donatists: these were the followers of Donat, a Bishop in Numidia, who had accused the regularly elected Bishop of Carthage, Cecilian, and his predecessor, of having betrayed Christianity by handing over sacred books and papers to the persecutors. They were a fanatical sect, allegedly prone to hasten their arrival in Paradise by indulging in mass suicide or otherwise procuring their own deaths; and the success which their movement enjoyed during the years to come suggested that their habits must have appealed to some trait in the Berber character.

Constantine, when he succeeded Diocletian, issued an Edict of Milan ending the persecution of heretics, and took the part of Cecilian against the Donatists. This did not, however, work out well, for during the fourth century the Romans found themselves confronted with three separate sources of disorder: one was the Donatists, whom the Catholics had taken advantage of Roman support to persecute; another was Firmus, a disgruntled Berber chieftain from the Kabylie mountains, who with his followers was in revolt; and the third was the Circoncelliones (which means 'prowlers round farms'): these were sedentary Berbers carrying on class warfare against the Roman landed proprietors, whose oppression of the peasantry, and insistence on concentrating production on olive oil, which could be profitably exported, instead of on cereals which the people could eat, had caused intolerable economic distress. Roman attempts to suppress these last two revolts merely drove the rebels into the arms of the Donatists, whose following became so strong that it was not until 395, when Augustine (the future Saint) became Bishop of his native Hippo (Bône, in Algeria) that the Church and the civil power, in close alliance, were able to organize effective resistance to the forces of schism and disorder. In 410 the Emperor Theodosius proclaimed freedom of religion, a measure which might have seemed to regularize the position of the Donatists, but it was quickly countered by Augustine's action in convening a Council in Carthage which was so heavily weighted in Catholic favour that it ended by ordering the Donatists to return to orthodoxy under pain of confiscation of their property and other sanctions. The order was followed by a renewed repression of Donatists, which largely stamped out the movement but left a legacy of smouldering hatred against the Catholics; this was to break out into flame after the Vandal occupation.

The Vandals when they took over at once began to persecute the Catholics because they themselves were supporters of the heretical Arian Church. In 484 they convened another Ecclesiastical Council which was as heavily weighted in favour of the Arians as, seventy years previously, Augustine's Council had been weighted in favour of the Catholics; its outcome was an edict by the Vandal King Hunseric which reproduced almost

Punic monument at Maktar, Tunisia

Timgad from the back of the theatre, Algeria
Roman mosaic at Volubilis, Morocco

word for word Augustine's anti-Donatist measures, this time directed against the Catholics, and this was followed by a persecution which was perhaps the worst that the Church of Carthage had ever suffered.

Then came a complete reversal of fortune, for the Vandals were expelled from the Maghrib by the Byzantine Emperor Justinian, whose burning desire it was to restore the Catholic Church to its primacy and who accordingly encouraged it to persecute not only the Arians but also the Jews and what remained of the Donatists. But this was its high point. Within ten years its leaders had fallen out with Justinian and been sanctioned, and in the next century it was racked with schisms.

Then came the Arab conquest, under the impact of which the Church of Carthage wilted rapidly. It took long to expire: even up to the twelfth century Christian Churches seem to have survived in several towns, but then the central Maghrib was conquered by the Almohads, fanatical Muslim Unitarians, and under their régime North African Christianity became extinct. Its inability to resist had been due partly to its own disunity, but more to its lack of support amongst the Berbers, in whose eyes it was overmuch identified with their Roman oppressors.

North of Tebessa, in the region of Ouenza and on both sides of the Algero-Tunisian frontier, lie the iron, lead, and tin-mines which produce much of the mineral wealth of both countries. I did not visit them, but instead turned west across the Algerian Tell in search of three Roman settlements once intimately linked with Thebeste and with each other: Mascula (now Khenchela), Thamugadi (now Timgad), and Lambaesis (now Lambesa). All were developed towards the end of the first century A.D., and a glance at the map will show why. This was the time when Rome, having taken over Numidia a century earlier and encouraged development of its arid northern plains, found herself obliged, in order to fulfil her evident duty of defending the farmers and settlers under her wing, to extend her *limes* towards the south, whence raiding Berbers might

G

come; and these three posts commanded the outlets from the
Aures *massif*, the haunts of particularly rapacious tribes. Accordingly the headquarters of the Legion were transferred
to Lambaesis, and Mascula and Thamugadi developed with
it into a fortified system whence control over intruders from the
Aures could be promptly exercised. All three were destroyed,
like the other Roman fortified points, by the Vandals, but
in the eighth century were restored by Justinian, only to be
destroyed again, partly by Berbers as Byzantium weakened,
finally by Arabs after their seventh-century conquest of the
Maghrib.

Their ruins have suffered different fates. Those of Mascula
have almost disappeared. Beside the present village of Lambesa,
overlooked by a frowning penitentiary, Lambaesis still dis-
plays a magnificent Praetorium, or headquarters building,
in which are a series of mess-rooms each marked with the rank
of the men using it, and a theatre, baths and an arch of
(once again) Septimius Severus. But those of Timgad, as I
saw them on a perfect spring afternoon in their setting of
green fields, almost rivalled Lepcis Magna in beauty, if not in
size.

Timgad was fortunate. Until 1881, when the French began
to excavate it, the ruins were so deeply embedded in sand and
debris that they had escaped the usual fate of ruins, of being
plundered for building-stone; and although much has been destroyed by time, by fire, and by earthquake, enough remains,
admirably restored as it has been, to present a living picture of
an important garrison town in this Roman colony. As at Lepcis, the back of the theatre provides the best viewpoint whence
to take in the design of the original rectangularly-planned city;
the *decumanus maximus*, bordered by rows of columns and with the
ruts of the chariot-wheels on its paving; the two transverse
cardos; Trajan's triumphal arch; the Capitol, where two tall
columns have been re-erected (and a stork was sitting on her nest
on the top of a broken third); the broad forum, with the plinths
of its statues still in place; the Catholic and Donatist Churches;
the foundations of the six sets of public baths and of innumerable villas; the market with its little shops – so like those of any

suq today – and their stone slabs for counters. I had the whole vast area to myself, and could linger or move on as I pleased.

I moved on that evening to Batna, a graceless rectangular town which seemed unique, in this land of antiquities, in having no history before 1844: for it had begun its life as a camp for a French expeditionary force pushing southwards to subdue the Aures and the desert beyond, and had subsequently been developed into the headquarters of a garrison. Now that the French Army had gone it looked shabby and down-at-heel, and the accommodation I found in it was on a par with its appearance, so that I was thankful to escape next day into the Aures and for the first time on this journey to find myself amongst high mountains.

The Aures *massif* rises to 7,500 feet, and its inhabitants the Chaouia, like those of all the most rugged parts of the Maghrib, are Berber-speaking and of almost unmixed Berber stock. They are also exceptionally tough. Throughout history they recur, always untameable, turbulent, and predatory: under Tacfarinas revolting against the Romans and forcing them to set up a screen of Legion posts to contain them; under their chieftainess El-Kohina throwing the invading Arabs out of their country; being a thorn in the side of the Turks; and rebelling so effectively against the French that twice, in 1849 and 1850, Aures oases were razed as a punishment. There can be no surprise that it was in the Aures, on November 1st 1954, that the rebellion began which, eight years later, was to drive the French from Algeria; nor that since independence the region has given trouble more than once.

My road was beautiful. It wound through ravines of spectacular rock scenery, and valleys with forest-covered peaks above and almonds in blossom round the rare farms below. It threaded its way at length through a narrow defile with precipitous walls, a gateway in a line of cliffs, which according to a Roman legend was kicked open by Hercules; the Arabs call it 'The Mouth of the Sahara', which is apt, for on its farther side the scenery changes abruptly from the mountains and the cultivation of the Aures valleys to the bare red rolling plains of

the region known as the Zab, where there is little rain but much
subsoil water, so that date-palms flourish but nomadism has
always been the way of life. It grew hotter, and dust-clouds
blew across my path as I approached a line of low hills; I crossed
a col, and before me the land stretched away to a distant horizon.

In the foreground were the walls and minarets of a town, set
in an immense palm-grove. It was Biskra, the capital of the
Zab, and here I had reached the farthest limit of Roman colonization, when in the third century A.D. their *limes* had been
pushed southwards so that they ran along the natural geographical division between the desert and the nomads to the
south, and the sown and the settlers, to the north. Vascera, as
they called it, was an important post, commanding the southern
exit from the Aures and situated on a main road which came
down from the north, round the western side of the Aures, and
went south into the Sahara, until it joined another main road
leading across to Kano.

But its importance in Roman times is not the only claim to
fame of this oasis. More decisive in the history of the Maghrib
was A.D. 683, when Oqba ibn Nafi, the Arab founder of Kairouan, was defeated and killed by the Berber hero Kusaila in a
battle rendered famous by Oqba's exhortation to his troops
'Break your sheaths, for your swords will never return to them'.
His tomb lies some twenty miles away, in a tiny village named
after him; I found it behind a carved wooden door in a primitive mosque with a squat minaret, of a pattern peculiar to the
villages fringing the Sahara, on its roof. In the Middle Ages
Biskra was occupied in succession by each of the Berber dynasties who had achieved paramountcy at the time, including the
Hafsids, whom we met at Madhiya, and the Merinids, whose
acquaintance we have still to make. The Turks, when they
occupied the coast, found it of sufficient strategic importance to
justify the installation of a garrison, and the French did the
same in the middle of last century, both adopting the same pro-
cedure of playing off the local tribes against each other in order
to ease their maintenance. In this century it became a favourite
resort of those who flee the northern winter, and Clare Sheridan,
the sculptress, long made it her home.

Today it looked hot, dusty, and almost repellent; but, as at Gabes, I found the surrounding palm-grove a place of gently rustling fronds and bird-song, in which white-clad peasants laboured unhurriedly and chanted in minor keys; and towards evening the lighting effects on the hills round about, those amethysts, mauves, purples, and finally indigoes which you seem to find only in the vicinity of deserts, explained the spell which the place has set on so many.

I returned to Batna by a road which wound through the heart of the Aures in a continuous series of whorls and was more of an Advanced Driving Test than a scenic wonder. I came out near Lambaesis, which I revisited; an owl was sitting on the arch, and proved to be for me, as it would have been for the Romans, an evil omen: for sitting in my car outside reading the guide-book (which seemed a sufficiently innocent occupation), I was sharply challenged by a motor-cyclist gendarme who, when I could not produce my car-papers which I had left in Batna, rudely directed me to follow him to the Batna police-station; and once there I was told by an even ruder superior that my offence in not having my papers with me was grave, that I must leave my car-keys on his table and proceed on foot to retrieve the papers from my hotel; and that even if they were in order (which he made clear he thought unlikely) I should be fined a substantial sum to teach me to respect the law. Indignation lent me eloquence with which to talk myself out of the fine and to give the police some ideas on the treatment of tourists, but I was glad to quit Batna at the earliest possible moment and could bear with fortitude the thought of never seeing it again.

CHAPTER 8

Constantine and the Kabylies

I went northwards, skirting a region of pasture and salt-marshes in which the Madjarda, the river which silted up Utica and Carthage, rises. Beyond it appeared on the horizon the walls and towers of a considerable town, crowning a precipice: this was Constantine, the second town of Algeria and the former capital of Numidia.

It must always have been a centre of power, for it is difficult to imagine a site better adapted to the needs of defence in the pre-cannon era. The original settlement, and the main part of the modern town, are perched on a lozenge of rock, of which three sides are sheer and have deep stream-beds along their feet, and the fourth is joined to the land outside by a narrow isthmus of rock which is also precipitous on both sides.

Under the name of Cirta, it first emerges just before the Second Punic War as one of two capitals of a band of territory running from the Moulouya River, near the Algero-Moroccan frontier, on the west, to the region which Carthage administered, on the east. This territory was shared between two Berber tribes ruled at this time by Kings named Syphax and Massinissa, the former of whom had married a Carthaginian wife, Sophonisbe, was allied to Carthage, and by virtue of this alliance had occupied most of Massinissa's territory. When Scipio landed in the Maghrib to attack Carthage, Massinissa, who had made a temporary alliance with Carthage, deserted to the Romans in the middle of the battle, as a result of which the Romans routed and slaughtered both the Carthaginians and Syphax's men. They then allowed Massinissa to enter ahead of them into Syphax's capital of Cirta, where he fell in love with Sophonisbe and went through a form of marriage with her, but on being told by the Romans that he must either give her up or renounce the Kingship of Numidia, he ungallantly chose the former and induced her to poison herself (the episode has inspired more than one dramatist). He thus became the master of all Numidia, and with the support of Rome held this position until his death in 148 B.C.

His successor Micipsa, not a forceful character, was content to carry on the development of Numidia which Massinissa had begun, under the aegis of Rome; but on his death thirty years later his throne was usurped by an illegitimate nephew, Jugurtha, whose rebelliousness made him a major headache for the Romans and who was finally suppressed after a three-year campaign. A confused period followed during which Numidia was divided between various conflicting chieftains, with Rome apparently mainly concerned to keep it in being as a buffer State between their Province of Africa and the tribes of the far-western Maghrib. In 46 B.C. it was, as we have seen, annexed by Rome and in 25 B.C. incorporated into the enlarged Province of Africa; and in the first century A.D. Cirta became the head of a consortium of four colonies, the other three being what are now Collo, Phillippeville, and Mila.

About A.D. 313 Cirta took the name which it has borne ever since when Constantine reunited the two halves into which Numidia had been divided in Diocletian's reorganization, and under the Byzantines it became a provincial capital. Through the centuries which followed the Arab conquest it was, like Biskra, occupied in succession by each of the dominant Berber dynasties. The Turks when they took over also made it a provincial capital, and its Bey was the only one of the three provincial Governors to offer serious resistance to the French when they invaded Algeria in 1830, so that Constantine was not finally brought under French control until 1848.

Since then it has grown in size, but without, I suspect, changing the essential independence of character which it has always borne; even a casual stroll through its crowded streets is sufficient to demonstrate that its people are in their own conviction not merely as good as, but definitely better than, the stranger within their gates.

Between Constantine and the Mediterranean coast lies the Petite Kabylie, the smaller of the two coastal ranges, extensions

of the Atlas Mountains of Morocco, which fill the whole of
northern Algeria from Phillippeville to just east of Algiers. This
range was the home of the Kutama tribe who, in the tenth century performed the remarkable exploit of conquering Egypt
under the leadership of the Fatimid El-Moizz; like the Aures it is
a Berber-speaking region into which neither the Arabs nor any
other overlords of the Maghrib made any permanent penetration. I decided to traverse it from Bône, the most easterly port
of Algeria, so on leaving Constantine I drove for a few miles
along the former Roman road which led back towards Tebessa,
and then, turning off it to the north-east, came to the coast
through the foothills of the Petite Kabylie. Along the latter part
of the road traces of Roman remains every few miles testified
to the density of the Roman colonization of Numidia, but it
would be wearisome to catalogue them all. Bône itself, beautifully situated on the side of a wooded mountain, is a busy port
through which most of the iron ore from Ouenza is shipped, and
its main street hums with activity. Two miles to its south are the
ruins of its ancestor Hippo Regius, on a site overgrown with the
jujube trees which give the place its Arabic name of Annaba:
for these trees, a species of zizyphus, have a fleshy fruit which
the Arabs liken to grapes and call by the same name, *'ainab.*

Between them Hippo Regius and Bône have a lengthy history. The former was a Phoenician station which according to
some authorities antedates Carthage; it became a favourite resort of Massinissa and the other Berber Kings of Numidia, was
annexed with the rest of Numidia by Caesar, and was a thriving Roman settlement until sacked by the Vandals. Its chief
claim to fame during this period was that it was the birthplace
of St. Augustine, who became its Bishop and died during the
Vandal attack on the town of which he, the arch-opponent of the
Arians whom they supported, was a main target. From that
time onwards Bône, which takes its name from a local holy
woman, Lella Bona, seems to have replaced Hippo. A Christian
community survived in it until at least the eleventh century, for
two letters dated 1076 from Pope Gregory VII, one to this
community and one to the local Berber chief, have been preserved. Like most neighbouring ports, it was occupied by Roger

II of Sicily and later by the Spaniards, until the Turks took over. The present town is modern, but at Hippo Regis the foundations of Augustine's Basilica have been discovered, and there are a number of Roman ruins, including those of baths dedicated – once again – to Septimius Severus.

East of Bône lies the cork-oak country which I had visited from Tunis, badly damaged on this side of the Tunisian frontier by clearances made by the French when they tried to prevent Algerian forces trained in Tunisia from infiltrating back into Algeria by building a wire fence along the frontier and patrolling it with helicopters. The road which runs westward from Bône passes close to a dried-up lake, Fetzara, now a rich grazing area, and then bends northwards to Phillippeville, which as Rusticade was one of the four colonies composing the Roman Confederation of Cirta and was the port of Cirta itself. Unlike Bône, it was spared by the Vandals in their first inrush because its Christianity was Donatist and therefore more akin to their Arianism than St. Augustine's forthright Catholicism. It was, however, destroyed by the Arabs and only revived after the French occupation, when its new name was taken from the then ruling French King. In 1914 both it and Bône had the distinction of being shelled by the famous German cruisers *Goeben* and *Breslau* when they broke through the Royal Navy's cordon and, by reaching Istanbul and thence shelling Odessa, involved Turkey in the First World War on the side of the Triple Alliance.

Phillippeville today is an ugly port. In 1960 I had landed there with my car from Tunis, the Tunisians having forbidden me to drive over the frontier into Algeria because they did not wish me to see what they were doing on their side to help the Algerian rebels; and it was on my arrival here that I realized for the first time how far the heads of the French in Algeria were still in the sand over the extent of the Algerian revolution and their chances of suppressing it. Over dinner they explained to me in detail how the rebels, a Communist- or Nasser-financed minority commanding no local support, were on the point of being finally routed; and a swarthy individual, introduced as an Algerian Deputy, was eloquent on the theme that the Algerian people only wished to remain permanently under French rule – but would have carried more conviction had I not discovered that he was married to a Frenchwoman and spoke no word of Arabic. Just two years later the French signed the agreements which gave Algeria its independence.

This time I by-passed Phillippeville and entered the Kabylie proper, a lovely jumble of steep hills, forests, and cultivated valleys. The road cuts across the base of the peninsula on which stands Collo, formerly, as Chullu, the second colony of the Cirta Confederation, and having joined the main road coming up from Constantine debouches on to the coast again just east of Djidjelli. For the next sixty miles thereafter it is a Riviera-like Corniche, which twists and turns round headlands and through tunnels, with high cliffs on one side and the Mediterranean on the other.

Djidjelli is the only town along this stretch, and beautifully situated it is, amongst the finest oak-forests in Algeria. It too began life as a Phoenician station, under the euphonious name of Igilgili, and had three moments of prominence in its history: one in 1134, when it was bombarded by Roger II of Sicily before he occupied Jerba and Mahdiya; one in 1514, when it became the first capital of the notorious corsairs Aruj and Khaireddin Barbarossa before they occupied all the central Maghrib on behalf of the Porte; and one in 1664, when the French became so incensed with corsair attacks on their shipping from Maghrib ports that, having bombarded Algiers without succeeding in abating the nuisance, they landed an expeditionary force at Djidjelli, only to find that it could make no headway against the Turks, with whom the Kabylie tribes made common cause, and was being decimated by fever, so that it had to be taken off again with heavy loss.

Time pressed, and I had to leave this glorious piece of wooded coastline. I turned inland along a winding secondary road, and after a tiring drive came at last to another of my main objectives, a cluster of ruins on a rocky spur ringed round by a horseshoe of hills and on terraces down the sides of it. This was Jemila, which under the name of Cuicul became an important Roman colony in the first century A.D., but, after a fairly tranquil four centuries of existence, was so completely destroyed by the Vandals that it never recovered. It has been magnificently restored, like Lepcis and Timgad; and it must rank after these as the third most impressive ruin in the Maghrib.

Being well inland, its form invites comparison with Timgad rather than with Lepcis; but whereas Timgad is built on a flat plain which allowed expansion in any direction and could therefore assume the rectangular form in which the Romans delighted, Jemila's somewhat curious site on a comparatively narrow spur with steep sides limited lateral expansion to what could be done by terracing; thus whilst the north-south *Cardo Maximus* runs from end to end of it, there is only room for two short *decumani* at right angles to it. The family of the almost inevitable Septimius Severus are well in evidence: the great temple, one of the finest in the Maghrib with its high perron, is dedicated to them, and the triumphal arch which dominates the Forum honours Septimius's son Caracalla. There is a good theatre, which could seat 3,000, and a market with stalls and a central pagoda, rather reminiscent of Lepcis, which according to an inscription on it was given to the town by one L. Cosinius I, apparently a rich merchant who held most municipal offices and eventually became High Priest. To the south-east of the main town is a Christian quarter, built later than the rest and often with materials taken from the ruins of earlier constructions, with an excellent circular Baptistery and two Basilicas, one of them built by the local Bishop to commemorate the 'Reunification of the Catholics and the Donatists'; this must have been soon after Augustine's manipulated Council of Carthage, and sounds a little like a tiger commemorating his unification with a goat. Perhaps the most notable relic is a mosaic taken from a villa, now in the little local museum; it is a 'Toilet of Venus' and is memorable even amongst all the fine mosaics which the Romans have bequeathed to us in the Maghrib and which adorn in particular the Tunis and Algiers Museums.

Again I had the ruins to myself, apart from some Bedouin children from a neighbouring black-tented encampment who tried to sell me Roman coins, and for hours I could enjoy the sheen of the sun on golden stone and the clean feel of the wind blowing over this upland place, so far from human habitation today.

I went on southwards, to arrive that night at Sétif, a shoddy contrast to the loveliness of the past two days, for although, as Sitifis, it was a Roman colony and the capital of one of the two halves into which Diocletian divided the province of Mauretania Caesariana – Numidia's western neighbour – it is today merely another dreary product of nineteenth-century French colonial construction. But here took place two decisive historical events. One was in 1152, when the Beni Hilal Arabs were totally defeated by the Berber Sultan Abdul Mumin and their hold on the central Maghrib permanently broken; the other in 1945, when it was the scene of a riot which seems in retrospect to have been a direct cause of the Muslim revolt which ended in Algeria securing its independence. The consequences of the latter were so far-reaching for the Algeria of today that its background is worth describing here.

The end of the Second World War found the Algerian Muslims more restive than at any time since the French had completed their pacification of the country a century earlier. The war and Allied occupation, combined with the complete suspension of trade with France, had dislocated the economy and caused bitter local distress; while the defeat of France, and the influx of Americans with their built-in anti-colonial prejudices, had had the inevitable effects of both weakening respect for the ruling Power and intensifying Nationalist sentiments and the Muslims' sense of grievance (to which I shall be reverting later). In this atmosphere a parade was held in Sétif on VE day during which a group of Muslims took the opportunity to shout, apparently quite good-humouredly, Nationalist slogans, and a policeman lost his head and fired on them. It was the spark which set alight the tinder of Muslim resentment and caused a disproportionate conflagration. Muslims ran amok and killed or wounded some eighty Europeans; in revenge, the French military authorities, using not only the Foreign Legion but also their deeply hated Senegalese troops and abetted by settler Vigilante organizations, indulged in what seems to have been an unbridled massacre of Muslims in the Constantine and Kabylie regions, while naval units bombarded coastal villages and aircraft strafed settlements. Estimates of the number of dead varied wildly, from the French official figure of 1,005 to those of Cy Sulzberger, the New York journalist (18,000) and the Muslims' (40,000 to 50,000); but what is certain is that from this moment the majority of Muslim political leaders became openly revolutionary, working not for an accommodation with the French, or even for any association with France, but for complete independence from her. Wartime security arrangements, still in force, enabled the French to keep the affair from the ears of the outside world, but it was known, and embroidered, throughout the Arab countries and set in train a series of events which could have only one outcome in the world of today.

When I turned northwards again from Sétif towards Bougie on the coast, I left behind me a region known as the Hodna, consisting of a deep depression, along which the Roman *limes* coming up from Vascera formerly ran, and on its northern side a range of hills which form part of the southern fringe of the Tell. In these hills lies a ruin which I was not able to visit (and of which I believe little is visible anyhow), called the Qala'at (castle) Beni Hammad. This place is closely linked with Bougie, and with another site which was somewhere in the mountains almost due south of Algiers, called Ashir, because the three were all at some time capitals of two linked Berber dynasties, the Zirids and the Beni Hammadids, who between them dominated the central Maghrib in the tenth and eleventh centuries and the coastal region even longer.

The Zirids belonged to the Sanhaja group of Berber tribes, which were situated both in the Kabylies and in the extreme south of Morocco. The founder of the dynasty, Ziri ibn Manad, came from Ashir and had rendered valuable service to the Fatimid Caliph by raising the siege of Mahdiya when it was on the point of being taken by 'The Man with the Donkey'. As a reward, the Caliph made his son Bolouggin ibn Ziri Governor of the Maghrib when, in 973, he transferred his capital to Egypt.

Bolouggin at first ruled in the Caliph's name from Mansuriya, his administrative centre alongside Kairouan, but he was given such wide powers by the Caliph that he assumed the title of 'Sultan' and, in the manner of successful rulers already noted, founded a new capital for himself at his native Ashir. In 1014 his brother Hammad broke away from him and made his own capital at Qala'at Beni Hammad in the Hodna (apparently in the place where the Man with the Donkey had been finished off fifty years before); and as the Zirids failed in two attempts to capture it, they and the Hammadids thenceforth ruled different parts of the country simultaneously. The Qala'at, according to such descriptions of it as have survived, was a notable piece of Arab-style architecture.

Meanwhile Bolouggin had been prospering. Acting in the name of the Caliph, he had captured the two important centres of Tlemsen and Tiaret in western Algeria and had made two fairly successful expeditions into Morocco, as a result of which the Caliph also made him Governor of Tripolitania. But his son Mansur, when he succeeded him, began to chafe under the Fatimid yoke and showed signs of rebellion, with the result that he found himself faced with two successive revolts of the Kutamas of the Petite Kabylie, evidently stirred up by the Fatimid against him, and had to suppress them; and Mansur's son El-Moizz, as we have seen, broke away altogether, and by so doing brought upon the Maghrib the second Arab invasion, that of the Beni Hilal and the Beni Sulaim. In the face of this danger, the Zirids evacuated Kairouan, which the Beni Hilal sacked, and Mansuriya, and took refuge in Mahdiya, where in 1146 Roger II of Sicily put an end to the dynasty.

The Hammadids lasted longer. They had initially escaped the fate of the Zirids by buying off the Beni Hilal, but nevertheless found the Qala'at Beni Hammad too exposed to the marauding nomads who were now dominating the interior, and transferred their capital to Bougie. Here they were able to rule unmolested, and an Arab historian who visited Bougie later in the century found that they had developed trade with West Africa and across the Sahara and were enjoying not only material prosperity but also intellectual progress, the town being full of doctors, lawyers, poets and divines – though it was also, in his ascetic view, a sink of loose morals. The twelfth century found the Hammadids still ruling from Bougie along the coast as far as Jerba, and westwards as far as the border of Morocco; but their time was running out, for in 1151 the Almohads from Morocco by a sudden onslaught captured both Bougie and the Qala'at and put an end to this dynasty also.

My road to Bougie was an ancient trade-route which led through the Grand Kabylie, the main coastal range, by the so-called Iron Gates, a ravine so obviously designed for guerrillas that it was no surprise to learn of the difficulties which the French had had in keeping it open during the rebellion. Bougie itself, when I reached it, proved to be, like Bône, delightfully situated on the side of a hill, with orchards and vineyards covering its open flank. Augustus had founded a colony called Saldae on the site, but otherwise it seems to have had little importance until it became the Hammadid capital. After the extinction of that dynasty it was constantly being involved in the interminable dynastic squabbles of the thirteenth and fourteenth centuries between the Hafsids from Tunis, the Abdul Wadids from Tlemsen in western Algeria, and the Merinids from Morocco; it was briefly occupied early in the sixteenth century by the Spaniards, and then by Charles V; but its trade was ruined by the Turkish occupation later in the century and it was only after the French occupation that the town began to recover.

My own visit brought me the acquaintance of an English missionary who had lived for thirty-five years amongst the Kabyls and spoke their language perfectly. His reputation amongst them stood so high that even in the worst moments of the rebellion, of which the ever-turbulent tribesmen were spearheads, he was never molested. Independence had decimated his little congregation and increased his isolation, but he and his wife were carrying on uncomplainingly and doing such good as they could.

I was now on the last lap of my journey to Algiers, which took me through the heart of the Grande Kabylie by way of that admirably-named village Tizi-Ouzou. It was a magnificent drive, much of the way through trees of the most varied, oak, ash, juniper, carob, olive, fig. The people I passed were equally varied, long- and broad-headed, tall and short, dark and fair, but were evidently all Berbers of entirely unmixed race, for here no conqueror had ever settled. Traditionally the Kabyls had always governed themselves through municipal councils under a headman, but the French in order to strengthen their authority changed the system by appointing the headmen from outside, and the independent Algerian Government, equally determined to establish a unified and centrally controlled régime, is perpetuating the idea. But it is difficult to imagine any method of administration which will tame these individualists in their wild and remote country.

CHAPTER 9

Algiers and the French

I came out of the mountains on to the coastal plain, and forced my way through teeming traffic and interminable suburbs into the centre of the metropolis itself. Thence, by a complicated network of steeply rising roads up the hill behind the port, I reached a hospitable house from which I could look down through conifers to the sea far below and, in the days that followed, penetrate into most parts of this beautifully situated, sprawling hotch-potch of styles and races which is Algiers, from the solid European-built commercial quarter by the quays, to the hillsides of ornate villas in their grounds and the evil-smelling Qasba, the original Berber town, with its *suqs* and brothels and variegated humanity.

A Roman settlement, Icosium, underlies Algiers, but hardly a trace of it remains and the Arab historians loftily ignore its existence. For them the founder of the city was Bolouggin ibn Ziri, which seems reasonable, for this great leader, having made his capital at Ashir about 974, no doubt felt the need for a port and was attracted by the possibilities presented by the string of islands off the coast, the 'Al-Jazair' from which Algiers takes its name. Its growth seems to have been fairly rapid, for within a century another Arab traveller was commenting on its prosperity. But then, early in the sixteenth century, the course of its history was changed by a series of events already touched on in connection with Tripoli, Mahdiya, and Tunis, but now to be described, namely the Spanish invasion of the Maghrib, followed by the Turkish occupation of it.

These events began in 1492 with the capture by the Spaniards of Granada, the last Arab kingdom on the Iberian Peninsula, and the consequent arrival in the Maghrib of a body of Muslim refugees who brought with them valuable resources and skills,

H

but also a venomous hatred of the Christians with whom, in their view, they had tried to live in peace only to be rewarded by unprovoked aggression and expulsion from their homes. From this time on piracy in the Mediterranean, which had long been prevalent – and of which the Christian Powers were far from guiltless – was intensified by the activities of what came to be known as the 'Barbary Corsairs', operating from North African ports. Resentment at their depredations combined in the mind of Ferdinand the Catholic, who sat on the throne of Spain, with a crusading spirit already woken in it by Cardinal Ximenes, that arch-enemy of Islam, and perhaps also with visions of plunder; so that he formed the resolve both to rid the seas of these pests and to convert their homeland to Christianity. Accordingly in 1509 and 1510 Spanish forces landed at and captured in succession Oran, Algiers, Bougie, Tripoli, and a string of other ports.

At Algiers the invaders, under Pedro Navarro, built a fort on one of the offshore islands and settled down to govern the town. Their Christian rule was, however, by no means to the liking of the predominantly Muslim population, who in 1516 appealed for deliverance to the brothers Barbarossa, Turkish corsairs of Albanian origin, who had made themselves a name by aiding Muslim refugees to escape from Spain and were already established at Djidjelli. The brothers were only too glad to extend their operations, and soon recaptured Algiers from the Spaniards, who however managed to hang on to their island fort. Two years later Aruj Barbarossa was killed in conflict with the Spaniards and the future of the foothold which the brothers had secured in the Maghrib seemed in jeopardy; but at this juncture Khaireddin, who had succeeded his brother, took the shrewd, and momentous, decision to make formal submission to the Sultan of Turkey, thus obtaining Turkish military backing without having to suffer any real control. From then onwards the Turks gradually extended their authority in the Maghrib at the expense of the Spaniards. The fort off Algiers fell in 1529; in 1541 an expedition under the famous Genoese Admiral, Andrea Doria, sent to Algiers by Charles V, failed to capture the town and was then wrecked in a storm with heavy loss of life; and by the middle of the century the Spaniards had virtually abandoned their ambitions.

During the next three centuries Algiers, with an improved port and fortifications, became a hive of commercial activity, in which local Arabs and Berbers mingled with Greeks, Jews, Sicilians, Maltese, and Levantines of all kinds. The wealth which flowed into it came partly from legitimate trade, but more from the cargoes of ships taken by the corsairs of which Algiers had now become the main centre, and the ransoms of their crews.

For, from the European point of view, the installation of the Turks in the Maghrib which had come about as a direct result of the Spanish adventure had greatly worsened the situation to which that adventure had been designed to put an end. The Turks, themselves freebooters by instinct, had soon seen the profits to be found in piracy and had more than condoned it, so that the corsairs operating from the ports under their control could be more accurately described as 'privateers', the definition of which is 'vessels owned or manned by private persons, but furnished with the authority of their Government to carry on hostilities against the shipping of States with which their own is at war'; and the Corsairs' Corporation in Algiers became an influential quasi-official body, which incidentally numbered amongst its members a high proportion of European renegades, some of them ex-slaves, others free men, but all attracted by the opportunities for rapid self-enrichment.

The European Powers were in no position to take moral exception to privateering, which Drake and Hawkins had developed in the Spanish Main and which many of them had long practised in the Mediterranean; in the eighteenth century, for example, the Knights of St. John in Malta seem to have preyed on Muslim shipping no less than the Turks on Christian, to judge from their reported holding of 10,000 Muslim slaves in 1720, and the 2,000 whom Napoleon released when he captured the island in 1798. But the Turks carried the practice a stage further by evolving their 'protection money' racket, under which they threatened Powers trading in the Mediterranean with a declaration of war, and the consequent exposure of their shipping to privateer attacks, unless they bought immunity for it; and this led to constant friction, for the embryo international law and the loose diplomatic arrangements of those days provided ample loopholes for extortion or chicanery in its operation. The American reaction in Libya described on page 13 above was only one of many expressions of foreign resentment during the next three centuries: Algiers was bombarded by the British on three separate occasions in the seventeenth century, and again attacked by them in 1820, while the French, Spanish, and Dutch – as well as the Americans – took forcible action at various times between the seventeenth and nineteenth centuries. These unco-ordinated efforts did little good; but during this period the Europeans gradually developed a superiority in sea-power which compelled the Turks to limit their aggressions, and the number of slaves in Algiers diminished correspondingly. The process became complete with the French occupation of Algiers in 1830.

Meanwhile, the Turks had organized their dominion in the Maghrib in their own fashion. After their division of the country into the three 'Regencies' of Libya, Tunisia, and Algeria (they never occupied Morocco) after 1587, they further divided Algeria into four provinces, those of Algiers, Constantine, Medea, and Oran. The office of Pasha, the original title of their representative, was soon supplanted first by that of Agha and then by that of Dey, the latter ruling the province of Algiers and having Beys under him in charge of the other three provinces. The position of the Deys, of whom there were twenty-three in succession, eventually approximated to that of the President of an oligarchic republic, for they had their own Ministers for Foreign Affairs and of War, Marine, and the Interior – the last-named being also Treasurer – and exchanged diplomatic representatives with several other countries, including Great Britain. They did not, however, become to any great extent identified with the country, as their colleagues in Tunisia did, but remained always aliens; and despite the wealth to be found in Algiers the interior of the country was undoubtedly as backward and poverty-stricken as every other part of the Ottoman Empire. The French, when they decided in 1830 to invade it, were under the impression that they would be welcomed as deliverers by the bulk of the people.

This belief was, however, wholly mistaken because it failed to take account of the particular character of the Berber-Arab people, who had never effectively resisted the Turkish assumption of control over them and for whom this control had one priceless advantage: it had left them alone to operate their own tribal customs and to live their own lives with a minimum of interference. The Turks were, in the first place, co-religionaries who, with the infinite tolerance of the Islamic faith, were prepared to respect the numerous special rites and deviations of the Berber form of that religion. Again, the Turks did not colonize, nor impose more than a minimum of officials, ruling almost exclusively through locally recruited personnel; and the conscription which made them greatly hated in the Middle Eastern territories of their Empire seems to have had no counterpart in the Maghrib; so that the Turkish role was in effect confined to keeping order, collecting taxes, and self-enrichment. The Turks did nothing for economic development, social services, or education, and their officials and Janissaries were shamelessly corrupt and grasping; but in the eyes of the local population these drawbacks were compensated by their non-interference. The Arabs and Berbers were not sorry to see the Turks go; but had they had the choice they would certainly have preferred them to stay rather than to be obliged to submit to new, infidel, and far more vigorous masters, especially had they known that the French occupation would result in many of them losing their lands.

The French occupation, which in the long run was to cost France so dear after bringing her so much profit, came about almost by chance. Its immediate cause is usually held to be the insult offered by the Dey of Algiers to the French Consul, for having not only failed to induce his Government to settle up for some quantities of wheat bought by them from two Algerian Jews but also maintained that to ask for payment would be 'a waste of time'. The Dey's account of the affair alleges that the Consul added some gratuitous remarks about the Islamic faith which infuriated him; be that as it may, he seems undoubtedly to have struck the Consul with a fly-whisk. What is less certain is whether the blow was the direct cause of the subsequent French intervention, for it was in fact three years before the French got around to collecting an expeditionary force, and it can hardly have been coincidence that the moment which they chose to launch it was when their Government, that of Charles X, was in the doldrums and badly needed some distraction to divert popular attention from its own shortcomings. In any event, the French disembarked without any clear idea of what Algeria was like or of what they proposed to do in it.

Within a few days of their initial landing at Sidi Farrukh, near Algiers (where the Americans also landed in 1942), they had swept aside the Janissaries, the militia which formed the only force at the Dey's command, and had received the submission of Algiers and of two out of three of the provincial Beys; and the French Commander, Marshal Louis de Bourmont, hazarded the opinion that the whole country would submit within a fortnight. He was wrong: Turkish resistance had been overborne (except in the Province of Constantine), but local resistance was only beginning. Three weeks later a French column thirty miles inland from Algiers was wiped out by Berber partisans; and then came the 'July Revolution' in Paris, which resulted in part of the expeditionary force being recalled to France and in doubts as to whether the rest would follow or stay. The decision to stay arrived; but the new French Government had no idea what to do with Algeria, and discussed seven alternative solutions, of which only one involved direct administration, all the others being based on evacuation on varying conditions. Clinching arguments for staying may have been provided by the discovery that the contents of the Dey's treasury had paid for the whole cost of the expedition and left a profit of seven million francs, and also by optimistic reports which filtered back to Paris about the economic potential of the country. In the meantime, however, the French military authorities in Algeria had made a series of mistakes, such as the appointment to municipal office of notoriously corrupt Jewish and Moroccan merchants (probably because they spoke French, an attribute to which French colonial administrators have always tended to attach exaggerated importance) and the execution of notables to whom protection had allegedly been promised; and the effect of these mistakes on a truculent people, already racially and religiously opposed to the alien and infidel invader, was profound. Within a year, at Mascara in western Algeria, the Muslims revolted and rallied behind Abdul Kader, a young man of good family who had made the pilgrimage to Mecca and was also a natural leader, and began to preach the *jihad* or Holy War against the French.

Abdul Kader's declared object was to organize Algeria on a national basis, with a central administration, a regular army supported by local levies, and the country divided into provinces which would have their own officials to collect taxes and dispense justice. He found more enthusiasm for resistance to the French than for his proposed organization, which ran too much counter to the independence of the Berbers and their parochial, or at best tribal, loyalties. But the French had little stomach for a prolonged campaign, and in 1834 made a vaguely-worded agreement with him, the purport of which was to set up a French Protectorate over the country whilst recognizing his sovereignty. This, however, only lasted a year before guerrilla warfare was resumed, and the French, having suffered a series of reverses, decided to make peace with Abdul Kader and appointed a bluff soldier, General Bugeaud, to negotiate it. The Treaty of Tafna, signed in 1837, granted Abdul Kader the Province of Oran and the ports of Arzew and Mostaganem, all in the west, and the French then attacked and conquered the only province which had not yet submitted, that of Constantine, and reluctantly began to administer it directly. But the irrepressible Abdul Kader tired of this situation and began operations anew, harassing the French settlers who had already installed themselves in the fertile Mitija Plain, inland from Algiers; and a conference of Muslim representatives which he convened at his capital at Bu Khersha pledged unity in defence of their liberties. In 1841 the French Government decided that he must be crushed and entrusted the task to General Bugeaud. The resulting war was brutal on both sides, and dragged on for six years before, in 1847, Abdul Kader gave in and was sent to honourable exile in Damascus. There were subsequent rebellions, two of which, in the Aures in 1849 and 1850, led to the razing of Berber villages already noted, and two others, in the Kabylies in 1857 and 1871, were also serious, the second of them spreading southwards as far as the desert oases and keeping the French forces at bay before being finally suppressed; but from 1848 onwards French possession of the country was unchallenged.

The French Government's change of policy which led to the complete occupation of Algeria was at least partly due to the speed with which French settlers had followed the flag. Land speculation had begun almost from the time of the first landings, and in the Mitija Plain in particular the French had acquired land from Muslims by methods which were even less scrupulous than those practised in other colonial territories. During the long struggle with Abdul Kader settlers were often murdered or driven out, but on the other hand Muslims tended to drift to the west where he ruled, so that by the end of the war good land was to be had in abundance, not to speak of the areas which French methods of agriculture rendered cultivable where the Muslims had not deemed them worth working. Between 1845 and 1853 the number of settlers increased from 46,000 to 140,000, and the lands round Algiers were almost entirely in French hands, with such of their former owners as had not moved elsewhere working for the Europeans as hired labourers.

From then onwards immigration into Algeria not only increased in volume but changed in character. The flood of newcomers which raised the European population to 781,000 by 1912 and to 960,000 by 1948 was by no means entirely composed of French agriculturalists. A high proportion were Spaniards, Italians, Greeks, Maltese, and other Mediterranean peoples, and a still higher proportion were soldiers, shopkeepers, political deportees, and artisans of all sorts, who found in Algeria either a refuge or a land of opportunity. To all of

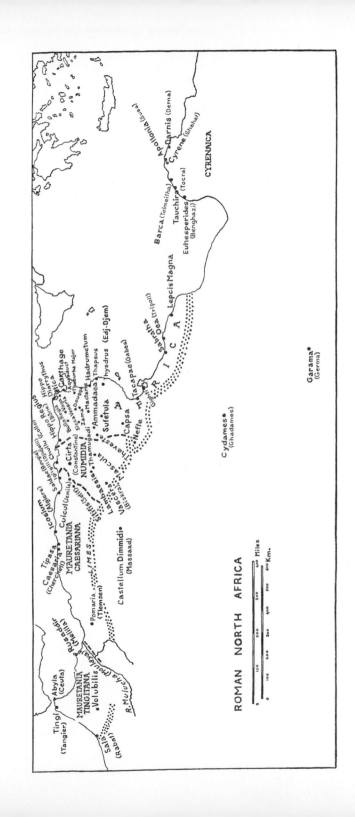

ROMAN NORTH AFRICA

Tingi (Tangier)
Abyla (Ceuta)
Rusaddir (Melilla)
MAURETANIA TINGITANA
Volubilis (Ksar Faraoun)
Sala (Rabat)
R. Muluc (Moulouya)

Tipasa
Cassaria (Cherchel)
Caesarea (Algiers)
MAURETANIA CAESARIANA
Icosium (Algiers)
Pomaria (Tlemsen)
Cuicul (Jemila)
Sitifis (Sétif)
Castellum Dimmidi (Messaad)
L I M E S

Rusicade (Philippeville)
Saldae (Bougie)
Hippo Regius (Bône)
Thibilis (Collo)
Hippo Diarrhytus
Utica
Carthage
Sicca Veneria (Le Kef)
Dougga
Thuburbo Major
Ammaedara
Hadrumetum
Thapsus
Thysdrus (Edj-Djem)
Cirta (Constantine)
Bulla Regia
Zama
Mactar
Sufetula
Capsa
NUMIDIA
Lambaesis
Thamugadi
Theveste
Vescera (Biskra)
Nefte
A F R I C A
Gigthis
Tacapae (Gabès)
Sabratha
Oea (Tripoli)
Lepcis Magna

Cydames (Ghadames)

Garama (Germa)

Euhesperides (Benghazi)
Tauchira (Tocra)
Barca (Tolmeitha)
Cyrene (Shahat)
Apollonia (Susa)
Darnis (Derna)
CYRENAICA

Miles
0   100   200   300   400
0   100   200   300   400   500   600   Km.

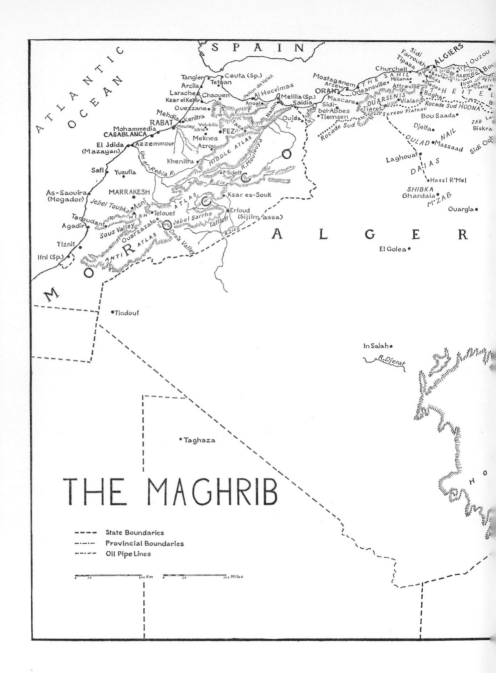

THE MAGHRIB

- - - - - State Boundaries
- · - · - Provincial Boundaries
- · · - · · Oil Pipe Lines

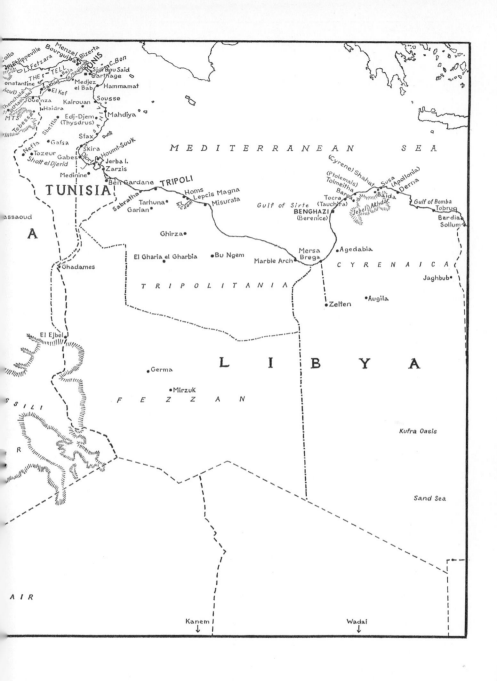

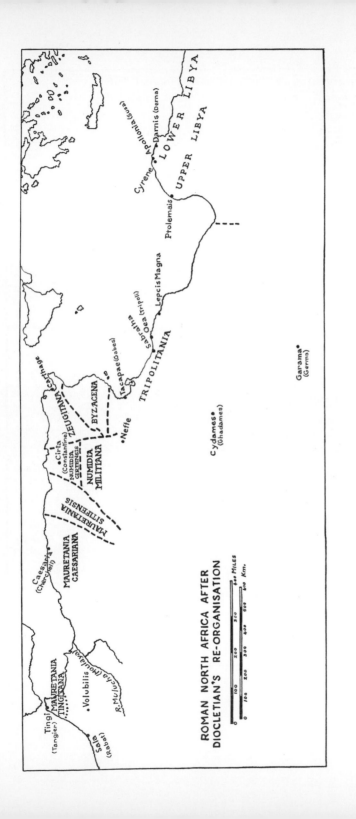

ROMAN NORTH AFRICA AFTER
DIOCLETIAN'S RE-ORGANISATION

LOWER LIBYA

UPPER LIBYA

Cyrene
Apollonia (Susa)
Darnis (derna)

Ptolemais

Lepcis Magna

Sabratha
Oea (tripoli)

TRIPOLITANIA

Garama
(Germa)

Cydames
(Ghadames)

Tacapae (Gabes)

BYZACENA

Nefte

ZEUGITANA

Carthage

Cirta
(Constantine)
NUMIDIA
CIRTENSIS

NUMIDIA
MILITANA

MAURETANIA
SITIFENSIS

MAURETANIA
CAESARIANA

Caesaria
(Cherchell)

MAURETANIA
TINGITANA

Tingi
(Tangier)

Volubilis

R. Mulucha (Moulouya)

Sala
(Rabat)

MILES
0   100   200   300   400

Km.
0   100   200   300   400   500   600

them, as to the Algerian Jews, the French Government granted French citizenship unconditionally, whereas Muslims could acquire it only by surrendering their right to be judged by their own religious courts in matters of personal status, a sacrifice which no reasonably devout Muslim was prepared to make.

Between 1830 and 1939 French methods of administering the country underwent many changes. Initially their régime was military, the country being divided into the three Provinces of Algiers, Oran, and Constantine and the Muslims being dealt with by their own chiefs under the close supervision of the 'Service des Bureaux Arabes', an organization staffed by officers who had made a special study of the country and its people. Under the Second Republic, this system was retained for the Muslims, but civil departments headed by a Préfet were created in each province to deal with the settlers. Under Napoleon III the French 'Senatus Consultus' in 1865 indicated that Algeria had been annexed to the French Crown and that all Algerians were thenceforward French subjects, but it did not make them French citizens and they had no political rights.

In 1870 the French Government under Thiers instituted a civil administration in Algeria in a form which in essence endured until 1947. The scope of the civil departments was extended, and the provinces were subdivided between 'Communes de Plein Exercise', in which the settlers were numerous and which were administered, as in France, by a Mayor (always French) and a Municipal Council, and 'Communes Mixtes', which were situated in the poorer parts of the country, mostly to the south, and had a minority of settlers: these were directly administered by a French official responsible to the Governor-General in Algiers through the Préfet of his province, assisted by a corps of local officials and by Municipal Councils, the members of which were nominated by the Préfet. Under this diarchic system the powers of the Governor-General, though they varied at different times, gradually became far-reaching in all fields and the administration was centralized – over-centralized as it eventually proved – in Algiers. Up to 1900 the

civil departments were controlled by the corresponding Minis-
try in Paris, but then Algeria was granted administrative and
financial autonomy, its budget being voted by Financial Delegations in which the Muslims had a one-third representation
and in the election of which, as from 1919, they could partici-
pate. But their status remained otherwise unchanged; even as
late as 1936 a proposal known as 'The Blum-Violette Reforms',
which would have increased their opportunities to acquire
French citizenship without having to surrender their rights of
personal status, had to be shelved in the face of a threatened
revolt of all the French Mayors of Algeria.

During the century which preceded the Second World War
the material condition of Algeria improved enormously. Agricultural development, mining of the country's not inconsiderable
supplies of iron-ore and other minerals, and the establishment
of light industries, all combined to increase its wealth. The
French administration provided law and order, a network of
excellent roads, railways, education, and at least the beginnings
of the medical and other social services which under the Turks
had been completely lacking. The Algerians benefited accordingly, and those prepared to forego their rights of personal
status and join their fortunes to the French could even acquire
wealth and some influence. Many tens of thousands of them,
too, were able to gain the livelihood which their own country
could not afford them by emigrating, temporarily or permanently, to France, where they became an essential part of the
labour force and whence their remittances became an essential
part of the economy of Algeria and especially of its poorer
regions.

But from the 1930's, and especially after 1946, the contention
of the Muslim Nationalists who had begun to emerge, that the
country was being run solely for the benefit of France and the
French settlers, had an uncomfortable ring of truth. The
settlers' lobby in Paris had become politically influential, and
through it the settlers could obtain such advantages as Government subsidies and preferential tariff-rates, and could block
industrial development, which they feared might raise wage-
levels, on the grounds that the existing levels, which they them-

selves were keeping unjustifiably low, would enable Algerian products to compete 'unfairly' with French. They could also ensure that Algerian agriculture was developed on lines which benefited themselves, and their business associates in France, rather than the people of the country: a notable example of this was wine, the vines for which took up a disproportionate acreage of the agricultural land, for the Muslims do not drink it but 95 per cent of it was exported to be sold cheaply to the French Army and other interests in France. (A similar grievance in the fourth century had produced the 'Circoncelliones'.)*

Another Muslim grievance was the 'Commune Mixte' system, or rather its shortcomings. In contrast to the overweighted central administration, the Service des Bureaux Arabes suffered from a chronic shortage of trained officers, so that many of the remoter districts were entrusted to French-nominated officials under no effective supervision, who were thus free to indulge in petty tyranny and corruption. In some purely Berber areas like the Kabylies the very presence of these officials was an offence because it ran directly counter to local custom.

More dangerous than the Muslim resentment thus created was the effect of the land-policy of the French administration. A law promulgated in 1865 by the 'Senatus Consultus' in Paris, which remained in force, had abolished tribal land ownership in favour of individual holdings, and the resulting fragmentation of the former tribal lands worked entirely in favour of the French settler, or land speculator, who had the ready money with which to tempt needy or improvident Berber smallholders. A landless class of former peasants was thus created, whose only recourses were either to drift into the towns or to work for their supplanters, and the pressures thus created were enhanced by the very success of the French medical services in reducing infant mortality and thus increasing the population. The employer or settler found this type of labour shiftless, lazy, unreliable, and potentially dangerous if not firmly kept under; yet little else could have been expected of men who had been

* See page 86.

deprived, or had seen their parents deprived, of their birth-right.

Against these practical resentments, the lack of a voice in the affairs of the country at first counted for comparatively little with the majority; but the first stirrings of political consciousness, brusquely repressed though they were, could not be stifled. They occurred soon after the First World War, and received a powerful impulse during the Second, by the fall of France and the arrival of American forces in Algeria. General de Gaulle, who as President of the French National Committee set up in Algiers in 1942 spent two years in the country, did not fail to observe the symptoms; but the remedies which he was able to carry through were inadequate, consisting as they did only of Ordinances extending the categories of Muslims permitted to acquire French citizenship without loss of personal status rights, and allowing the Muslims to elect fifteen Deputies and seven Senators to the French Assembly. In 1947 a more far-reaching reform was proposed, in the form of a Statute which for the first time included the conception of the 'integration' of Algeria with France; the Statute also created an Algerian Assembly of 120 members, half of them elected by a College composed of male Muslims who had acquired French citizenship (the so-called 'assimilés') and Europeans, the other half by a College composed of non-assimilated male Muslims; merged the Communes Mixtes with the Communes de Plein Exercise; gave Muslims the right to acquire French citizenship without renouncing their rights of personal status; and reaffirmed assurances, first given in 1832, about non-interference with the Islamic religion and the teaching of Arabic in schools. The Statute was voted in the French Assembly by a narrow majority, and Liberals hoped that it would solve the problem of Algeria's future by removing the major Muslim grievances and satisfying at least some of their aspirations.

The hope was forlorn. The Muslim sense of injury over past French policy and actions, and the differences of culture, language, and above all religion, between them and the Europeans, were too deep to be bridged by legislation, even had the

Algerian French been wholeheartedly determined to make the reforms work. But they were not: the vast majority were unshakeably convinced that, as was taught in their schools, 'Algeria was French', and that the Muslims were inherently inferior and must therefore be ruled in perpetuity by France – or rather by themselves. Moreover the incorrigible habit of the French administration of relying on obsequious French-speaking 'assimilés' (such as the Deputy whom I had met in Phillippeville), who were hated by the local population and whose advice was invariably coloured by the desire to say what would please, resulted in even those officials whose duty it was to know the people being often, and sometimes ludicrously, out of touch with Muslim feeling.

Thus the Statute was never applied. The provisions regarding the teaching of Arabic remained a dead letter. Worse, the elections for the new Assembly, in a desperate attempt to ensure the return of a docile body free from any taint of Nationalism, were so blatantly rigged as to embitter the Nationalists and to destroy any faith they may have had in the electoral system, so long as the French were able to operate it without supervision. As for the general state of the country, an official report published in 1955 stated that 90 per cent of its wealth was in the hands of 10 per cent of its inhabitants (the Europeans); that a million Algerians were unemployed and two million seriously under-employed; that the average yearly income of the Muslims was £45 per head in the towns and £16 per head in the country districts; and that 75 per cent of the Muslims were illiterate.

The revolt which broke out in 1954 was in such circumstances inevitable. Its simultaneous flare-up in several places, followed by the wide distribution of an inflammatory pamphlet, suggested careful planning, but it did not become countrywide until 1956. By that time Algeria's neighbours Morocco and Tunisia had become independent and were supporting the rebels, at first clandestinely but later openly after the French military had committed the folly of intercepting an aeroplane in which five Algerian leaders, including Ben Bella the future President, were flying to a meeting in Tunis with King Muhammad V

of Morocco (whose guests they were) and President Bourguiba, and imprisoning them. French suppressive measures
were at first accompanied by some attempts at liberalization,
but apart from the creation of a corps of officers (the S.A.S.)
intended to serve as District Officers in the remoter areas and
thus to remedy the shortage of French administrators, these
efforts were mostly blocked by settler intransigence; in any
case, Soustelle, the Governor-General, was soon converted by
evidence of Muslim atrocities against Europeans to an anti-
Muslim attitude which resulted in his becoming, after his replacement in 1955, the Paris mouthpiece of the extremist settler
viewpoint. With this encouragement, the settlers became increasingly violent, and in January 1956 they succeeded by a
noisy demonstration against the new Governor-General, the
venerable General Catroux, whom they suspected of overmuch
sympathy with the Muslims, in frightening the Socialist French
Government into cancelling his appointment.

His successor, Lacoste, gave *carte blanche* to the French military to 'restore order', and from then onwards the revolt
entered into its most acute, and most hopeless, phase. The
Front de Libération Nationale (F.L.N.), as the rebels by that
time called themselves, were operating on the classic guerrilla
lines of ambush, murder, and sabotage; they were gradually
arming themselves with captured weapons and with supplies
received from Egypt and other sympathizers, and at first derived
great benefit from the use of Tunisian and Moroccan territory,
both as a refuge from pursuit and as training grounds for their
recruits. Against them the French forces, originally 50,000
strong, were successively reinforced until they reached a figure
of nearly 500,000 – a greater number, as de Gaulle had occasion
to remind them later, than Napoleon had needed to conquer
Europe – and they used any and every method to stamp out
opposition. They could defeat the F.L.N. in the field whenever
they could bring them to battle, and succeeded in cutting off
most of their reinforcements by their helicopter-patrolled fences
along the frontiers; and they dealt with the civilian population
by systematically 'scorching' areas known to be, or suspected
of being, sympathetic to the F.L.N., herding their populations

into internment camps in conditions which brought a steady stream of appeals from charitable societies in the British Press, and according to reliable evidence resorting to the torture of captives and of civilians accused of helping, or even of possessing information about, the F.L.N.

But their best efforts were inadequate. When I passed through Algeria in 1960, few organized F.L.N. forces were operating, but terror reigned in many country regions, the Kabylie and Aures regions were almost entirely out of French control, and incidents, mainly bomb-throwing, were occurring every few days in most of the towns. The situation was in fact another example of the powerlessness of an army, however efficient and ruthless, to prevail against a rebellion which enjoys at least the tacit support of the local population.

Meanwhile world opinion was beginning to become aware of it. As early as September 1958 the F.L.N. leaders in Tunis had set up a 'Provisional Government of the Algerian Republic' (G.P.R.A.), which had been fully recognized by Red China and several Afro-Asian States, and later by the U.S.S.R. and Yugoslavia. The United Nations Assembly had, on the application of the Afro-Asians with the usual Iron Curtain backing, inscribed the 'Algerian question' on its agenda, and despite a French refusal to discuss the matter the United States and other friends of France were beginning to express disquiet.

It is ironic that de Gaulle, who was brought to power on May 13th, 1958, by a *coup d'état* staged by the French military leaders in Algeria because they saw in him the one leader who could be trusted to give them the firmness of policy and the support which they thought would enable them to 'suppress the revolt', was in fact the one French political leader possessed of both the acumen to perceive that the French position in Algeria was untenable and was costing her more, in terms of both money and world esteem, than she could afford, and the authority to induce the French people to accept the inevitable. He was helped by the fact that opinion in Metropolitan France was already wearying of the cost of the Algerian 'war'; and once a referendum had confirmed his position he proceeded step by step, making skilful use of his gift of ambiguity of phrase, to liquidate the commitment.

He began by announcing the so-called 'Constantine Plan' for increased industrialization of Algeria, designed to create work for 400,000 more Algerians and thus, it was hoped, to soak up potential F.L.N. recruits. This, as he probably expected, proved a failure; but it had not gone unnoticed that his announcement had avoided the use of the phrase 'Algérie Française', which was the settlers' watchword, and had included a passage which could be read as a hint of possible self-determination for Algeria. This latter principle he formally enunciated in a major speech in September 1959, which offered the Algerians internationally supervised elections (to meet the distrust which previous rigging had created) and the choice between complete separation from France, complete integration with her, or an independent federal-type government closely linked with her in the fields of economy and education as well as in foreign affairs and defence. The speech roused furious settler hostility and much military resentment, but de Gaulle stood firm and in January 1960 coolly mastered a serious European revolt in Algiers. In June 1960 an initial attempt at unofficial talks between French and F.L.N. delegations broke down owing to mutual distrust, and when in December of that year de Gaulle visited Algeria he was met with hostile European demonstrations and Nationalist counter-demonstrations by the Muslims, the strength of which latter showed how firm a hold the F.L.N. now had over the population as a whole.

After some preliminary sparring, Franco-Algerian negotiations were resumed in May 1961, and went on intermittently for nine months. A referendum had already given de Gaulle a mandate to negotiate with the F.L.N. on the basis that there would be an Algerian State of their own choosing, and he brushed aside another, and this time wholly abortive, attempt at a coup by a group of French officers in Algiers. With the Algerians, difficulties centred on three points. The first, which had to be cleared before the talks could start, was F.L.N. insistence that they alone should represent the Algerians, thus excluding a formerly important rival party, the Mouvement

National Algerian (M.N.A.), to which a high proportion of the Algerian workers in France belonged but which later faded out. The second was the status of the Saharan province of Algeria, which the French had previously incorporated in the 'Organization Communale des Regions Sahariennes, (an administrative grouping of all the Saharan territories formerly, or still, in French possession); they sought to exclude this from the scope of the negotiations in the hopes of being able to retain exclusive control over the oil-production which, begun by a French group in 1953, was already bringing in substantial revenues and would obviously bring more in the future. The third difficulty was the desire of the French to retain military forces and bases on Algerian soil and nuclear testing-grounds in the Sahara.

On the first two of the difficulties, the French found it necessary to let the F.L.N. have their way; over the oil, it was agreed that the Algerian Sahara should form part of independent Algeria but that for six years there should be joint Franco-Algerian exploitation of its resources, with provision for review thereafter. (It was first reviewed in 1965.) On the bases, the Algerians finally agreed that France might under certain conditions keep her naval base at Oran for fifteen years, troops and nuclear sites at selected places in the Sahara, and landing-rights at certain aerodromes, but that all other French forces and bases should be evacuated. Agreement was reached at Evian in February 1962, to take effect the following July, and a cease-fire was proclaimed in March.

The next few months were critical and bloody, for an extremist settler organization, the 'Secret Army' (O.A.S.), committed a series of outrages against both Muslims and Europeans, apparently hoping to stampede the Muslims into reprisals and the French Government into re-intervention; on the other hand, in many of the out-districts Muslim terrorist gangs were ranging unchecked. But the F.L.N. rapidly established control in the towns and as a result the Muslims bore the O.A.S. outrages with exemplary discipline, while order was gradually restored in the more open districts. As the time for independence drew near, there was a mass exodus of the French

1

residents, who abandoned houses, estates, vineyards, factories, and even cars in a frenzied rush to save themselves, and as much of their effects as they could transport, from the revenge which they were convinced the Muslims would wreak the moment the French troops left: in fact it never took place.

Thus ended 132 years of French occupation, and the French attempt to turn Algeria into part of France and the Algerians into second-class (latterly, almost first-class) French citizens. In retrospect, it could never have succeeded, at least in the present-day world climate. Once a Nationalist spirit had arisen in Algeria, the French had three alternatives. One, repression, was tried and, inevitably, failed. Another, assimilation, was equally ruled out by the profound differences between the French and the Algerians which I have already noted. The third, partnership, has not really worked anywhere yet, and in Algeria was vitiated from the start by the resentments aroused by previous French policies and actions and by the support which the Nationalists could now command in the United Nations and elsewhere. So the French had to go, retaining – or developing – such economic and cultural links as they could. They could take pride, as we British have had to do in far larger areas, in having endowed their former subjects with a rich heritage.

Nevertheless the new Algerian Government was faced with as difficult a task as can ever have confronted an inexperienced team. The departure of the French had denuded the country of the majority not only of its trained administrators (a legitimate criticism of French colonial administration is that it failed to train its subjects adequately or to give them responsibility sufficiently quickly), but also of its doctors, lawyers and technicians of every sort. The security situation was bad in the countryside, especially in permanent trouble-spots like the Kabylies, where during the long years of struggle against the French the local F.L.N. commanders had been in the habit of operating independently and at first saw no reason to defer to a body in far-off Algiers which throughout the fighting had been outside the country and whose authority and competence remained to be demonstrated. The abandoned French houses had been grabbed by individuals, and their agricultural and industrial enterprises taken over by committees of their former employees, of varying degrees of competence, so that production was threatening to nose-dive. Something like 200,000 Algerians had taken refuge in Tunisia or Morocco, and another 485,000 were in the French Army's segregation centres; all of these had somehow to be returned to their homes, which as often as not they found damaged or destroyed in the French 'scorched earth' operations, while everywhere agriculture had inevitably been neglected. Finally, in the face of these and innumerable other problems, the Algerian leaders were by no means a harmonious body; those who had first come into prominence had been found too 'moderate' and had been superseded by the group who had concluded the Evian Agreements, but these in their turn were under fire from Ben Bella, perhaps the most forceful character of them all, who had been in French prisons (after his kidnapping in 1956) until after the agreements had been signed and had returned full of criticisms of their shortcomings.

A tumultuous period followed, during which the French Government proved themselves commendably scrupulous in carrying out the terms of the Evian Agreements and helpful in providing badly-needed financial and economic aid; so that in the minds of the Algerians a distinction gradually arose between the French, who might be their friends provided that they did not attempt to exert, or rather reassert, any form of pressure or control, and the Algerian French (or *pieds-noirs*), of whom they wished to see no more. By the time of my next arrival, twenty-one months after independence, a certain amount had been done to restore the situation. Apart from sporadic outbreaks in the mountains, the country was orderly; most of the property stolen by individuals after the French exodus had been taken over by the Government, and the 'management committees' running the factories, farms, vineyards, and hotels had been given official recognition and in most cases had been stiffened by the inclusion of officially appointed managers and technicians; a good beginning had been made in the repatriation and resettlement of the refugees; technicians were gradually obtained from abroad (including French, who were welcome provided that they were not *pieds-noirs*) and medical teams borrowed from such unlikely sources as Bulgaria and Yugoslavia; and finally Ben Bella, having ousted his political rivals for the moment, and suppressed dissidence in the Aures and elsewhere, was thrusting ahead with a programme designed to convert Algeria into a modern Socialist State.

Algiers itself showed few of the stresses through which it had passed, and at first sight its people looked much the same as before, partly no doubt because most of the 60,000 Europeans who still remained in the country – the comparative handful to which Algeria's million had dwindled – are mostly concentrated here, and have been reinforced by foreign diplomatic staffs and imported technicians, partly because there is not all that difference in appearance between an educated Algerian and a southern European. But as I went round, I became conscious of two major changes since my 1960 visit.

One was that the crowds in the streets and cafés now seemed to be composed entirely of young men in European clothes, speaking French or, more usually, the patois of the Bab-el-Oued quarter, which is more than half Arabic. I had noticed this in other towns: Algeria seemed to have become a country of youth, and their elders, when visible, looked bewildered, as well they might after the two dislocations which their country and society had undergone, the eviction of the French and then the swift transformation of the social structure. In a few years these young men would be speaking only Arabic, and might be accompanied by their womenfolk, for the emancipation of women is now a principle of general acceptance in the Arab world and is also in conformity with Berber tradition, so that it is likely sooner or later to sweep aside any Islamic objections which may still subsist.

The other change was in the atmosphere. The undertones of fear which I remembered, deriving from latent terrorism, had gone, but in their place was a different form of tension caused by poverty and unemployment. The régime, dedicated and hardworking though its leaders and officials were, had clearly failed to convince the bulk of the people that Utopia was round the corner, and on every side was visible the contrast – I had almost said conflict – between the activity of the government and the apathy of the governed; between enthusiasm, on the one hand, and disillusionment and bitterness on the other.

CHAPTER 10

Southern Algeria and the Kharijïtes

In Algiers I had suffered from the cold (the southern shores of the Mediterranean can have exceedingly cold spells in winter and spring, but are compensated by having comparatively moderate summers); and I decided to go southwards by a road which follows a traditional caravan-route into the Sahara, partly to get warm and partly because by so doing I should pass through a cross-section of the geography of Algeria, and arrive at an unusual destination.

My way led out across the Mitija, the colonization of which had cost so much French blood and Muslim bitterness, to Boufariq, a small town standing on what was once a marsh infamous for an incurable brand of malaria but is now an exceptionally productive plain; and then to Blida, another and much larger town known as 'The Little Rose' from its incomparable setting amongst orchards and mimosas, which has orange-trees lining its streets and was, not surprisingly, a favourite resort of the Turks. Beyond it the road winds through a long monkey-infested defile, by which the River Chiffa penetrates a chain of hills, and then uphill on to the Tell, that jumble of plateaux and hills and valleys which stretches from Tunisia to western Algeria and is a continuation of the Atlas. Immediately over the brow is Medea, a rather nondescript market-town which began as a Roman settlement and was one of three strongholds founded, or rather refounded, by Bolouggin ibn Ziri in the tenth century, Algiers being another and Miliana the third; under the Turks it was the capital of their province of Central Algeria. The road continues to rise through pleasant Provençal-like scenery until it crosses a 4,000-foot col; but here comes a change as abrupt as occurs on the way to Biskra, for this is the 'Rocade Sud', the edge of the Tell, a great natural east–west dividing-line along which the Roman

limes ran, and south of it the rich agriculture of the Tell is replaced by bare steppe on which alfalfa grass flourishes. Just
south of the col is another village, Boghar, which is aptly known
as 'The Balcony of the Sahara', for from it you can look south
on to the beginnings of the desert.

About eighty miles farther on comes another line of hills,
the 'Mountains of the Oulad-Nail', named after a tribe of
whose women I shall be speaking later. On their southern
slopes, rather to the east of my road, the Romans established
what was, I believe, the most southerly of all their posts, the
Castellum Dimmidi, now Massaad; it lay well outside the
limes, and although Septimius Severus, the most active pro-
moter of defence against the nomad marauders, is believed to
have considered extending the *limes* even farther south, he does
not seem to have managed to do so. From here onwards the
alfalfa dies away and bare yellow earth takes its place. Next
comes Laghouat, a little town in an oasis, which rather resembles Biskra and serves the same function, that of a 'port of the
desert', whence the caravans set forth into the Sahara and
where they find relaxation on their return. Through both of
them roads go south, to join at El Golea and thence to cross
the Sahara to Nigeria; though their chief function nowadays
is to service the rapidly expanding Saharan oil industry, as the
traffic on them shows. Like Biskra, Laghouat is built in what is
known as the 'French-Saharan' style, with massive crenellated
white walls and gateways, and arcades which give shade from
the glare of the Saharan sun; but its palm-grove, unusually
favoured with clear running water, is its chief beauty.

Unless, of course, one counts the Oulad Nail girls. These
strapping wenches, from a large tribe of the region, have for
generations been accredited purveyors of entertainment and
pleasure to Saharan travellers, and are found in all the 'desert
ports', where their performances were between the world wars
an essential item on tourists' itineraries. They are unveiled and
wear brightly-coloured dresses, sashes, and bandeaux, and
necklaces of silver coins; they used to carry their savings in the
form of gold coins sewn into their headdresses or on their
breasts, but in these days of grubby notes are compelled to

make do with costume jewellery and keep their hoards elsewhere. Their dancing has little in common with the 'belly-
dance' of Egypt, which I personally find repulsive, but rather
resembles the style of contortion to be seen in Black Africa, the
art of which seems to consist in causing successive sections of
the body to vibrate independently of the neighbouring parts;
it is frankly erotic and is understandably successful with men
just in from weeks in the arid desert. It may seem strange to
find the women of a Muslim tribe permitted to leave it and live
a life of complete freedom – and licence; but such is the Berber
tradition: Berber women have always enjoyed a far greater
measure of sex-equality than their sisters in the towns or in
other Muslim countries, having often taken over the headship
of their families on their husbands' death, and to their menfolk
there is nothing repugnant in the idea of these girls going out
to earn their dowries in this manner, on the understanding
that, having done so, they will return to a normal married life.

When I resumed my journey south, I had no reason to complain of cold. Directly after Laghouat lies the region known as
'the *daias*', a plateau sprinkled with hollows which become
morasses after rain and support groves of pistachio and jujube
trees, and on it today the sun beat down. Even hotter was the
next section, known as the '*shibka*', or net, from the multitude
of water-channels, all dry now, which divide it into a labyrinth.
Beyond this useless country, where nothing grows, I came suddenly to the crest of a ridge, and looked over it to one of the
most remarkable sights of my whole journey.

I was on the lip of a deep depression, the walls and floor of
which were of perfectly bare brick-red earth. In the middle of
it lay a string of villages, each surrounded by a containing wall
of the same colour, over which I could see buildings and minarets of dazzling white, but also houses of the same brick-red.
Beyond the villages lay an immense palm-grove: so that in the
hot clear air the whole formed a colour-scheme of red, white,
and green, of a vividness which I cannot remember having
seen equalled.

I went down into the depression and came to the largest of the villages, Ghardaia, where I found, for the first and the last time in provincial Algeria, a hotel still run by a French couple and preserving the standards of another era; and in its olean-der-shaded garden, beside a blue pool with bulbuls giving tongue in the pepper-trees around, I was able to recharge after the stresses of Algiers.

In the next two days I went through the whole area, which is called the Mzab, and came to the conclusion that it was unique in every way, situation, people, economy, and above all origin.

It was this last which I found particularly fascinating. The community would in all probability never have existed had the great schismatic movement of Kharijism not swept through the Maghrib in the eleventh century. This movement, which I mentioned as having been embraced by the majority of the people of Jerba, began in the Middle East in the seventh century A.D., when 12,000 of the troops of Ali, the Prophet's son-in-law, walked out on him (the word 'Kharijite' means 'walker-out') in disgust because, when his claims to the Cali-phate were disputed by a rival, Muawiya, whom they regarded as a usurper, Ali accepted arbitration instead of fighting him. Since then the descendants of the original schismatics have declined to recognize any of the succeeding Caliphs, and elect their own leader, or 'Imam'. We do not know exactly how or when the schism first came to the Maghrib; all that is reason-ably sure is that about 742 a revolt of Berbers, professing Kharijism but probably animated by patriotic as well as re-ligious zeal, broke out in Tangier against the Arabs who by that time were supreme in the Maghrib, and in two pitched battles in Morocco defeated the Arab forces. The revolt spread across the central Maghrib; and although defeated with great slaughter by the Arabs at El Qarn, near Kairouan, the same year, the moderate wing of the movement, the Ibadites, in 758 captured Tripoli, while its more extreme wing, the Sufrites, represented by the Ourfedjouma branch of the Nefzawa tribe of southern Tunisia*, captured Kairouan. In doing so,

* See Page 57.

however, the Ourfedjouma committed such excesses that the Imam of the movement, Abul Khattab, at the head of the Ibadites from Tripoli, expelled them from Kairouan and installed his own Governor, Abdurrahman ibn Rostem, who was of Persian origin.

In 761 the Arabs surged back from Egypt and recaptured Kairouan, whereupon Rostem came across to what is now western Algeria and made his capital at Tahert, near the modern Tiaret; here he founded a dynasty (thus adding to the number of such founders who were not themselves of Berber origin) and was appointed Imam of the movement. In the next few years there was fierce fighting between Arabs and Kharijites, during which the Ourfedjouma were virtually wiped out and disappear from history, but in 787 Rostem made overtures of peace to the Arab Governor of Kairouan, who accepted them, so that for more than a century there was relative tranquillity in the central Maghrib, the Arabs, and later their nominees the Aghlabids, ruling Tripoli and the settled areas of Ifriqiya (i.e. the Tell and the Sahil of Tunisia and Eastern Algeria), and the Rostemid State controlling the belt of territory which lies between the Tell and the desert, from Morocco to the Jebel Nafusa of Tripolitania, where incidentally they commanded the lines of communication between Tripoli itself and Egypt. The Rostemid State was a theocracy, ruled by its Imam and attracting adherents from all over the Islamic world; but its interests lay more in the realms of religious controversy than in those of defence, and in 911 it was conquered by a more martial dynasty, the Fatimids from Mahdiya, and its Ibadite adherents driven into the desert.

The more extreme form of Kharijism had one more moment of vitality, when 'The Man with the Donkey' led them in revolt against the Fatimids. Their leader, evidently a cruel and lascivious adventurer, came from the Shott al Djerid in southern Tunisia and had been a teacher under the Rostemid régime in Tiaret. In 929 he began preaching insurrection against the Fatimids, using the inflammatory denunciation of the Sufrite creed which he professed, and by 934 was followed by a considerable host of nomad Berbers, originally drawn from the

Luata and the Huwara, apparently a tribe of the northern
Aures, but later augmented by other tribes attracted by the
prospect of being able to pillage the sedentaries who formed the
supporters of the Fatimids. They took and duly sacked Beja,
Tunis, and later Kairouan, which they also burnt, but as already related failed before Mahdiya and were dispersed after
their leader's death in the Hodna. Thereafter Kharijite adherents within the Maghrib proper were confined to communities
in the Jefara and Jebel Nafusa regions of Tripolitania and in
Jerba.

The Ibadites chased out of Tiaret initially took refuge in
Ouargla, which lies on the trunk route running south in to the
desert from Biskra, but even here found themselves harassed by
their implacable orthodox Muslim enemies and were forced to
seek a safer habitat. Their choice fell on the Mzab region,
which seemed to them, lying as it did between the Sahara and
the *Shibka*, too barren to tempt anyone, whereas they hoped
that by skill and hard work they could find water and make it
habitable. They succeeded; ample water was found in the subsoil and they now have three thousand wells from which to
supply the 270,000 palms in their groves and the fruit-trees
and vegetable gardens under them.

But as their community throve and multiplied, agriculture
alone could not suffice for its needs, and when time had somewhat blunted the original hostility of the orthodox Muslims
their young men were able to travel in search of trade. In due
course they developed specialities: in some regions they acquired
almost a monopoly of the sale of certain types of cloth, and of
the trades of butcher and grocer, so that the Mzabites became
familiar figures not only in all the main towns of Algeria but
as far afield as the Sudan.

I spoke to some of them (their native tongue is Berber, of a
brand similar to, but distinct from, the dialect of the Kabyls,
but they have found it profitable to learn French) and found
that, despite the long absences which their trades force on them
(and which, I was told, has led to a local religious ruling that
a child born within two years of its parents' last contact should
be regarded as legitimate), they retained a strong sense of

solidarity with the community which their remittances largely supported, and regarded it as normal to return at regular intervals in order to keep in touch with family affairs, to re-steep themselves in their native atmosphere, and above all to die. A Mzabite would, it appeared, go to any lengths to reach his home if he felt himself failing, and should he expire *en route* his companions would bring back the body for burial in a sack packed round with salt; and respect for the dead is manifested in elaborate ceremonies held in the cemeteries more than once a year. I also found that these former victims of Muslim persecution not surprisingly took little interest in the New Algeria; indeed I suspected that they probably regretted the departure of the French, whose protection they had specifically sought in the 1880's and with whom they had lived in amity ever since.

Ghardaia itself, apart from an untidy collection of former French buildings, shops, and petrol-stations on the outskirts, has much charm. Its real centre is the market-place, an acre of open space surrounded by irregular arcades in which no one pillar or arch matches another. It contains two unusual features: one is the *msallah*, a fifteen-foot-square enclosure reached by a flight of worn steps, which is an open-air place of prayer for those who do not wish to climb the hill to the mosque; the other is the *hwaita*, a semicircle of twenty-six stones on which the elders of the town sit in conclave to adjudicate its affairs and to hear disputes. Their powers, I was told, extended to the award of punishments up to and including prohibition to trade, which is almost the equivalent of a sentence of death since no one may help the guilty party in any way. On most of my several visits I found the market-place a hive of activity, with grain and animals the chief wares on sale and the buyers in their off-white cloaks and turbans thronging round the vendors crouched over their stalls and forming an ever-changing pattern against the glaring white of the arcades. From beside the *msallah* the view across this throng was artistically right, for behind it the hill, covered with a tightly-packed muddle of red and white hovels, rose to a summit on which stood a minaret, white, tall, and tapering, with an opening in its top like the eye of a needle in which the muezzin could stand to give the call to prayer. Nowhere else in the Islamic world have I seen a minaret of this shape, and nowhere else a minaret which so well illustrates its name, a derivative of the word for 'light-house'.

The other villages of the Mzab each had its own individual-ity: Melika, a natural citadel perched on a cliff, which claims never to have been captured by an enemy; El Atheuf, which has two minarets and two mosques separated by a high wall, because its people have since time immemorial been divided into two warring factions; and Beni Isguem, which is so holy that a special permit must be obtained to enter it, and where the French could never set up a school within its walls but had to put it outside the gate. Finally there is the palm-grove, full of walled enclosures in which the women spend the heat of the summer, where at all times, above the rustling of the fronds, you can hear what they call 'The Song of the Mzab', the squeaking of the innumerable pulleys on the walls as the don-keys raise the water on which life depends.

I turned my back on the Mzab and drove northwards again, through the *shibka* and the *daias*, until I reached the Oulad Nail hills and, at the little poet of Djelfa, turned north-west. Seventy miles of fast going across the steppe brought me to a region of pure sand-dunes, the first I had seen since leaving Libya; and soon across them rose the palms of another large oasis, that of Bou Saada, their vivid green contrasting gloriously with the gold of the sand around. In its midst lay the town, displaying all the characteristics of a 'desert port', including the camels and the Bedouin from the black-tented encamp-ments beyond, obviously in to shop; though in fact Bou Saada is rather part of the Hodna, that deep depression which lies below the edge of the Tell, and the Roman *limes* seem to have passed well to the south of its site. Not that the place, so far as I could gather, had existed in Roman times; local legend attri-butes its foundation to a *marabout*, or holy man, called Sliman ibn Rabia, who in the twelfth century is said to have arrived from no one knew where and camped in the oasis; here he was joined by a bandit, Si Tamer, whom he reformed and with whom he performed works of piety amongst the local population; but his saintliness was not realized until one day, walking near a stream in the grove, the two men came upon a female jackal with young, who instead of attacking them licked their hands; and this demonstrated that Allah wished them to remain in that place and to build a town in His honour, and thus Bou Saada was founded.

I would remark here that the *marabout*, or local saint, though not unknown elsewhere in the Islamic world, is a peculiarly Maghribi institution, probably because it suits the Berber temperament; for, as I shall be showing later, the Berbers when they embraced Islam imported into the Faith not a few of their previous pagan practices, including that of venerating men whom they deemed to be holy or, more often, possessed of magical powers. As a result, the Maghrib is dotted with *marabouts'* tombs, little whitewashed enclosures round a *qubba*, or domed building, which serve as an object of worship to the neighbouring peasantry or to passers-by; and more than once in the history of Morocco in particular, when a strong central authority has been lacking, the country has tended to break up into sections each dominated by a *zawiya* dedicated to a particular *marabout*.

From Bou Saada my road bent northwestwards and climbed the 'Rocade Sud' on to the Tell. Thence it took me by a 6,000-foot pass, a fine piece of engineering, with innumerable hairpin bends, over an extension of the Kabylie massif, tortured country clothed in fine trees; and so down to the Mitija and back to Algiers.

In the south I had heard much of oil, because the road which I had followed to Ghardaia is nowadays a main artery feeding the oil-producing areas; and in Algiers I inquired about the state of the industry. It was less spectacular than that of Libya, partly because the promising areas were farther from the coast and more expensive to develop, partly because, I gathered, the oil so far found was somewhat light in quality and therefore less profitable. But Algeria had little reason to complain, especially as her two immediate neighbours Morocco, so far at least, had found no oil and Tunisia very little. The proved reserves of the Algerian Sahara together totalled 1,500 million metric tons, and in 1963 the revenue accruing to the Algerian Government from the two fields already in production, Hassi Massaoud and El-Ejbel, had amounted to $70m., a figure not then reached (though since surpassed) in Libya. Pipe-lines already ran from Hassi Massaoud to Bougie, and from El-Ejbel to Skira, on the eastern coast of Tunisia, and during my stay in Algiers the Algerian Government awarded to a British firm a contract worth some £25m. for the construction of another pipeline from Hassi Massaoud to Arzew, on the north coast; in so doing, they brushed aside French objections that the contract should have been given to a French firm, and made clear their determination in future to throw open contracting opportunities to all possible international competition – a reaction against their former subservient state which was entirely natural, if disappointing to those French who still hoped that by lavish aid France could retain a position of special privilege in Algeria.

Thus Algeria is already assured of substantial revenues for the foreseeable future, which may well multiply if one or other of the oil companies, not all French, which are at present exploring the Algerian desert, by virtue of concessions previously granted, make important strikes. Moreover oil is not the only potential benefit from these regions: at Hassi Massaoud, and perhaps elsewhere, are huge deposits of natural gas, and already some two-thirds of the production is being bought by Great Britain and shipped in liquified form from Arzew to Canvey Island in Essex, constituting an important part of the total gas supplies of this country.

CHAPTER 11

Western Algeria

The time had come to leave Algiers. From it I drove westwards along the Sahil, which like its counterpart in Tunisia is a narrow plain between the Tell and the sea. It is thickly populated and closely cultivated, as it must have been in Roman times, for all along it are Roman sites, two of which, Tipasa and Cherchell, are noteworthy even by the high standards of the Maghrib.

Before reaching Tipasa, the first of them, the road passes close under a curious monument, one of several in Algeria (there are others in the Hodna, and near Tiaret): it is a huge circular pile of stone, surrounded by a containing wall in which are sixty Ionic-type pilasters, and surmounted by a stepped dome. Locally it is known as 'The Tomb of the Christian Lady', probably because at each of the points of the compass are false doors in the containing wall, thus forming a cross; but it certainly antedates Christianity in the region and in all probability was built, perhaps by an imported Greek architect, to serve as the mausoleum of some important Berber family. At intervals in the past it was vainly ransacked for hidden treasure, and its interior, which contains various passages and chambers, was explored by a team sent out by Napoleon III.

Tipasa lies on the coast and must have been a Phoenician site, as the prefix 'ti' is Punic: there are two columns of place-names beginning thus in the index to the Guide Bleu. It was a big place, within the most solid of all the ramparts that I saw in the Maghrib; this bears an inscription to Antoninus Pius, who seems to have been the main creator of the city. The forum, theatre, baths, and temples have been well restored and are of a high standard, but most appealing, to me at least, is the Basilica dedicated to St. Salsa; for this child of fourteen, who was torn to pieces in A.D. 320 by a pagan mob for having pushed their idol, a bronze dragon, into the sea, is the subject of a macabre legend. According to this, her remains were also thrown into the sea, which had been flat calm but which thereupon erupted into so violent a storm that a ship just arrived from Gaul was in danger of foundering at its moorings. Its captain, Saturninus, fell into a deep sleep during which voices told him that the remains of the young martyr were under his keel and that if he did not raise them and see that they were given decent burial his ship would perish. Not until the storm had raged for three days was he convinced that the warning was serious, but he then plunged into the sea, where he found himself divinely guided to the remains and pulled them out; on the instant the sea became calm, the witnesses of the miracle surged forward in repentance, and the remains were duly buried in a chapel erected for the purpose, the ruins of which are said to have been since identified. The chapel is the subject of another legend: it is said that Firmus, the Kabyl rebel who made common cause with the Donatists, prayed at it before attacking Tipasa, but in vain, for not only did he fail to take the city but on leaving it he fell down in a fit from which he never recovered. Even these are not the only miracles connected with Tipasa: a third relates how Hunseric the Vandal when he captured it put out the tongues of its inhabitants because they would not embrace Arianism, but they nevertheless continued to speak. (I find this easy to credit; the mere loss of their tongues would assuredly not silence some conversationalists of my acquaintance.) Apart from its legends, the most attractive feature of Tipasa is the garden which the original excavator of the ruins created round them, so that, in contrast to the bareness of Timgad and Jemila, the site is embowered in trees in which the birds and the cicadas provide background music for your wanderings.

Cherchell, the former Caesaria, lies a little farther to the west and has a longer history. As Iol, it was a Phoenician station, and in 25 B.C. became the capital of the Mauretania of Juba II, the Berber, who, having been installed there by Augustus, named the place after him; but in A.D. 40, after the death of Juba and the assassination by Caligula of his son

K

Ptolemy, Mauretania was annexed by Rome and Caesaria became its capital, and also the main Roman naval base. Its
subsequent history was much the same as that of the other
Roman sites in the central Maghrib: it was sacked by Firmus
(lacking a St. Salsa to protect it), had its fortifications destroyed by the Vandals, was restored by the Byzantines, and
was subsequently occupied by a series of Berber dynasties, by
the Spaniards in their sixteenth century 'crusade', and by the
Turkish corsair Khaireddin Barbarossa. Today its ruins are
scattered in the fields round the modern village, under which
many more must lie, and its chief asset is its museum, which
contains, apart from some lovely mosaics, two exceptionally
interesting statues: one is of Cleopatra Selene, the daughter of
Antony and Cleopatra who married Juba II and who, if not
libelled by the sculptor, looks exceedingly coarse, while the
other has been identified as Cleopatra herself and suggests, if
this identification is correct, that the Serpent of Old Nile was
far more of a power-thirsty politician, and far less of a siren or
courtesan, than most authorities have deemed her.

At Cherchell I left the coast and went southwards to Miliana,
a Roman site refounded by Bolouggin ibn Ziri in the tenth
century but now a rather featureless little town; and thence via
Affreville to Orleansville, a town which was totally destroyed
by an earthquake in 1954 and has been rebuilt in a singularly
charmless manner. All this part of the Tell was intensively
colonized by the French and these towns, the villages between
them, the roads and railway which join them, and indeed the
whole aspect of the country, would recall southern France
were it not for the ragged Arabs (they seem to be Arabs rather
than Berbers here) at every corner – and the incipient ragged-
ness of the properties and villas by the way.

For this region constituted a particular test of the new
Government's ability to tackle the problem of the 'biens
vacants', the properties left behind by the departed French;
and from what I heard in Orleansville the 'management committee' system was not so far working too well. The effectiveness of the committees seemed to depend almost entirely on the
quality of their individual members, employees stiffened with

Algiers nominees, and the general opinion seemed to be that
an overall drop in production of at least 20 per cent was to be
expected that year, with the probability of a further drop as the
momentum on which many of the properties were still running
began to slow down. It could hardly be otherwise, unless an
exceptionally effective control could be exercised by the central
Government; and this seemed unlikely in view of the desperate
shortage of trained men which I have already mentioned. In
an attempt to help a British charitable organization which was
trying to succour the children of the region but had run into
trouble with the local authorities, I interviewed several local
officials, whom I found hardworking and conscientious, but
inexperienced and inclined to be bureaucratic; so that it
appeared to me doubtful how far they would be able to deal
with the pressing exigencies facing them, not least of which,
here as in Algiers, was unemployment.

My next journey was lovely. I drove south from Orleansville
over the massif of the Ouarsenis, one of the folds of high ground
which run across the Tell from west-south-west to east-north-
east, and for hours the road snaked along ridges and between
crests, most of the time through superb cedar-forest, with
views back on to the Sahil and the coast beyond, and later on
views forward on to the Sersou Plateau ahead. At Vialar, a
little town on the edge of this plateau, I turned south-west
across its undulating expanses of cornfields, where only a kestrel
or a wheatear gave life to an otherwise deserted landscape.
These uplands were immemorially the summer pastures of the
nomads who wintered in the Laghouat region and who came
up to them via the Zab and the Hodna, and the French, when
they developed it into cultivation, had trouble with the nomads
from then on. As night fell I came to Tiaret, a town on the
southern slope of the Ouarsenis which today is of no interest,
but which has a notable past: for it was at Tahert, its predecessor, the ruins of which lie five miles away, that the Kharijite Abdurrahman ibn Rostem in 761 made his capital and
founded the dynasty which dominated the interior of the central

Maghrib for nearly 150 years, until they were driven into the desert and, eventually, created the Mzab community.

Tahert even in those days was renowned for a bad climate. A contemporary Arabic rhyme exists which may be rendered thus:

> 'The bitter cold is hard to bear;
> The sun through mist doth scarce appear
>   As though from under ground he came;
> But we, the men of Arab race
> With gladness greet his fleeting face
>   As Jews their Sabbath Day acclaim.'

I was therefore the less surprised next morning to find Tiaret under a blanket of fog which persisted all day, and the cold of which, in an unheated hotel, I found extremely 'hard to bear'; it also frustrated my intention of visiting a group of 'djedars', Berber monuments similar to the 'Christian Lady's tomb' near Tipasa, which stand on a hill in the vicinity. But it cleared overnight, and under bright sunshine I left Tiaret by a road which followed the top of the Rocade Sud for some distance and then turned northwards into an extremely populous valley full of vineyards, the wine from which I discovered later to be celebrated. Across this I came to Mascara, a small town having no connection that I could find with eye-black but much with agriculture. All this country recalls Abdul Kader, the warrior who here raised his standard against the French in 1832; his family tomb lies near Tiaret, and near Mascara is a *zawiya* named after his father, in which he himself at one time lived and near which a monument to him was erected in 1949.

From Mascara I went on towards the coast, which I had left at Cherchell, and recrossed the Sahil. It looked much the same as farther east, and indeed there is little variation in the coastal belt of Algeria and Tunisia, though all of it is pleasant, and much of it highly productive, country. I reached the sea at Mostaganem, a fair-sized port which claims to have been founded in the eleventh century by a monarch of whom we shall hear much later, Yusuf bin Tashfin the Almoravid, from

Morocco; it was also a Turkish naval base, and was the birth-place of the founder of the Sanusi movement. From here I followed the coast westwards to Arzew, a tiny but well-sheltered little place which is acquiring a new importance as the terminal of the latest oil pipeline; and then cut across the base of a peninsula until I saw below me the roofs and port of Oran.

I had last been here in 1960, when de Gaulle's 'Constantine Plan' for depriving the F.L.N. of recruits by tempting them into new industries was not yet dead, and had listened with some amusement to a hard-bitten group of industrialists from France being assured by local French officials, to their patent disbelief, that the rebellion was 'all but over' and that the Golden Age for an industrialized French Algeria was about to begin. At that time the town looked mainly European, with a definite Spanish tinge; and this was natural, for in 1509 the Spaniards had made it their base for their 'crusade' in the Maghrib and had hung on to it even after they had been expelled from Algiers, Bougie, and the other ports by the Turks. They were chased out of it in 1708, but in 1732 returned for another sixty years, only evacuating finally after the town had been largely destroyed by an earthquake. There is still an enchanting Spanish quarter, which with its narrow streets and high walls and ornamented gates and cool patios glimpsed through wrought-iron grilles recalls the Arab quarter of Cordova and should be able with ease to reorientate itself to a new period of Muslim domination. A high proportion of the settlers who came here during the nineteenth and early twentieth centuries were of Spanish origin, a fact sometimes held by French apologists to explain why, during the last desperate days of 1962 before French forces were finally withdrawn, Oran Europeans were the most fanatically aggressive against the Muslims and some of the worst O.A.S. excesses were committed here. The town at that time had a population of 300,000, but it must be much less now and a good deal of readjustment is having to be done; but Oran is the natural port not only for the rich western region of Algeria but also for eastern Morocco, which has minerals, so should have no difficulty in keeping going.

Beside the busy commercial port is the French naval base of Mers-el-Kebir, the scene of that tragic episode in 1940 when Churchill was compelled to order the Royal Navy to sink a French fleet because its officers, under a mixture of emotions which included Gallic pride, dislike of the British, and bitter shame at their country's defeat, had refused all his alternative offers – to join us, to neutralize their ships in a British, American, or French West Indian port, or to scuttle them. Under the Evian Agreements the French may keep the base for fifteen years, after which it becomes Algerian.

My next destination after Oran was inspired by curiosity alone: it was Sidi-bel-Abbes, for so long the home base of that toughest, most celebrated, and most misrepresented of all fighting forces, the French Foreign Legion. I had read much of this force: of its formation by Louis-Phillippe in 1831; of the battle-honours it had won, first against Abdul Kader at Mostaganem in 1833, then in the Crimea, in Mexico in 1863 (where the last stand of a small detachment against overwhelming odds at Camerone created its most cherished legend), in Tonkin and Dahomey and Madagascar, during the pacification of Morocco and the Rif War of 1925, in both world wars, especially at Bir Hakeim in the Western Desert in 1942, and in Indo-China before the humiliating French withdrawal therefrom in 1955. It was a fine record; wherever France fought, the Legion had been in the van. Yet it had never been a large corps, averaging 30,000, of whom 70 per cent were German, 10 per cent French, and the rest of every sort of nationality, background, and upbringing, all fused together by iron discipline and a deep-rooted tradition. In Morocco thirty years before I had known two very different Legionnaires, one a Scandinavian Prince, a magnificent physical specimen who evidently liked the life, the other an engaging British character who was serving a prison sentence. This latter may fairly claim to have been unlucky: having deserted from the Legion and bluffed his way back to England, he had then gone to the United States, had got himself deported therefrom on a French vessel which called at Cherbourg, and had there been promptly arrested as a deserter. Having influential friends, he had induced the French Government to pardon him for the desertion, only to find himself serving precisely the same sentence for having in his desertion made away with French military property, to wit one cap and one belt.

But Sidi-bel-Abbes was a disappointment; the Legion (now, I believe, reduced to 9,000) had gone to its new base near Marseilles, after ceremonially burning a trophy which, by its deed of gift, might not be taken out of Algeria; its barracks had become Algerian; and only a monument or two in the typically ugly little garrison town remained to show that for nearly a century it had contained the main pillar of French control of Algeria, and a famous legend.

I went on to my last stop in Algeria, Tlemsen, near the Moroccan frontier. This is a place with a long history, mainly due to its position at the crossing of two important trade-routes, one north–south from the coast into the Sahara, the other east–west connecting the thickly populated central regions of Algeria and Morocco. To judge from the accounts of Arab historians, and especially that of Leo Africanus, an Arab who was captured off Jerba by a Christian galley about 1520 and sent to the Medici Pope Leo X, the first of these routes was particularly important to Tlemsen because it connected the city, through Sijilmassa in south Morocco, with the western Saharan regions whence came those priceless commodities gold and salt, and also with northern Nigeria through In Salah and the so-called Hoggar route, the trade along these routes being organized between the merchants of the coast and the trans-Saharan caravaners by middlemen residing in Tlemsen itself. But for the development of the city the connection with Morocco was also important: for by bringing it within the sphere of the powerful dynasties which evolved there it enabled Tlemsen, alone amongst Algerian cities, to acquire examples of the striking school of architecture which grew up between Andalusia and Morocco and by which Morocco, as we shall see, has been so notably enriched.

Tlemsen had many masters. Prehistoric man lived in the caves round it, and a Roman camp, called Pomaria after the numerous orchards which are still a feature of the area, was

established at Agadir (a Berber word meaning 'escarpment')
to the north-east of the present town. On this, in the eighth
century, a Berber dynasty called the Idrisids, from Fez in
Morocco, founded a settlement; and in the eleventh century
the great Almoravid Yusuf bin Tashfin, the founder of Mostaganem, founded another town on the present site. His successors endowed it with its superb Great Mosque, which in
style recalls the Mosque of Cordova and was clearly inspired
by it; and the town developed further under the Almohads,
the dynasty which succeeded the Almoravids. But Tlemsen's
real period of glory began in 1235, when it became the capital
of an independent dynasty, the Abdul Wadids (sometimes
known as the Zianids), whose founder Yaghmorasen enlarged
the mosque whilst his successors built other mosques and several
medersas or religious schools. The Abdul Wadids belonged to
the Zenata group of tribes, as did the Merinids, another dynasty who almost simultaneously established themselves in Fez,
but despite this tribal relationship the two were almost perpetu-
ally in conflict. In 1302 the Merinid ruler Abu Yaqub el Mansur came to besiege Tlemsen and set up a permanent camp at
Mansura, two miles to the west, in which he built another fine
mosque, while his son built an equally fine mausoleum at another suburb of Tlemsen, Bou Medien, in honour of a *marabout*
who died there. In 1337 the Merinids at last captured Tlemsen
and ruled it from Mansura for the next twenty-five years, but
in 1359 another Abdul Wadid, with the help of the Beni Hilal
Arabs who were still dominating the centre of Algeria by playing off one set of Berbers against another, recaptured Tlemsen.
His dynasty were, however, unable to maintain their independence, probably because the coastal belt between it and Oran
is so narrow that its sedentary population were too few in numbers to support them, and from then onwards Tlemsen was
ruled alternately by the Merinids and by the Hafsids from Tunis,
until finally engulfed by the Turkish occupation in 1554, when
it became the capital of a 'Beylik' or province.

Incidentally Tlemsen is the only former dynastic capital which
still exists in Algeria: in Tunisia, Kairouan, Mahdiya, and
Tunis, the capitals of the Aghlabids, Fatimids, and Hafsids

respectively, have all remained in being, whereas in Algeria
Ashir, Qala'at Beni Hammad, and Tahert, the capitals of the
Zirids, Hammadids, and Rostemids respectively, are all in
ruins.

During the Turkish occupation, Tlemsen retained its ties
with Morocco, which had remained independent, and in 1830,
when the French expelled the Turks, gave a further demonstration of its western-looking sentiments by attempting to have
itself incorporated in Morocco. When this failed, the population
split between supporters of Abdul Kader's resistance movement
and the advocates of submission to France, and it was not until
1842 that the latter prevailed and Tlemsen became a normal
part of French Algeria.

It is perhaps the most attractive town of Algeria, beautifully
situated on the side of a hill with steep cliffs behind and a wide
valley in front, sloping down to a gap in a range of hills through
which the River Tafna flows to the sea. All down the valley
are the orchards which inspired its Roman name, and carobs
and terebinths and olive-trees; and in the town itself, which
has overflowed its walls, are the mosques and *medersas* with
which the Moroccan dynasties embellished it. Less pleasing
are the quarters of former French villas, now being 'managed'
by committees and showing signs of neglect, and the throngs
of obviously un- or underemployed youths in the streets and
the cafés; in a year or two the town would probably look as
shabby as many quarters of Algiers and Oran and other towns
already do.

On this my last night in Algeria, I looked back on my experi-
ences of the preceding weeks and tried to imagine what the
future of this difficult country was likely to be. Clearly it ought
to have no difficulty in providing for itself, blessed as it is with
oil and gas and iron-ore to supplement the produce of a rich
countryside. It had no real enemies, and was receiving a good
deal of aid without any need to incur obligations in return.
But the departure of the French had not only crippled the administrative machine but had distorted the whole structure
of the country; and the present rulers had still to produce

convincing evidence that the 'Arab Socialism' which was their declared policy was restoring the position and curing the manifold ills, notably unemployment. Failing such evidence, they could only hope to survive by continued authoritarianism, which would perpetuate the present tension and uncertainty and risk periodical upheavals; whereas the only hope of stability, to my mind, lay in a régime able to win sufficient public confidence to enable democratic processes gradually to be introduced. The Algerians, after all that they had suffered, deserved a period of calm in which to find themselves; but, as I left, the prospects of their enjoying one looked to be remote.

CHAPTER 12

Fez and the Middle Atlas

Morocco, in which I found myself after the now familiar frontier struggle, is geographically and racially part of the Maghrib, but has a rather different history, because it has undergone less foreign domination than the rest.

It began similarly, with settlement by Berbers; but the Carthaginians contented themselves with setting up a string of stations along its Atlantic seaboard to serve the traffic which they later developed with West Africa, and never attempted to rule the interior; the Romans ruled most of its northern half, their *limes* almost bisecting the country, but left its southern half alone; the Vandals and Byzantines barely touched its northern coast; and the Arabs occupied the lowlands but hardly penetrated into the mountain regions which make up almost half the total area, so that a high proportion of the autochthonous Berbers have remained unmixed and Berber-speaking. In the sixteenth century the Turks more than once threatened it from Algeria, but neither they nor the Spaniards nor the Portuguese, who made lodgements on its coasts in the seventeenth and eighteenth centuries, achieved any domination over the successive dynasties which during those centuries ruled – or at least were predominant in – the country. The history of Morocco from the eighth to the twentieth century is in fact the history of these dynasties, Idrisid, Almoravid, Almohad, Merinid, Wattasid, Sa'adian, Alawi; but in 1912 this last, which has been paramount since 1660, all but disintegrated and brought the country to chaos and near-bankruptcy, so that the French and Spaniards were moved to step in and set up a Protectorate over it. In 1956, however, Morocco recovered its independence and began a new existence.

I passed through the French-built frontier town of Oujda and made fast time along a highway which led arrowlike across a perfectly flat and highly cultivated plain. This eastern region of Morocco is its least attractive scenically, but has importance because it contains most of the coal, lead, and zinc which, with the phosphates to which I shall be referring later, make up the mineral wealth of the country. It would indeed contain even more such wealth if Morocco had succeeded in 1963 in wresting from Algeria the iron-ore deposits at Tindouf, in the far south, which she claims are hers by right and were allotted unjustly to Algeria by the French when they controlled both countries; but her attempt to seize them by force was frustrated when Egypt came militarily to the help of the sister 'Arab-Socialist' State, and the Organization of African States eventually negoti-ated a settlement which, for the present at least, seems to have put them out of her reach.

As I drove, ranges of hills along both the northern and southern horizons gradually closed in on one another, so that as I approached the next town along the road, Taza, they left only a comparatively narrow passage through which the road ran. This was the 'Taza Gap', which through the centuries served as a gateway to the plains beyond for nomad tribes and Arab invaders; and through it, too, but in the reverse direction, must have come the Kharijites in the eighth century when they extended their revolt against the Arabs into Algeria, for two tribes which seem to have been its backbone, the Mashgara and the Beni Ifren, were apparently based on this region. It has indeed a tradition of revolt against authority, notably between 1902 and 1908, when a pretender to the throne, whose nick-name, Bou Hamara, means 'The Father of the She-Ass', held it against the reigning Sultan until suppressed by his successor.

Taza today is of no interest; but seventy miles farther to the west, as the plain opens out to the north and the mountains rise ever higher to the south, is one of the two most lovely cities of the Maghrib, Fez. I came to it in late afternoon, when the sun was throwing long shadows across the fields and the crenellated walls of the Old City stood up dark red against it; and I realized then how fortunate Morocco had been to have for its first Resident-General after the institution of the Pro-tectorate a man of imagination: for Marshal Lyautey, as he became, ordained that whenever one of the old cities was in danger of overflowing its walls (as so often happened in Algeria), a new town should be built, but not less than five kilometres from the old. At this distance, therefore, from the old city of Fez is an agglomeration of modern boulevards and blocks of flats and French-colonial public buildings, but the space round the old walls has been left inviolate, with olive-trees growing up to them and streams and woods within five minutes' walk. Within the walls no car is allowed, nor indeed could cars easily thread that labyrinth of narrow streets, which continually turn at right angles and are often roofed over, down the steep slope to the River Fez at the bottom and up the farther side. You force a way through hurrying pedestrians and laden donkeys, past unending rows of tiny shops whose patient owners sit cross-legged behind their wares; and you will be lucky not to get lost now and then. If you do, there is one landmark (apart from the river) which you can hardly miss, for it is audible about a quarter of a mile away: this is the quarter of the brassmakers and the coppersmiths, leather-aproned craftsmen who unendingly beat these metals into kettles and trays and bowls.

When I first knew Fez, thirty years ago, another feature of the *suq* was the leather-work, which you saw being fashioned by small boys sitting round tiny rooms below street-level and pricking the gold leaf into the soft surface with needles, and outside these rooms you walked on skins which had been thrown into the street to be softened by the feet of the passers-by; but nowadays the work seems to have been transferred to 'artisanats' where child-labour is strictly regulated and conditions are better all round. Today my favourite quarter is the dyers', where men stir skeins of yarn in big pots of crude blues and yellows and reds, their own arms tinted to the elbow, and under the roofs above are bright patches of colour where the dyed skeins are hanging out to dry. Down by the river mills grind corn, and in sheds carpenters are busy with power-lathes, and black-smiths with forges and odd pieces of iron.

But not all is commerce and craftsmanship: every now and then you will come upon the portal of a mosque, with a beggar outside turning his sightless eyes to the sky and croaking the traditional supplication, or the entrance to a *medersa* or religious college, through which comes a hum of voices repeating the Quran or the Sayings of the Prophet to remind you that Fez is also a University town and a renowned centre of Islamic studies. These *medersas* incidentally contain some of the finest and most intricate plaster-work and woodcarving to be found outside Andalusia, whence its inspiration came when both countries were Arab. Bigger business may be done in the town-planned surroundings of the New City; but as a pulsating ant-heap of human activity the Old City is unrivalled in the Maghrib and must have few rivals anywhere.

It was, so to speak, founded twice over. The first time was about A.D. 789 when an Arab from the Levant, Idris ibn Abdullah, who claimed direct descent from the Prophet but was a fugitive from the Abbassid Caliph at that time ruling in Baghdad, came to the Maghrib and after a brief stay in Tangier, and a rather longer one in the former Roman city of Volubilis, just north of where Fez now stands, founded a settlement on the left bank of the River Fez and used it as a base from which to carve out a kingdom in north Morocco. He was soon afterwards poisoned by an emissary of the Caliph, but twenty years later his posthumous son Idris II, having decided in the manner of Maghribi rulers to found his own capital and made two false starts, established another settlement on the right bank of the river just opposite his father's. For many generations the two settlements were at loggerheads; in the meantime the former had been enlarged by an influx of refugees driven out of Kairouan during the Kharijite troubles, and the latter by a similar influx from Andalusia, so that the two main quarters of Fez el Bali, as the Old City is known, are called the 'Kairouani' and the 'Andalous'. Many Jews, too, were attracted by trade possibilities, though their community has now migrated to a different part of the city known as the 'Mellah': this is a generic name for ghettoes throughout Morocco, derived from the Arabic word for 'salt', allegedly because a traditional occupation of the Jews of Morocco was salting corpses.

In choosing these sites both the Idrises seem to have been attracted by the plentiful water-supplies available, since the sites stand at the confluence of two rivers and a main reason for quitting Walila (Volubilis) had been lack of water; but they must also have appreciated the commercial advantages of a site which commanded both the route eastwards through the 'Taza Gap', and a main north–south road, known as 'The Sultan's Way', which led from the Mediterranean coast through the Atlas range to Sijilmassa in Taroudant and thence linked up with the Trans-Saharan tracks.

The Idrisids, who incidentally suppressed Kharijism in their realm, ruled until smashed by the Fatimids about 921, and thereafter Fez seems to have languished for a century until another dynasty, the Almoravids from south Morocco, conquered the whole country and went on to take over the Arab possessions in Spain, the intellectual and artistic resources of which flowed into Fez during the next century; hence, *inter alia*, the Qarawin *medersa* which is one of its greatest treasures. The Almoravids were then succeeded by another Moroccan dynasty, the Almohads, who ruled for the best part of another century until in 1248 they in their turn gave way to the Merinids. From that moment the growth of Fez was resumed, for the Merinid ruler, Abu Yusuf, having evicted the Almohads from the whole of Morocco and being desirous of founding a new capital for himself, decided to put an end to the constant strife between the existing quarters of Fez, which had plagued him, by founding an administrative centre alongside them, which he called 'Fez el Jdid' (The New City – not to be confused with the French-built Ville Nouvelle).

The Merinids, unlike the Almoravids and the Almohads, who both belonged to the Sanhaja* group of tribes, were Zenata* from the Zab and Biskra regions of Algeria, who during the period when the two former had dominated the central Maghrib had withdrawn to the confines of the Sahara, but as the Almohad power gradually waned had infiltrated back into eastern Morocco and reoccupied Meknes, whence they went on to take Fez and Marrakesh. During the next

* See note 1.

hundred years their power fluctuated. As already mentioned, they were intermittently at war with their Zenata cousins, the Abdul Wadids of Tlemsen, and captured the latter's capital only to lose it again; and expeditions which they made against both the Christians in Spain and the Hafsids in Tunis were costly failures. By 1420 the dynasty was extinct, its last years having been overshadowed by Portuguese and Castilian attacks on Morocco which I will record later; but its achievements had been great. It had restored the orthodoxy of Islam, which had been vitiated by the heretical form of Shi'ism professed by their predecessors the Almohads; and had made a notable contribution to the civilization of the Maghrib by endowing Fez with more marvels of Andalusian-Arab art in its later *medersas*, the Tlemsen region with the now ruined but excellent mosque at Mansura and the *medersa* at Bou Medien, and Rabat with that best of all its monuments, the necropolis of Shella, to which we shall come later.

For rather more than a century after the end of the Merinids, another Zenata dynasty, the Beni Wattas, or Wattasids, based on Fez, precariously held the northern part of Morocco against a new peril, the Portuguese who were establishing themselves along the Atlantic coast and were seeking to turn Morocco into a base for their transatlantic commercial ventures. The failure of the Wattasids to contain them led to the growth of a new tendency amongst the Berbers of Morocco which was to manifest itself prominently in the future, namely the spread of *maraboutism*, or the cult of local 'saints', and the proliferation of *zawiyas* dedicated to such saints and other politico-religious confraternities, which had substantial power and influence in limited areas. This fragmentation of the country led to the final extinction of the Wattasids and their replacement by a new dynasty, this time Arab, the Sa'adians, who will be dealt with later.

Meanwhile Fez, while retaining its religious and intellectual reputation and its commercial importance, declined in political power and never again held the dominating position which it had held as the Merinid capital.

Ghardaia, Algeria
The village of Moulay-Idris, Morocco

Decorative plaster-work in a Fez *medersa*

I spent many days in Fez. I had kept some acquaintance from my previous service, which procured me access to a different life from that of the streets, the life that is lived behind the blank walls which so often border them. A small door opens into a garden, with big trees and flowering shrubs, in which stands an immense mansion, built round a patio on to which all the main rooms open, with a fountain in its centre; and there, over meals of *pastilla* and *cous-cous* and other products of the incomparable Moroccan cuisine, followed by the mint tea which is the national drink and the making of which is a lengthy rite entrusted only to members of the family or guests to be specially honoured, I was told much of the New Morocco, and believed some of it. Many different viewpoints could be gathered in the one building, which usually housed an entire clan: in one room the head of the family would be entertaining his European guests, in another his brother concluding a business deal, in a third his wife receiving women friends, in a fourth his married daughter with her children; and so on. I found one point in common with all whom I met: a belief in the future of the country, and an intense desire to see it transformed into a twentieth-century State with all the trappings of modernity; of feeling for the past there seemed little, apart from the wistful desire to prove that pre-Protectorate Morocco had a glorious history of independence.

One change from thirty years previously was the emancipation of women, begun by the previous King, Muhammad V, when he made his own daughter appear unveiled on a public platform at the age of seventeen, and carried on by the present King and his unveiled sisters, who were active in many fields and one of whom has since become Moroccan Ambassador at the Court of St. James. My Moroccan hosts would now introduce their wives and daughters, and at a party in a European house a young girl of good family, who had come alone, spoke to me without shyness of her charitable committees and political ambitions and even invited me to her home to meet her mother – who also received me unveiled, but with a constraint which indicated unfamiliarity. The Berber tradition of sex-equality, which had given the Maghrib at least two heroines*

* Kohina and Zainab.

L

but had been overlain by Islamic rigidity, was in fact re-asserting itself under the impulse of westernization, and seemed to be manifesting itself in the right avenues of approach, those of social work and child-welfare.

Following the 'Sultan's Way' south from Fez, I was immediately in the foothills of the Middle Atlas, which are more richly beautiful, if less lofty, than the High Atlas farther west. From the little summer station of Azrou, where I watched Berber teenage girls weaving rugs in a Government 'artisanat' and chattering like magpies as they worked, the road rose into magnificent cedar-forest; it was probably from this region that Hannibal obtained his elephants, but now it is given over to birds and woodcutters. I went on past skiing grounds, now deserted, and over a wide, rolling plain, in the midst of which stood the forlorn relic of a French military station, Midelt, with its tennis-club derelict, its hotel-restaurant closed, and its shops catering only for the local Bedouin; and finally by a high col over a line of crests, the watershed between the Mediterranean and the Sahara, into the long sinuous palm-filled gorge of the River Zizz. This led out into a new world, the raw red country which lies beyond the Atlas and is the threshold of the desert.

As the road emerges from the southern foothills on to the plain beyond, it crosses, at a horrible little red town called Ksar es-Souk, an equally important trade-route connecting the southern Oran Province of Algeria with the Sous Valley, which runs to the sea along the southern side of the High Atlas chain; and then proceeds to Erfoud, a little desert town where the Moroccan Government are carrying out an irrigation scheme with a view to restoring to this region, Tafilelt, some of the commercial importance which it had in the Middle Ages.

For in the vicinity of Erfoud lay a rather shadowy place called Sijilmassa, which occurs more than once in the history of the Maghrib. It was apparently founded about A.D. 757 by the Kharijites during their revolt, just before they established the Kingdom of Tiaret, and Kharijite skill in palm-growing, which has been so convincingly demonstrated in the Mzab and is said to have been responsible for the development of many of the oases along the northern edge of the Sahara, made it a great exporter of dates. It was also, by virtue of its commanding position at the gates of Morocco and at the same time on the line of the east–west caravan routes, a noted commercial centre, trafficking in particular in gold from Black Africa and in that essential of the desert, salt, from Taghaza in the Sahara. It was here that the Mahdi Obaidullah took refuge before being brought to Raqqada to found the Fatimid dynasty; and on it the Almoravids based themselves before embarking on the conquest of Morocco. Under the Merinids, and on occasion later, it became a centre of dissidence, but for some reason – probably a change in trade routes – it began to decay in the eighteenth century and fell into ruins in the nineteenth.

From here I turned westwards along the line of the Atlas, which showed vivid violet on the northern horizon as I went towards the distant sea. To the south, on my left, was a line of lower hills, the Jebel Sarrho: this was the last region of all Morocco to be pacified by the French, who only completed its occupation in 1934. Here, as everywhere else, they had adopted a policy of diplomacy backed by inducements, their political officers infiltrating the dissident tribes and gradually winning over the more moderate elements to the idea of negotiation, the armed forces only being used as a last resort against the obdurate.

I remember being told at the time of a setback to their efforts unwittingly caused by an eccentric Irishwoman who ran a dispensary for sick animals in Marrakesh. After months of patient striving the French had succeeded in inducing the paramount Sheikhs of one such tribe to attend a conference, which was held in a marquee pitched outside the walls of Marrakesh. During the first session the lady came by, observed that three of the Sheikhs' horses tethered outside were in what she regarded as a disgracefully galled condition, and being an exceedingly strong personality browbeat the grooms into leading them to her dispensary for treatment; but when the Sheikhs emerged from their meeting and found their animals gone, they rounded on the French, accused them of having stolen them, and stormed off into the mountains; whence it took months more effort to cajole them anew.

Before evening I was at Ouarzazate, where there is a tourist hotel, built in the architectural style of the region; and very distinctive that style is. The constant threat of nomad raids from the desert has resulted in even farmhouses being built like fortresses, with battlements and towers at each corner, but in dried red earth, no doubt effective up to the appearance of cannon but merely picturesque now. Near Ouarzazate is a particularly fine Qasba called Taourirt, which must house a whole clan, so extensive are its ramifications; and smaller versions of it are scattered amongst the palms of the oasis in which it stands.

The colours of the Maghrib have always entranced me, but this spring evening beyond the Atlas provided a spectacle which I never saw equalled anywhere. In the foreground the brilliant green of the young barley, speckled with the black and white of the migrating storks which prowled in the fields, contrasted with the darker green of the palms and the dull red of the battlements behind. On the horizon the long line of the Atlas changed imperceptibly, as dusk approached, from its day-time violet through purple to deepest indigo. Over the western horizon, which was clear, the sun went down in a blaze of gold, leaving a great cone of amethyst light stretching from its point of disappearance to high in the upper sky; while to the south a bank of clouds flushed from primrose yellow to crimson which faded to grey as night fell and the stars came out.

Very different was my journey next day, when I turned northwards to recross the Atlas at their highest part by the Tizi n'Tishka. For nearly two hours I drove uphill in a series of loops across bleak hillsides, the prevailing lead-colour of which was relieved only by occasional almond-trees blossoming before flat mud hovels where Berber mountaineers were scratching a livelihood in conditions of bitter hardship.

Just before the pass which takes the road over the crest of the range, a signpost points to 'Telouet' and recalls one of the more curious episodes in the last stage of Morocco's struggle for liberation from the French Protectorate. The place is a Berber castle, the largest and finest of several in the trans-Atlas region, and like all of them the seat of a great Berber family. The El-Glawis of Telouet are of no great antiquity by Berber standards, but during the nineteenth and early twentieth centuries amassed a fortune by levying tolls on caravans, thereafter increasing it to impressive proportions by a number of methods which, unless popular rumour lies, were not over-scrupulous. The French Protectorate authorities, in their efforts to pacify and then to hold the country, were not averse to enlisting the support of powerful barons like this, and during the post-war years their alliance with the El-Glawi family was cemented by a common opposition to the Nationalist movement, which both rightly saw as a potential threat to their respective interests. The Glawi of the day thus became a creature of the French, entertaining almost royally in his mountain fastness and his city houses and receiving deference from the French representatives, and their guests. But in 1953 came a crisis. The Sultan (as he then was) Muhammad V had come to the conclusion that his duty lay in co-operation with the now powerful Nationalists, and the French decided that he must either be coerced into withdrawing this co-operation or be unseated. In an effort to mobilize all available local support against him, they induced the Glawi, in conjunction with a religious leader, to convene a meeting of rural notables and to persuade them to take an oath of solidarity on the tomb of that great leader of the past Moulay Idris; and then to demand the deposition of the Sultan. With this doubtful encouragement they duly deposed the Sultan and exiled him to Madagascar. Two years later, when the inevitable came about and they had to restore him, the Glawi hastily rallied to his cause and, after his return, made an act of grovelling submission which was recorded by hidden cameras and publicized; his prestige thus destroyed, he soon afterwards died. He had become an anachronism in the progressive Morocco of today; but his real error lay in backing the wrong horse.

The col, something over 7,000 feet, was clear and provided a long view backwards over a patchwork of beige and green, the desert and the sown. Then I wound on downwards, through country which became progressively greener and more wooded, until I came on to the immense flat plain which stretches from the north side of the Atlas chain to the Atlantic. Donkey-traffic gradually gave place to lorries and cars, and scrub-oak and olives to palms; and at length appeared across my front a long low red wall with towers and a horseshoe gate; and thus I came to Marrakesh, the capital of the south and, the second loveliest city of the Maghrib.

CHAPTER 13

Marrakesh and the High Atlas

It invites comparison with Fez. Both are ancient capitals; both have outstanding charm. But they are totally different. Fez, cloistered in its walls, with its vibrant life concentrated in endless narrow *suqs* and the houses hidden behind them, is the city of a long-settled community. Marrakesh, though also walled, is open; like Biskra or Laghouat, it is a city of the desert, journey's end for caravans; and although its *suqs* are extensive too, and stocked with all that travellers or peasants need, the real life of Marrakesh is not in them but in the Jama'a Fna, the great space below the minaret of the Kutubia, where from dawn to long after dusk little booths supply food and drink and sweets to the passers-by while musicians and jugglers and snake-charmers and story-tellers cater for their amusement, before they again face the road out to the mountains or the desert.

The difference between the two cities becomes more understandable when one considers their origin. No one is certain who were the followers of the two Idrises when they founded Fez, but all the evidence suggests that they were the inhabitants of what the Romans called Mauretania Tingitana, or northern Morocco, a region which had long been inhabited by a sedentary population and where nomadism hardly existed; whereas Marrakesh was founded by the Almoravids, who were dyed-in-the-wool nomads from the Sahara.

The name of these Almoravids has already cropped up several times and their story must now be told. It began in the middle of the eleventh century, when Yahya ibn Ibrahim, the chieftain of two Sanhaja tribes who roamed the desert south of the High Atlas, the Lemtouna and Jedala, visited Kairouan on his way back from a pilgrimage to Mecca and after talking to the religious leaders there realized how ignorant he and his people were of Islamic doctrine. At their suggestion he engaged Abdullah ibn Yasin, a divine living in the Sous (a fertile south Moroccan valley to which we shall come presently) to visit him and instruct his tribe. Ibn Yasin seems to have been a powerful personality who combined a marked taste for women with a gift of leadership, and his religious knowledge, although limited, was at least extensive enough to impress the tribesmen; but they disliked the austerity which he preached without practising, and he therefore induced some of their chiefs to found a *ribat*, which is best described as a 'military monastery', on an island somewhere in the south (it may have been off the coast, or in the Niger or Senegal Rivers), where he could inculcate in them a severe monastic discipline and thus equip them to battle for the faith. It is a tribute to his persuasiveness that he managed to enrol a thousand or more *murabitin*, or people of the *ribat*, as they came to be called (the word 'Almoravid' is a corruption of it); and after instruction they so much impressed the tribesmen with their fanaticism and piety that they were able to weld them into a formidable fighting force. The first test of strength of this force came about when the inhabitants of Sijilmassa in the Tafilelt appealed to them for help against a Zenata tribe who had expelled its original Kharijite founders and occupied it. The Almoravids duly came and expelled the Zenatas, but, as always seemed to happen in the Maghrib, the people soon found that their régime was no improvement and from then onwards periodically made trouble in their rear as they advanced elsewhere.

But nothing could now arrest this advance. The Almoravids occupied all the Sous valley, whence their preceptor had come, and penetrated into the High Atlas, where they put an end to a small Shi'a Kingdom, centred on a place called Aghmat, which had been founded by the Fatimids in one of their expeditions into Morocco. Here their temporal leader, Abu Bakr, who was a brother of the original Yahya, married Zainab, widow of the local King, who is the second Berber woman, after Kohina, to achieve lasting fame as a leader or a witch; but she seems to have been too much for him, for two years later he handed her over to his cousin Yusuf ibn Tashfin, who had become the military leader of the Almoravids and who, thanks to her guidance (or so it is related), twenty years later succeeded Abu Bakr as their chieftain.

About 1060 Yusuf ibn Tashfin, following precedent, founded his own capital at the foot of the Atlas, and planted round it the palms which he and his followers, being nomads, thought essential; and thus Marrakesh was born, and from it as a base the Almoravids moved forward. In 1069 they took Fez, and in the next few years Oujda, Tlemsen, and the Ouarsenis plateau; they even laid siege to Algiers, but here their attention was distracted elsewhere.

From the time when the Arabs in their first onrush through the Maghrib had crossed over into Spain, until 1031, when the last representative of the Omayyad Caliphate which they had established there was expelled by his own followers, the greater part of the Iberian Peninsula had passed a relatively peaceful and prosperous existence under tolerant Muslim rule, and it was then that the arts developed which were to bring so much to the cities of Morocco. But once the Omayyads had gone, the Muslim-ruled area had broken up into a number of mutually antagonistic principalities, on which the Christian rulers of northern Spain were beginning to exert ever-increasing pressure. They would have exerted even more had they been united amongst themselves and had the best general of their chief protagonist, Alphonse VI of Castille, not changed sides from time to time: he was Diaz de Vivar, better known by his sobriquet of 'The Cid', a word which comes from the Arabic 'Sayyid', Lord. Nevertheless by 1083 Alphonse had occupied Toledo and was bearing so heavily on the remaining princes that they felt impelled to seek help from their co-religionists in the Maghrib. The two possible sources were the Beni Hilal, at that time supreme in the centre, or the growing power of the Almoravids in the west, and they chose the latter as being less likely to prove a menace later on. Yusuf ibn Tashfin responded to the appeal, and having landed at Algeciras in 1083 he had succeeded, when he died a centenarian in 1106, in consolidating the whole of the southern half of the Peninsula, and the Balearic Islands, under his rule.

But this was the zenith of Almoravid power. Under the impulse of the militant spirit engendered by the success of the First Crusade, the Christians were constantly, if irregularly, advancing in Spain, and the reign of Yusuf's son Ali saw the Almoravid Empire gradually whittled away. The dynasty was ended in 1148 by other Sanhajas, the Almohads. Its lasting memorial was its creation of a cultural and intellectual bridge with Muslim Spain, whence came the inspiration for such masterpieces as the Great Mosques in Tlemsen and Algiers and the Qarawin *medersa* in Fez.

The Almohad dynasty which succeeded was also centred on Marrakesh, so it will be convenient to tell its story now also. The name means 'Unitarian', from the reformist creed which the founder, Ibn Toumert, developed after leaving his native Sous and travelling extensively in the Middle East and Muslim Spain. This man on his travels met near Mahdiya a Berber from Tlemsen called Abdul Mumin, and the association between the two was to have important results. Together, with a few followers, they came through the Taza Gap into the High Atlas, where their creed appealed to a Sanhaja tribe of the region, the Masmuda, so that they were able to found a small mountain State. In 1122 Ibn Toumert died, but Abdul Mumin took over the movement and proclaimed himself Caliph. He set out on the conquest of the Maghrib, and by keeping to the uplands and avoiding a direct clash with the Almoravid plainsmen he had succeeded by 1148 in occupying the whole of Morocco and the Tlemsen region, Tashfin ibn Ali, the last of the Almoravids, having in the meantime been accidentally killed. Next he passed into Spain and established a sort of Protectorate over the Muslim States there, and then pushed eastwards in the Maghrib and assailed the Hammadids, who had by that time transferred their capital from the Qala'a Beni Hammad to Bougie; he captured both in 1151. Then he took on the Beni Hilal and smashed them in a notable victory near Sétif, whence they retired in confusion beyond Tebessa.

After a quick visit to Marrakesh to consolidate, Abdul Mumin set out again in 1159. In a rapid campaign he captured

Mahdiya from Roger II of Sicily and expelled him and his
Normans finally from all the coastal towns from Tunis to
Tripoli in which they had been established for the past fifteen
years, and from the Island of Jerba. This done, and the whole
of Ifriqiya occupied, he proceeded to organize his domains and
to institute a system of land-survey and taxation which, according to Arab historians, prevailed from the Atlantic coast to
Cyrenaica. He also took a step which changed the racial composition of Morocco, for in the hopes of diluting the strength
of the Beni Hilal Arabs he transferred some of their tribes to
the plains of western Morocco, which they 'arabized'. He died
in 1163 in Rabat, which he had founded thirteen years earlier.

His son Abu Yaqub managed to bring all Muslim Spain
under his hegemony, but he then died and his successor Yaqub
al Mansur was faced with several rebellions, notably a curious
come-back by an Almoravid group from the Balearic Islands,
who landed at Bougie and made a temporary alliance with
the Beni Hilal, so that between 1184 and 1204 they succeeded
in occupying all Ifriqiya, the Biskra area, and the Jebel
Nafusa of Tripolitania. Al Mansur was at first too much tied up
in Spain to be able to deal with them, but in 1196 his hands
were freed by a notable victory which he won over the Spaniards at Alarcos, with enormous booty; it was in commemora-
tion of this that he endowed Morocco with two of its finest
monuments, the Kutubia Mosque at Marrakesh and the Tour
Hassan at Rabat, and Seville with a third, the Giralda. His
son An-Nasir was now able to reoccupy Ifriqiya and expel the
Almoravids, who disappear from history.

The Almohads thus ruled over the whole Maghrib, which
no other Berber dynasty had ever done or ever would do in the
future. They found it too big to control, and were obliged to
institute the Hafsids* in Tunis with such widely delegated
powers that a dynasty was established. In any event, they were
entering on their last phase. There were difficulties of succession, rebellions of the Zenata and the Merinids, and disasters
in Spain, where by 1248 all but Granada had been taken by
the Christians. By 1269 the Almohad Empire had been split

* See page 77.

into three, with the Merinids taking over Morocco, the Abdul
Wadids, based on Tlemsen, the central Maghrib, and the Hafsids the east. Its disintegration demonstrated once again the
inability of the Berber peoples to form a nation, mainly because
of the cleavage between the sedentaries of the mountains and
the nomads of the plains, which has proved too deep to be
bridged by even the most masterful ruler.

For three centuries Marrakesh was politically in eclipse
whilst the Merinids and the Wattasids ruled from Fez; but by
the middle of the sixteenth century the picture had radically
changed, with the Portuguese already established on the Atlantic coast, the Spaniards in Oran, and the Turks thrusting inward from their footholds on the Mediterranean coast. The
Wattasids were still engaged with the Portuguese when a new
enemy appeared: this was the Beni Sa'ad, or Sa'adians, an
Arab tribe who seem to have come from Arabia about the
thirteenth century and since then had been quietly occupying
the Sous and Dra'a valleys south of the Atlas. They claimed
direct descent from the Prophet, and by 1541 had begun to
make themselves felt by expelling the Portuguese from the ports
of Agadir, Safi, and Azzemour which they had founded and
fortified. They then took the offensive against the waning
power of the Wattasids, capturing Fez in 1545, and by 1554
had occupied the whole of Morocco.

Not surprisingly the desert-dwelling chief of the Sa'adians
Muhammad esh-Sheikh, who had taken the title of Caliph,
felt uncomfortable in the shut-in city of Fez and preferred the
oasis-city of Marrakesh, which he made his capital. Of the three
dangers at that time threatening Morocco, the Turks, the
Spaniards, and the Portuguese, he feared the Turks most; but
when he tried to intrigue against them with the Spaniards in
Oran, the Turks sent against him a long-range commando who
succeeded in murdering him and taking his head to Constantinople. His sons Abdul Malik and Ahmad had reinsured with
the Turks by taking service with them, and with their aid the
former managed to depose Al-Mutawakil, his third son, who
had succeeded to the throne; but in 1578 the Portuguese came
into the picture in an attempt to conquer Morocco and a battle,

known as 'The Battle of the Three Kings', was fought near Ksar el Kebir, in north Morocco, in which the Portuguese lost 60,000 killed and the dead included not only their King Sebastian, but also Al-Mutawakil, who was allied with him, and Abdul Malik, who was opposing him. Portugal, thus enfeebled, soon afterwards came under Spanish domination; and with their pressure removed Muhammad's surviving son Ahmad, who took the title of 'Al-Mansur', was able to rule Morocco peacefully for the next twenty-five years.

Al-Mansur seems to have been an exceptional monarch, for not only did he manage to master constant tribal revolts, and to restrain the growing penchant of the Moroccans towards *'maraboutism'*, or the veneration of local saints, but the general lines of administration which he laid down endured until the French occupation, over three hundred years later. Under it, Moroccan tribes were divided into three categories: those from whom his armed forces were drawn and who paid no taxes (the so-called *gaish*); those who recognized his authority and paid taxes, whose areas constituted the so-called *Bled-el-Makhzen*, or Royal Domain; and those who did not recognize his authority, whose areas were known as the *Bled-es-Siba*, or Domain of Dissidence; the areas of these latter domains varying from reign to reign with the strength of the ruling Sultan. He showed considerable commercial enterprise: he carried on a brisk trade with Elizabeth's England, bartering the saltpetre and sugar which the English needed for the timber and cannonballs which he needed; and with armies composed mainly of European mercenaries he embarked on a series of expeditions across the Sahara to Taghaza, whence the salt came, and the countries of the Niger, whence for centuries gold had flowed to the Maghrib. He was unsuccessful in discovering the actual sources of the gold, and unable to hold these countries in subjection, but he obtained from them considerable wealth, with which he embellished Marrakesh and increased the general strength of his realm. His enemies, too, were diminishing: the Portuguese were under the Spaniards, the Spaniards were too heavily engaged in the Low Countries to plan aggression in Morocco, and the Turks were similarly bogged down in Persia.

Al Mansur, who had also become known as 'Adh-Dhahabi' –
the Golden – was thus able to bequeath to his successor when
he died a rich and comparatively peaceful country, and a
capital in which, although the grandiose palace which he built
for himself was subsequently destroyed, the tombs of his dynasty,
including his own, are masterpieces of delicate, if slightly deca-
dent, Moorish art. It was to be another three hundred years
before Morocco again became as stable.

After his death his dynasty rapidly decayed in the manner
of all such dynasties in the Maghrib, through internal dissensions aggravated by renewed pressure from the Spaniards in
the north, and the last Sa'adian Sultan was assassinated in
Marrakesh in 1659. Eighteen years later the successor dynasty,
the Alawis, of whom we shall be hearing later, deprived Marrakesh of its title of 'Capital of the South' by transferring the
capital to Meknes and thereafter Marrakesh, while retaining
its commercial and regional importance, ceased to be the political centre of the country.

I first came to it in 1928, on a fine winter afternoon; and I can
still remember the patches of glistening white, which were the
snow-capped Atlas peaks, taking shape in the air above the
ground-mist which masked the horizon, so that they seemed to
have no connection with the earth; the glorious blue and silver
of the whole chain, seen closer from across the orange-trees
when I awoke next morning; and the salmon-coloured sunflush
on them in the stillness which comes before sunset, when the
smoke rises straight in the air and the sparrows chatter from
every palm. I have seen that wonderful chain many times since,
each time after a long absence, and each time with a fresh stab
of pleasure; and if I shut my eyes I can see it now.

On this occasion I spent many hours, as I had so often done
before, in making my way slowly round the city. It had changed
relatively little in thirty years. The *suqs*, which are as extensive
and almost as confusing a ramification as those of Fez, had
unhappily been hygienically rebuilt after a disastrous fire and
seemed somehow less authentic; but in the quiet courtyard of
the Sa'adian Tombs a pair of storks nesting on a wall were lak-

lakking together as I remembered their predecessors doing, and in the Jama'a Fna the crowds of countrymen still gazed with awe and delight at the marvels spread before them and the emotions still played like sunlight and shade across the faces of the story-tellers' audiences as the tales unfolded themselves. Always I was conscious of the minaret of the Kutubia, that supreme achievement of Andalusian-Arab architecture, standing massive and splendid over the city which it seemed to hold in its care.

From Marrakesh I went up into the High Atlas again, retracing a route of my youth. On that long-past occasion, two of us had boarded a native bus full of veiled women, with bundles of chickens and sheep tied by the legs festooning its top, at 5 a.m. on a hot May morning, and had been carried across the plain to the distant foothills and up the road that leads to the hill-village of Asni. From there we had struck off into the recesses of the mountains, our baggage on mules convoyed by lithe little dark-eyed, hook-nosed Berbers who shuffled over the stones of the rough track in broken slippers. We had passed through tiny hamlets round which the almonds were in bloom, and the path had led higher, round the sides of hills above a deep gorge, across which we could hear, above the thunder of a torrent below, the chanting of the hillmen on the farther side. We had come to a village of Jews, distinctive in their black caftans and skull-caps, probably descendants of Berbers who had been Judaized in Cyrenaica and had migrated after the suppression of the second century Jewish revolt there. We had made camp at 10,000 feet in a stony amphitheatre of mountains, up and down which a great golden eagle patrolled morning and evening, and the muleteer whom we had kept with us insisted on sleeping outside, wrapped only in his brown woollen cloak, while our water froze in the bucket inside our tent. For the next week we had explored the heights around, until one morning we stood on the summit of Jebel Toubkal, which at 13,666 feet is the highest point of all North Africa, and had seen the contrast between the green of the spring fields to the north and the beige and yellow and brown of the desert to the south.

This time I did not stop in Asni, but continued upwards towards the crest of the range. Just off the road was the site of Aghmat, where Zainab was Queen and the Almoravids gained their first foothold, but nothing is visible now. For two hours I saw no one except little gangs of roadworkers conscientiously cleaning the verges – one of many signs that the Moroccan administration is efficiently carrying on where the French left off – but above the scrub-covered hillsides (the northern side of the Atlas is far greener than the stark southern) I could see snow-peaks looming ever nearer, until I came at last to the Tizi n'Test, the twin of the Tizi n'Tishka by which I had crossed before and at about the same height, and from here I could look down into the broad fertile Sous Valley.

Another hour of steep hairpin bends brought me down into this valley, where I at once ran into an unexpected hazard, a swarm of locusts, like a red-flaked snowstorm, which covered the car and smashed themselves on the windscreen; three months later, when in a Cambridge garden I unrolled a coil of chicken-wire which I had carried along the front bumper in case I might run into soft sand, I found a dozen dried Moroccan locusts in it. Locusts are a scourge in Morocco when they come, which fortunately is not often, as they breed in the Sahara and can only cross the Atlas under a particular combination of wind and early snowmelt which occurs only once in every few years. George Borrow in *The Bible in Spain* describes a big swarm in Tangier about 1840, and in 1929 I myself experienced another in Casablanca, when the streets were covered with a red carpet which the wheels of cars crushed into a paste and the small Berber boys swept them up joyfully to fry and eat, for they are said to taste like shrimps.

I came soon to Taroudant, the capital of the Sous province and an old town which was occupied in turn by Almoravids, Almohads, and Merinids. In the seventeenth century it was for some years the capital of an independent principality, and in 1912, after the French had established the Protectorate, it became a base for a Berber divine from the far south called El-Hiba, when he declared a Holy War against them and had to be suppressed by a full-scale military operation. Round it are

Berber castle beyond the Atlas Mountains, Morocco
Berber powder-play at the Feast of Moulay-Idris, Morocco

King Hassan II rides to the Friday Prayer

the crenellated ramparts of trans-Atlas architecture, with five gates, and within them the town is busy enough; though not apparently on the scale of the sixteenth century, when the sugar of the province, exported by way of the port of Agadir at the valley's end, was a prime source of wealth. A British charitable organization was working amongst the children here; and I carried away a welter of impressions: of the scent of syringa and orange-blossom in shady courtyards; of wastrel boys in a dormitory above the teeming *suq*; of blind children doing Braille in Arabic; of little dark-eyed Berber beauties romping in the grounds of a Franciscan school.

The Sous valley, as I drove on down it, was patently rich, with orchards and olive-groves, and fields of sugar-cane and grain between them; but it seemed also remote and shut-off between the Atlas on the one side and the lower anti-Atlas on the other – and yet from it had come the founder of the Almoravids, who had ruled half Spain, and the Almohads, who had ruled all the Maghrib. As I advanced, the mountains receded, and ahead I could catch glimpses of the distant Atlantic, until I came out on a bluff from which I could look down upon Agadir, the obscure little fishing-port which twice in its short history has made the headlines of the world Press.

We first hear of it in 1505, when the Portuguese bought it during their original penetration of Morocco, and its capture by the Sa'adians in 1541* was the first step forward by that dynasty. Under them its trade must have increased greatly as the cultivation of sugar-cane up the valley developed, but in 1765 the then Sultan of Morocco, Moulay Muhammad ibn Abdullah, partly in order to revenge himself on the Sous for having revolted against him and partly because he wanted to have his own base for corsair operations, favoured the rival port of Es-Saouira, farther to the north, to a point where it effectively killed the trade of Agadir. In 1911, however, the first of its moments came. The French had been increasingly involving themselves in the affairs of Morocco, which was sliding into near-anarchy under the rule of an exceptionally incompetent Sultan, because of their need to prevent his unruly tribesmen

* See page 162.

M

from raiding into Algeria. Kaiser Wilhelm II had observed their activities with jealousy, the more so as he had not been consulted when, in 1904, the British and French had under the terms of the *Entente Cordiale* allowed each other a free hand in Morocco and Egypt respectively; in 1905 he had made a loudly-trumpeted visit to Tangier, but this had merely led to a diplomatic defeat for Germany at the Conference of Algeciras held the following year. He therefore decided to dispatch a gunboat, the *Panther*, to Agadir as a warning to France that any further forward movement by her in Morocco might provoke a German counter-move into the Sous Valley. There was an immediate British reaction on the side of France and the peace seemed in danger, but intense diplomatic activity ended in Germany acquiescing in France's free hand in Morocco in exchange for a concession in the Cameroons, on the understanding that freedom of trade would be preserved. The incident had, however, another and different consequence: by creating the impression that Germany might be preparing to interest herself in North Africa it spurred the rulers of Italy to mount the expedition which, the same year, wrested Libya from the Turks.

Agadir's second moment, a sadder one, came fifty years later. Until the 1930's the French had strictly controlled access to it, allegedly on security grounds, with the result that land-speculators had, if rumour is to be believed, made fortunes by selling to the credulous unseen plots of land which turned out to be situated out to sea or to have been measured up the faces of cliffs; but in the 1950's a French company began to develop it as a winter resort, and when I visited it in February 1960 had already built a Casino and fine hotels. Exactly four weeks after I left, an earthquake destroyed it, and many villages in its hinterland, with a completeness which must be unique in history. No one will ever know how many bodies lay under the ruins when they were finally sealed off and bulldozed, but 15,000 is probably a conservative estimate; and I was told of an aeroplane which, flying over the ruins the next day, reported that the hotel on the third floor of which I had stayed was intact, whereas the roof which the pilot saw was in fact resting on the ground and of the 150 people who had been under it hardly one escaped uninjured. It was a hard test for a newly independent Government, not overblessed with money, but its resolution never faltered: the place must be rebuilt and must develop as planned. Now, four years later, I found a mass of bulldozers, concrete-mixers, and dust, as on a site lying rather to the south of the original (now grassgrown) town large buildings were rising and streets being laid out. Economic justification seemed to me doubtful; the spirit behind it was not.

I spent several days in the Sous, visiting a series of red-walled villages (one of them being Tiznit, which was the last refuge of the agitator El-Hiba before the French captured him in 1912) and once ranging as far as the frontier of Ifni, a tiny enclave of Spanish territory towards the southern extremity of Morocco which is all that remains of a formerly extensive Spanish territorial claim on south Morocco. It is fine open country with much agriculture, and the people looked happy, if poor. I remember most sharply a tiny school in the most remote of all the villages, where ten-year-olds in blue robes shyly kissed the palms of our hands whilst their master dilated on their keenness and his need of more books and better premises.

This thirst for education I found throughout the country; in this young country, determined to prove its fitness for independence, youth has been quick to realize that education is a first priority and the combined efforts of the Government, French, and Mission schools are insufficient to meet the demand.

CHAPTER 14

The Heart of Morocco

I turned northwards up the coast, and rounded a series of head-lands where the Atlas comes down to the Atlantic. This brought me on to the great central plain, which at this season was a miracle of flowers: most resplendent were the orange marigolds which lined the roadsides, but mimosa was in bloom in every gully and the fields were a blaze of diversified colour on which the storks strode. On that day of warm sunshine the road was a motorist's Paradise, for its surface was, as everywhere, perfect and I met little traffic apart from occasional trade lorries, strings of donkeys attended by Berbers in their hooded cloaks and their womenfolk in striped red dresses and shawls with dark cloaks over them, or a line of camels preceded by a stout Moor sitting sideways on a donkey and urging it forward with scissor-motions of his legs.

This part of the Atlantic coast is a constant reminder of the Portuguese penetration which came to an abrupt halt with the Battle of the Three Kings in 1578, for the first four ports up it, As-Saouira, Safi, Al-Jdida, and Azzemmour, were all founded by the Portuguese during this phase and all bear obvious traces of their origin. The first, and to my mind the best, is As-Saouira, until a few years ago known as Mogador. It has a superb line of battlements, against which the sea beats and through which rows of Spanish cannon still point outwards, and a busy little port where the fishing-boats lie and red nets dry; not to mention an admirable plage opposite its hotel. Offshore is an island on which Drake and his companions on Christmas Day 1577 made their first landfall since leaving Plymouth on their journey round the world in the 'Golden Hind' squadron. When I first knew the place, as Mogador, the population was largely composed of the Jews who had flooded in when Moulay Muhammad founded it in the eighteenth century, and amongst them were many who had trading connections with Great Britain (particularly, of course, in Manchester cottons) and enjoyed a limited measure of protection under the Capitulations system then still in force; but this no longer exists, and the attraction of Israel, as at Jerba, has decimated the community, so that Berbers now seemed to predominate in a smaller population today.

Next, another hundred miles northwards, is Safi, where another impressive Portuguese castle, with the remains of a Berber palace inside it, stands in ruins on the shore and from its battlements gives an unrivalled view of the sea and the coast in both directions. In the last few years Safi has achieved some prosperity by becoming the main port of export for the vast fields of natural phosphates which lie inland near Yusufia and provide Morocco with over a quarter of its export earnings, and on the coast just north of the town a vast chemical complex, opened in 1965, will substantially increase those earnings by producing superphosphates. For me, however, the great attraction of Safi is the pottery-market just outside the walls, for the local product is brightly coloured and distinctive, and in the mass makes a pleasant sight.

Then comes Mazagan, or rather Al-Jdida as it is now called, with another solid Portuguese keep in its centre: this has four bastions named after St. Sebastian, St. Antonio, 'The Angel', and the 'Holy Spirit', and a water-gate which gives on to an active little fishing-port. Mazagan had the distinction of being the last Portuguese foothold in Morocco, for it was only evacuated in 1769, or two centuries after the 'Battle of the Three Kings'.

Lastly Azzemmour, again with a Portuguese fort, this time with six bastions, and a similar battlemented wall, commands the mouth of the Um ar-Rabia, the 'Mother of Fertility' as the main river of south Morocco is called; like Safi and Agadir, it was captured from the Portuguese by the Sa'adians in their campaign of 1541. Anyone who has inspected these four massive strongholds must wonder at the resolution displayed by the Portuguese in building them and feel some regret that their efforts to maintain themselves on this hostile shore came so quickly to disaster.

After Azzemmour you are at the gates of Casablanca, the huge commercial centre, which with its million inhabitants is by far the largest city in the Maghrib, and nowadays the richest too. It is of no great antiquity: the Portuguese held it from 1575 to 1755, but it then relapsed into obscurity until in 1862 the Compagnie Paquet decided to run a shipping service to it from Marseilles. In 1906 the Sultan granted a concession to a French company to build a port, but the following year a riot resulted in the death of several French workers and led to direct French military intervention on Moroccan soil. From the time Lyautey assumed the direction of the French Protectorate and made Casablanca the base from which his columns operated to pacify the countryside, its importance increased, and the decision after the First World War to make it into a major port assured its future. Its history since then has been one of uninterrupted growth, almost unaffected by the abrogation of the Protectorate and Morocco's resumption of full sovereignty, and it has become a rather shapeless agglomeration of European buildings and boulevards surrounding the remains of the formerly walled native town, now largely a slum. Here is concentrated, much of it in French hands, most of Morocco's industry (mining apart), and in its neighbourhood, and up the coast as far as Rabat, sixty miles away, much of the agricultural land is owned by French settlers, whose superior agricultural skills enable them to produce between 75 per cent and 80 per cent of the country's valuable cash crops – citrus, tobacco, wine, and primeurs – from about an eighth of the total cultivable area. Casablanca has little to offer the sightseer; much, in the way of commonplace entertainment, to offer the tourist. Its appearance is shoddy southern European rather than Maghribi; but it is the commercial capital of the country, and its labour force, better organized than in most developing countries, is already an important, and could be a determining, political factor in the country's future.

Just north of it is Mohammedia, a small watering-place which in 1942 achieved unexpected notoriety when it became the scene of the first landing of the American troops executing Operation 'Torch'. Immense luck they had, to choose a day when the Atlantic surf allowed landings on the beach, for only one day in five will provide these conditions and on the other four the huge breakers which crash on to the rocks are a sufficient warning to keep off.

As I drove along this stretch of coast, I recognized a headland on which, in 1929, I had taken a party of Moroccan Boy Scouts for a week-end camp; and near it the farm from which a local landowner, an elderly Moor, who had strolled over to our tents with a tiny black-eyed daughter clinging to the skirt of his jellaba, had invited us for a mint-tea session. I could recall being surprised at the vehemence with which, even in those early days, he had inveighed against the French occupation; and I hoped that his descendants were now enjoying their independence.

From this point I turned inland, across the undulating plain with the wild flowers and the donkey- and camel-trains, and occasionally on the horizon the silhouette of a horseman with high-pommelled saddle and broad stirrups: the Moroccan Berbers are inveterate horsemen, and a 'fantasia', or charge of riders firing rifles in the air at full gallop, is still a feature of most ceremonies. It was of course from the Barbary Coast that 'barbs' took their name.

After three hours or so, another line of battlements rose before me, and the road circled round them to a very fine gate, of the horseshoe shape already familiar from Fez and Marrakesh, leading into Meknes. This is the fourth of the capitals of Morocco, and takes its name from a Zenata tribe, the Miknasi, but is more closely connected with the Alawi dynasty which rules Morocco today; and I will at this point complete the history of the country, which we left at the end of the Sa'adian régime in the mid-seventeenth century.

By this time the country had almost disintegrated. In the Sous, a certain Abul Hassan al Somlali had set up an independent principality. The Marrakesh region was ruled by an independent Sheikh. In the north and centre, a college of Sanhaja *marabouts*, centred on a *zawiya* at Dila, near Khenifra in the centre of the country, had extended their influence over the Berbers as far as Fez, but were already being challenged by a new power, that of the *Shorfa* (descendants of the Prophet) of Tafilelt, an Arab tribe from Yanbu on the Red Sea, who had migrated to that trans-Atlas region just after the Sa'adians had arrived in the Dra'a. Moreover Europe was active: the English, through the 'Barbary Company', were busily extending their trade and their influence, and in 1661 had acquired Tangier from the Portuguese; the Spaniards had seized the ports of Larache, Ceuta, and Melilla; the Portuguese were still in Mazagan and Casablanca; and the Dutch were commercially active. With all these mutually conflicting forces operating, it seemed as though Morocco was doomed to be irrevocably pulled to pieces.

That it was not, and that it succeeded for another two centuries in maintaining its independence, was due primarily to Moulay Rashid, a younger son of the leader of the Shorfa of Tafilelt, who rebelled against his elder brother, broke out from Tafilelt, and with irregularly-acquired funds managed to buy enough followers to enable him to defeat his brother, who died in the battle, and thereafter to occupy in succession the Rif Mountains in the north, the region (though not the town) of Tangier, the Atlantic coast, Marrakesh, and finally the Sous, breaking in the process the power of the *marabouts* of Dila and of Al Somlali's Sous principality. But it was his brother Moulay Ismail, who succeeded him at the age of twenty-eight, who became the most famous, or rather the most infamous, of his dynasty, the Alawi, which still rules Morocco today. During his long reign, which lasted from 1672 to 1727, he dominated and controlled Morocco as no sovereign had done before and few did afterwards; and having decided to transfer his capital to Meknes he spent most of his reign building a palace there which was intended to rival Versailles, using for the purpose 30,000 prisoners and a number which has been given as 25,000 (though this is probably exaggerated) of Christian captives or renegades. It was these immense buildings, now mostly in ruins, which confronted me as I arrived; inside you can walk through acres of courts and stables and the ghosts of gardens, once intended to provide an immortal memorial to a man who seems to have been a monster of cruelty and of most other vices, but now rather suggesting Ozymandias, or a Warning Against Vanity.

More sensible were his security measures. Having discovered in the Dra'a Valley in the extreme south an army of 150,000 Negroes from the Sudan who had originally been brought in by a rival claimant to the throne and then demobilized there, he recruited them, installed 70,000 of them in a sort of studfarm which he established at Mashra'a ar-Remel, near Meknes, to breed up the next generation of recruits, and garrisoned the remainder either in Meknes or in a chain of forts which he built along the main roads and in potentially dissident areas like the Middle Atlas. The country once subjugated, he attempted, with mixed success, to rid it of foreign domination. He failed to storm Tangier, but by destroying its trade induced the English to evacuate it. He took Larache from the Spaniards, but failed against their other fortresses of Ceuta and Melilla, nor could he reduce the Portuguese garrison of Mazagan. He succeeded in holding the Turks, by now well established in Algeria, on the farther side of the River Tafna, which runs from Tlemsen to the sea, and his commandoes even penetrated into southern Algeria as far as Laghouat, though they could not hold it. He encouraged trade with Europe, and also corsair operations from his Atlantic ports, both of which brought him great profit; and his personal courage in battle and frugality of life were unquestioned. His private life, however, seems to have been appalling by any standards. His harem numbered 500 at a time, and he had at least 700 sons and uncounted daughters, the majority of whom were strangled at birth as unwanted; and the stories of his brutality – that he would test a new sword by striking off the head of the nearest slave, and always insisted on demolitions of masonry being done from the bottom so that some workmen were bound to be crushed under its fall – seem too numerous to have been all inventions.

The removal of his controlling hand by his death in 1727 was, however, followed by thirty years of anarchy whilst his sons disputed the succession, but in 1757 his grandson Moulay Muhammad ibn Abdullah came to the throne and ruled for

thirty-two years, during which time he expelled the Portuguese
from Mazagan, their last foothold, and also ruined Agadir by
promoting As-Saouira. For the next century after his death the
country remained much the same. Three Sultans of note,
Moulays Sulaiman, who ruled from 1792 to 1822, Abdurrahman (1822–59), and Al Hasan (1873–94), at least managed to
keep it independent, though Moulay Abdurrahman came to
blows with the French in 1844 for having tried to help Abdul
Kader against them in Algeria, and Morocco and Spain came to
blows in 1860 over Ceuta; but internally these Sultans were no
more able than the less illustrious tenants of the throne to provide even the rudiments of a competent administration, even
in the *Bled al Makhzen* which they controlled.

After Moulay al Hasan's death in 1894 the state of the
country deteriorated rapidly. A weak and prodigal Sultan,
Moulay Abdul Aziz, was on the throne, but his authority was
virtually limited to the towns, and in the east the Pretender
Bou Hamara was supreme; while the backwardness, cruelty,
and corruption of his régime horrified foreign observers. The
French, with their now large commitment in Algeria, were
anxious to secure its western frontier by controlling Morocco, as
they had already secured its eastern frontier by occupying
Tunisia; the British wanted settled conditions for the trade
which they had built up over the years, but did not want to see
Morocco, and thus the Straits of Gibraltar, controlled by any
potentially hostile Power; the Spaniards, who still held Ceuta
and Melilla (as they do today) had territorial claims on both the
north and the south of the country; and the Kaiser was envisaging
staking a claim too as a move in the European diplomatic game.

But it was the French who proved to be the best players, for by
a series of astute diplomatic moves they gradually won a free
hand for themselves in Morocco. In 1904 the *Entente Cordiale*
eliminated Great Britain as a rival; in the same year a secret
agreement with Spain laid down respective spheres of interest;
in 1906 the Act of Algeciras, issued at the outcome of the Conference called as a result of the Kaiser's Tangier visit of the
previous year, recognized the independence and sovereignty of
Morocco but also, by implication, French predominance and

Spanish interests in it; and in 1909 Germany, as a result of a dispute with France about Foreign Legion deserters, recognized France's special interests there. Meanwhile from 1907 onwards France had had to intervene directly, first in the Oujda area, then in Casablanca and the Atlantic province, to quell disorders which were affecting French interests; while the Sultan's prestige, already low because of the opposition of vested interests to certain tax reforms, sensible in themselves, which he wished to introduce, was further sapped by his inability to prevent these foreign incursions. In 1908 his unpopularity led to his brother Moulay Hafidh being proclaimed as a rival Sultan in Marrakesh, and as the French, after some hesitation, pronounced themselves neutral in this dynastic conflict, he was able within a year to oust his brother and secure international recognition as Sultan.

Moulay Hafidh managed to suppress Bou Hamara's revolt, but internal disorders soon broke out elsewhere, for no effective reforms or redress of grievances had been accomplished. In 1910 another Pretender to the throne was proclaimed in Meknes and Fez was beleagured by the rebels, so that the Sultan was obliged to appeal to France for help, which was granted, a French column relieving Fez. In 1911 Spain, in pursuance of her 1904 agreement with France, occupied Larache and Ksar el Kebir in the north; and when in 1911 the Kaiser's thrust to Agadir was parried, while the internal state of Morocco became more and more hopeless, the way was clear for the assumption of responsibility by France which obviously alone could save the country.

By 1912 it was settled. The Sultan was induced to sign a Treaty of Fez, which established a French Protectorate over Morocco and also laid down the principle that Tangier should have an international status; while a separate Franco-Spanish Convention concluded the same year set up a Spanish Zone of Morocco under Spanish Protection in which the Sultan's authority would be delegated to a 'Khalifa' or Viceroy. Thus, for the time being, Moroccan independence was suspended and the country given the opportunity to recover and develop.

.   .   .   .   .

Mcknes is the fifth city of Morocco (after Casablanca, Marrakesh, Rabat, and Fez), and although a busy commercial
centre is the least sophisticated of them. It is overshadowed by
the great deserted palace, and has perhaps less charm than
most Moroccan sites; but it contains one thing of beauty, the
Medersa Bou Ananiya, which it owes not to the Alawis but to
their predecessors-but-two the Merinids – one more treasure
which those great artists have bequeathed. Outside it are a
pair of fine bronze doors; within, as in the Fez *medersas* which
it much resembles, intricate cedar-carving, delicate plaster-
work, and enamelled tiles in soft shades of colour; and here,
as in them, is the feeling of a retreat from the world outside,
of a quiet which the street noises hardly disturb.

But as I walked round the walls and through the full streets,
I was recalling another memory of thirty years back. I had
come over to Meknes from Fez one hot Sunday morning in
August to see the *moussem* or annual festival of the Aissaoua:
these are the followers of a *marabout* named Sidi Aissa, who
died in 1523 leaving a reputation for saintliness and has his
tomb in the city, and are (or were at that time) found all over
Morocco and in Kairouan, where they still have two *zawiyas*.
On a day corresponding to the Birthday of the Prophet, con-
tingents of them numbering something like 200,000, who had
started from their homes several days before and had marched
across the land under the burning summer sun, assembled outside one of the great gates of Meknes and, on an open space
kept inviolate for this, spent three days dancing themselves
into ecstasy and the three following nights in orgies so barbaric
that the whole ceremony has, I believe, now been banned by
the Moroccan Government as being incompatible with the
manners of a civilized State.

What I saw myself was striking enough. When I arrived,
bands of the faithful, in the dingy white cloaks and turbans of
the Moroccan peasant, were converging from all directions on
the space outside the gates, all across which rings of fifty or
more, their cloaks laid aside, were performing in their shirts
and drawers a knee-bending, body-contorting dance to the
wild music of the piper within each ring. Gradually the whole

plain became a sea of swaying figures and the air filled with
the shrilling of the pipes; and all through the heat of the day
the dance went on, with only brief pauses for the pipers to
draw breath, while the dancers streamed sweat and their eyes
glazed into unconsciousness. Sundown was the signal for the
evening prayer, after which the dancers surged into the town
for the next, orgiastic, phase. The French had surrounded the
Mellah, the Jewish quarter, with Foreign Legion troops with
fixed bayonets lest the celebrants might go berserk and attack
these infidels, who in those days were easily distinguishable
by the black clothing which they always wore. I did not
witness what went on thereafter; but that night after I had
returned home the rhythm of the dancing which I had watched
all day was still drumming in my head, and I can recall it
now.

It was, of course, a naked pagan survival from pre-Islamic
days; and that summer I witnessed another, still more naked,
in a small and beautiful village in the Jebel Zerhoun, north of
Meknes, which is called Moulay Idris after the original founder
of Fez. It was the annual ceremony of another and grimmer
sect called the Hamadcha, now also suppressed, and I went to
it on an even hotter day, all unsuspecting (I was very young)
what lay before me. I reached the village, and walked through
streets which seemed curiously deserted until through a low
archway I came out into the central square, and into a scene
lifted directly from a horror-film. Along the walls and on the
low roofs a line of villagers gazed intently at a swirling group
of perhaps fifty men in the middle. Most of these carried what
looked like medieval battle-axes, curved blades attached to
short handles, with which they were slashing their own faces
until the blood ran down their clothing; others had earthen
water-jars, which they were throwing in the air and heading
as one heads a football, until they broke and cut their foreheads
to the bone. Shouting and shrieking they swayed up and down,
arms flailing, battle-axes whirling, like some infernal ballet,
and looking as remote from reality; but as I watched the scene
changed and became all too real, for of a sudden they abandoned the open space and ran round the walls, so that they

pushed by mc as I stood, and for an instant I looked into eyes charged with such fanaticism as I never saw before, or have since. At that moment I realized my danger, of which no one had warned me – there seemed to be no one in authority in the place – and I slid away as unostentatiously as I could to the archway, outside which I went down in so complete a faint that my head hit the ground and brought me to again. Had I been wearing black and thus, to fanatical eyes, had the appearance of a Jew, I must have been cut to pieces.

I revisited Moulay Idris this time from Meknes. It looked peaceful, and as I walked through its streets the eyes of those I met looked only mildly curious. From the top of the steeply rising main street I gained a flat roof-top from which I could look out over the clustered houses of the village on to a vista of olive-covered Zerhoun hills, line upon line, with the snows of the Middle Atlas rising above them in the far distance.

I went on through these hills, and on emerging from their northern fringe saw before me, on a vast green plain stretching to the horizon, a triumphal arch and a large area of ruins. This was Volubilis, the only considerable Roman site in Morocco, which I have already mentioned as being the first capital of Idris before he founded Fez.

The Roman occupation of Morocco was a partial and brief affair compared with their settlement and development of the more easterly parts of the Maghrib, and we are far from sure of its details. We know that before 49 B.C., when the war between Caesar and Pompey was at its height, 'Mauretania', which could be defined as a strip of territory extending from the Atlantic coast to the Constantine area, was divided between two Berber monarchs, Bogud to the west and Bocchus II to the east, and that when, in A.D. 42, Caligula annexed Mauretania; he divided it into two provinces, corresponding to these two kingdoms, which he called 'Mauretania Tingitana' ('Tingi' was Tangier) and 'Mauretania Caesariana' respectively, the boundary between them being the Moulouya, the large river which runs from between Oujda and Taza to the Mediterranean just east of Melilla. At first Mauretania Tingitana seems in practice to have been no more than a strip of territory running down the Atlantic coast from Tingi to Sala (Rabat), but later the Roman occupation seems to have been extended as far south as the general line Rabat-Meknes-Fez; and although we do not know the exact location of the *limes* – nor indeed whether they were as continuous at this end of the Maghrib as at the other – it is reasonable to suppose that they went through the 'Taza Gap', that traditional highway, to join the *limes* coming through from Tlemsen from the direction of Tiaret, the line of which is more accurately known. In this form the province lasted no longer than the fourth century A.D., for under Diocletian's great reorganization it was detached from its sister province, attached to the Province of Spain, and apparently reduced to an even narrower area than at first so that it extended only from Tingi as far as the Oued Loukkos near Larache, Volubilis being evacuated; and in the fifth century, when the Romans were being pressed by the Vandals, even this strip was abandoned, though the Vandals seem never to have occupied it. When the Byzantines entered the Maghrib in the sixth century, by which time Spain was occupied by the Visigoths, they probably reattached the two Mauretanias, but do not seem to have occupied any part of Morocco.

Until its evacuation Volubilis, and not Tingi, seems to have been the capital of Mauretania Tingitana; and indeed its site was infinitely superior for the control of the *limes*. It must in fact have been a garrison town of some importance, as its numerous opulent villas testify; and the inscriptions dating as late as the latter half of the seventh century show that it remained in effective Byzantine occupation well after the time of the first Arab incursion into the Maghrib. Its Christian community seems to have existed even longer, for Idris I found Christians there in the late eighth century. As a spectacle, its ruins are far less impressive than those of several of the other sites I had visited, consisting as they do of one triumphal arch, of Caracalla, and the foundations of numerous villas and baths; but one mosaic, beautifully restored, of Orpheus surrounded by a most varied, and vividly depicted, collection of North African fanna stays in the memory.

I returned to Meknes and, striking westwards through the cork-oak forest of Mamora, which according to Pliny the Elder was in his time infested with elephants, I reached the coast again where the twin cities of Rabat and Salé stand on either side of the estuary of the Bou Regreg, the 'Glittering River'.

Rabat has been the capital of Morocco since Lyautey made it so in 1912, and without rivalling Fez or Marrakesh it still has a respectably long history. Some kind of settlement must have existed from early days at the mouth of the Bou Regreg, for although now largely silted up and accessible only to fishing vessels, it was a natural haven for vessels coasting southwards, as the Carthaginians did, in search of gold and ivory in West Africa; certainly the Romans established a station, Sala, there and retained it until their fourth century reorganization. But the real development of Rabat followed the foundation in the tenth century of a *ribat* or fortified monastery (whence its name comes) on the superb seacoast site now occupied by the castle of the Oudaiyas, and this was enlarged into a town by the Almohad Abdul Mumin and embellished in the eleventh century by his grandson Yaqub al Mansur, who built that admirable example of Andalusian-Arab work the Tour Hassan. The Merinids added to it by founding, on the site of Roman Sala, a necropolis called Shella which is one of the loveliest things in Morocco, for it is a quiet enclosed garden containing two little gems of mosques and a sacred spring, with carved Muslim tombs amongst the flowers.

Meanwhile Salé, a settlement on the opposite side of the river, which had been founded in the eleventh century and briefly held by the Spaniards in the thirteenth, had become a flourishing commercial entrepot. Early in the seventeenth century both sides of the river received a large influx of Muslims forced out of Spain by Philip III's general order of expulsion and thirsting for revenge against the Christians, with the result that the corsairs which they manned, known under the general name of 'Sally Rovers', became if anything a greater scourge of Mediterranean shipping than those based on Algiers, and caused French, British, Dutch, and Spanish warships to bombard Salé at intervals, with little success. The corsairs at first operated independently, as the Sa'adian dynasty at that time predominant in Morocco had become too weak to be able to control them, but Moulay Rashid, when he came to power, organized them on privateer lines and he and his successors profited from their ventures. In the latter half of the eighteenth century, however, Moulay Muhammad ibn Abdullah limited their activities, which in any case were becoming increasingly hazardous in the Mediterranean owing to the rise of European seapower, and by the early nineteenth century they were extinct.

Thereafter both Rabat and Salé sank into a torpor from which Rabat was woken by Lyautey but from which Salé has not entirely woken to this day; though it is in fact the eleventh in size of the Moroccan towns and does a good deal of business, it still preserves an air of antiquity. It contains at least one monument of note, the *medersa* built by the Merinid Abul Hassan, and two ancient *zawiyas*; and they still point out the gate through which Defoe made Robinson Crusoe enter the town before escaping to begin his adventures.

Rabat owes much, perhaps too much, to Lyautey. Its exquisite monuments, the Oudaiyas and the Tour Hassan of the Almohads and the Shella of the Merinids, have been well preserved for our enjoyment; the *medina*, or original town, with its mosques and crowds, remains much as it always has been except that handicrafts are rarer than in pre-mechanization days; and from the enormous palace the young King still rides out in traditional style to the Friday prayer in the Great Mosque, in a red-painted Cinderella coach one way and on a white horse under a scarlet umbrella the other, flanked in both directions by his personal bodyguard in their scarlet uniforms. But the city has indulged in an urban sprawl outside its former limits, with quarters of commonplace European villas and shopping-streets, and one whole area of grandiose public buildings in Franco-Moorish style. It is here, however, that the present Kingdom of Morocco was forged, and here that its future is being worked out.

Lyautey, whose name will always be linked, at least in European memories, with Morocco, was undoubtedly a great colonialist, and even if that word is nowadays blown upon he had

N

qualities which must be admired. Chief amongst them was courage. The Morocco of which he became the first Resident-General when the Protectorate was set up in 1912 had sunk very low, and was a sad contrast to its vigorously evolving neighbour Algeria. Moulay Abdul Hafidh, having signed the Treaty of Fez by virtue of which the Protectorate was instituted, had abdicated in favour of his younger brother Muhammad ben Yusuf, whose writ on accession hardly ran in the centre and south of the country; Fez was besieged by Berber tribes, and Marrakesh was soon afterwards threatened by El-Hiba's Holy Warriors. Even in the much reduced *Bled-al Makhzen*, the area which officially owed him allegiance, the taxes were not being collected, so that the treasury, already drained by the gross extravagances of earlier Sultans, was all but empty, and the administration was chaotic. There was hardly a doctor or an engineer in the country; hardly a school, apart from the few Quranic schools in the cities; hardly a road, or a vehicle; only a barbaric luxury for the rich, and bitter poverty and oppression for the poor.

Lyautey's first task was to restore law and order. Before he had succeeded, the First World War broke out and he found himself confronted with a French Government order to repatriate the bulk of his troops and to withdraw what remained to the coast. It was then that he showed his mettle: for, having complied with the first, he resisted the second, and during the war succeeded not only in preserving the French presence in Morocco but even in enlarging the area of French authority. His method of dealing with dissidents, using a minimum of force at the right time and place as an adjunct to patient diplomacy and negotiation, was eminently successful and economical, and set the pattern which the French followed thereafter. He himself would probably have brought about the complete pacification of Morocco, had he not had to contend with a serious revolt which broke out in the Rif Mountains of the Spanish Zone in 1925 and spilt over into the French Zone; and before it had been mastered Lyautey had been shabbily dismissed by his Government. He had given Morocco the benefit, so long denied, of a strong central administration, had extended the authority of that administration over the greater part of it, and had made at least a beginning with the provision of some of its more salient needs, notably medical services – supplied at first by the Army – and education.

It is, however, questionable whether Lyautey's ultimate aim was an independent and integrated Morocco, or a Morocco dependent on France and with its resources enriching French settlers and industrialists; certainly his successors gave the impression that they were working rather for the latter. This impression was intensified in the eyes of the incipient Nationalist movement, centred on Fez, which had come into being in the early twenties, by a decree promulgated in 1931 which allowed the Berbers to be governed by their own tribal customs in a wide range of matters of personal status, for this measure ran directly counter to the policy which successive Sultans had pursued for a century or more, of integrating the Arabs with the Berbers by making them all subject to the same Islamic Law for these purposes. From then onwards Nationalism became a live force; and it was fed by the unwillingness of the French to entrust responsible posts to the Moroccan products of their own educational system – the besetting fault of French colonial administration – which created a disgruntled white-collared class. Less justifiable was the complaint, still more widely voiced, that the French farmers and industrialists were 'robbing the Moroccan people' : for while abuses occurred in the allocation of tribal lands to French settlers, most French property seems to have been regularly acquired and French capital, skills, and industry undoubtedly enormously enriched the country and thus contributed to the relative stability which it achieved after pacification was completed in 1934.

Justified or not, Nationalist opposition to French rule grew. As in Algeria, it was nourished by the events of the Second World War, and as early as 1944 a manifesto issued by a group of leading Nationalists for the first time demanded independence. By 1947 the Sultan Muhammad V, formerly the faithful friend and ally of France, had felt compelled, lest he become fatally estranged from his people, publicly to proclaim Morocco's affiliation with the Arab world and to demand the fulfilment of its 'legitimate aspirations'. A bellicose Resident-General, having tried in vain to browbeat him into disowning the Independence Party, staged the gathering of sycophant Moroccan leaders described on page 155 and on the strength of the resolutions there expressed persuaded the French Government that French interests required the deportation of the Sultan, who was thereupon exiled to Madagascar. But such measures seldom work, and this was no exception: the puppet Sultan installed in his stead could command neither authority nor respect, and within two years the Nationalist movement had spread so widely, and was showing such menacing signs of becoming violent, that in 1955 a more liberal-minded French Government overrode the Cassandra outpourings of the French settler and commercial communities in Morocco and declared their intention of ending the Protectorate and recognizing full Moroccan independence. Within a few days the Sultan was brought back amidst countrywide rejoicing, assuming the title of King in celebration of his restoration, and in March 1956 a Franco-Moroccan Agreement was signed giving effect to the French declaration and restoring Moroccan sovereignty. Within the same year the Spanish Zone and the International City of Tangier, the evolution of which will be described when we come to them, had been incorporated into the new State, the integration of which became thus complete.

The transition had been relatively easy and friendly; yet the problems facing the country were numerous enough. The King, as the traditional repository of absolute power and also the head of the State religion, commanded considerable prestige, to which were added veneration for his direct descent from the Prophet and admiration for his sturdy stand for independence. But the nation was young, half its population being under twenty-one, and the Nationalists were growing in strength; they were also in a hurry. They wished to see Morocco transformed as speedily as might be into a modern, democratic, unitary State, entirely free of foreign commitments. There was therefore demand for a Constitution providing for an electoral system; for the subordination of the Berbers' tribal customs to the common law – which risked alienating the powerful Berber tribal elements; for the replacement of the French officials, and for those Moroccans who had made common cause with the French, by Moroccans of proved loyalty – though competent men were in desperately short supply; for the adoption of a foreign policy of 'non-alignment', and for the withdrawal of French, American, and Spanish bases from Moroccan soil – although France and the United States were the most likely sources for the economic and technical aid which Morocco so badly needed. They began, too, to cast covetous eyes on the large areas of the best land in the possession of the French settlers – although any abrupt measures of dispossession or expropriation (such as were taken later in Tunisia) would be likely to cause grave harm to a not too healthy economy.

The King trod warily. His task was not helped by the situation in Algeria, on which subject feelings ran high in Morocco, especially after his own guest Ben Bella had been kidnapped by the French; but by displaying studious moderation over this and over the other contentious issues affecting French interests in Morocco he managed to preserve good relations with the French and was rewarded by a generous measure of French aid. He handled his Nationalists with equal success, and the first five years of independence thus passed without any major trouble and showed satisfactory progress.

King Muhammad then unexpectedly died; but his son Hassan, on succeeding to the Throne, continued his policies. He faced new difficulties, for Nasser's ideas of 'Arab Socialism' were by now gaining adherents amongst the younger Nationalists, and an unusually well-organized Trades Union Movement was always liable to create political complications. On the other hand, he was helped by circumstances in some of the more thorny problems: the United States voluntarily surrendered their bases, thus making it impossible for the French not to do the same, and also raised no objection when, having accepted their economic aid, he balanced it by accepting Soviet military aid; and support for the more extreme Nationalists markedly decreased after a conflict which broke out with Algeria in 1963 over the possession of the Tindouf iron-ore deposits, in which Ben Bella was saved from defeat by the Moroccans by the dispatch of Egyptian military aid, thus damning both Nasser and Ben Bella, and by association their Moroccan admirers, in the eyes of the Moroccan people. But the King's greatest achievement was his enactment, and triumphant carrying-through by referendum, of a new Constitution under which he abrogated his absolute powers in favour of an ostensibly advisory function, thus creating a façade of democracy while preserving his power of decision in all important matters. The integration of the three Zones of the country was completed, and the integration of the Berber and Arab communities pushed ahead without undue precipitation or friction. It could at least be said that the country had got off to a good start.

CHAPTER 15

The Spaniards in Morocco

Just north of Rabat, where the signs of European farming die away and the country becomes bare and windswept, lies Kenitra, a small port on the estuary of the Oued Sebou, which the French called Port Lyautey but which since independence has reverted to its old name; and on a peninsula, where the Sebou meets the sea, is Mehdia. This tiny place, nowadays known chiefly for its bathing beach, has an interesting history: for it has been identified with Thymiaterium, a Carthaginian colony founded in about the fifth century B.C. by Hanno, one of the two *suffetes*, or Chief Magistrates, of Carthage, in the course of a voyage of exploration down this coast. The voyage was commemorated in the so-called 'Periplus of Hanno', an inscription in a temple at Carthage which the Romans destroyed with the city but of which copies survive; it suggests that Hanno reached Gambia and the Cameroons before turning back. The site of Thymiaterium was apparently abandoned when the Carthaginians disappeared, but was reoccupied later on and in the time of the Almohads became a naval station under the name of Al Mamora. In 1614 it was garrisoned by the Spaniards so as to serve as an observation-post on the piracy developing from Rabat and Salé, but by the end of the century had been retaken by Moulay Ismail and given its present name.

From here northwards the signs of French occupation cease but those of the Portuguese and Spaniards, especially Spaniards, multiply. Larache, the next port up the coast, which was in Spanish hands from 1610, and Arcila, which at different times was held by both Portuguese and Spaniards, were both retaken, like Mehdia, by Moulay Ismail, but Larache was reoccupied by the Spaniards in 1911 and became one of the three bridgeheads (Ceuta and Melilla being the other two) from which Spanish forces debouched to occupy what became the

Spanish Protectorate of Morocco; the boundary between it and
the French Zone ran immediately south of the town. Larache,
however, lies on a much older site, that of Lixus, a Carthaginian station reputed to have been founded in 1110 B.C., or even
before Utica; and the River Loukkos on which it stands seems
to have formed the southern boundary of Mauretania Tingitana
after Diocletian's fourth century reorganization. Inland from it is
Ksar el-Kebir, a large market-town where in 1578 the 'Battle
of the Three Kings' extinguished Portuguese aspirations in
Morocco.

From Larache I struck inland again, across the neck of the
peninsula on which Tangier lies, and came to Tetuan, a town
of some importance which was the capital of the Spanish Zone
and is now a provincial centre. It is a place of great charm,
standing in a broad valley which slopes down gradually from
the Rif Mountains, through orchards and olive-groves, to the
distant sea. Above it on a rock stands the old Qasba; and although the town has naturally overflowed its original walls,
Spanish urban development – as you can see in Cordova –
blends a good deal more sympathetically with Andalusian-Arab
than does French, so that the general aspect is extremely
pleasing. The old quarter still within the walls is a smaller
version of Fez, being a similar jumble of narrow, twisting *suqs*,
often lattice-roofed, with a similar throng of pedestrians and
donkeys. Tetuan will always be overshadowed by Tangier,
now that the two places are on the same footing, but it will
always have its admirers and some commercial importance.

By the standards of the Maghrib it is not old, having been
founded in 1306 by one of the Merinids, Abu Thabit, as a base
from which to attack a rival who had proclaimed himself Sultan
in Ceuta. In 1399 it was destroyed by Henry III of Castille for
its piracy, but in 1610 was refounded by a group of refugee
Muslims and Jews who, like those who simultaneously flooded
into Rabat and Salé, had been driven out of Spain by Philip
III's edict; like those towns, it became, once again, a lair of
corsairs, but also an important trading centre. In the eighteenth
century Moulay Ismail built the battlements which are still a
feature of the old town. From that time onwards its connection

with Spain gradually increased, geographical proximity and
lucrative trade having softened the former Muslim resentment
against the Spaniards, to a point where even religious orders
were able to set up foundations within the walls; and it was
thus natural that it should become the capital of the Spanish
Protectorate after its establishment in 1912.

This Protectorate began in circumstances almost as difficult
as those which faced Lyautey in the French Zone. The Spaniards had three solid bases from which to operate, the enclaves
of Ceuta and Melilla, which had been their property since the
sixteenth century, and Larache, which they had occupied in
1911; but inland they had to contend with a completely re-
bellious area covering the whole of the Rif massif, the eastern
districts north of Taza, which were controlled by the pretender
Bou Hamara, and a western district under an adventurer called
Sharif Moulay Ahmad ar-Raisuni (often known as Raisuli),
who had been the Sultan's Governor of the Atlantic Province
but had come out in opposition to him because he had not been
appointed Viceroy for the Spanish Zone. Once the outbreak of
the first World War had brought Lyautey's operations in the
French Zone almost to a standstill, the Spaniards decided to
restrict their own action to the holding of the regions which
recognized the Sultan's authority and to the institution of an
embryo administration in them. They therefore judged it pru-
dent to come to an accommodation with Raisuli and to leave
him undisturbed in the area of which he was the undisputed
master.

In 1920, however, they began active pacification measures
which in the west had some success and enabled them to occupy
Chaouen, an important hill-town in the Rif itself to which we
shall presently come. But in the east matters went otherwise.
In 1921 a new and tougher rebel leader appeared in the person
of Abdul Krim al Khattabi, a Berber from Ajdir, who had
formerly been a judge in Melilla and friendly to the Spaniards,
but had been alienated by their having imprisoned him,
allegedly at the behest of the French to whom he had always
been openly and bitterly opposed. Having escaped and raised
the Rif tribes, he inflicted on the Spaniards a severe defeat at

Anual, near Al Hoceimas on the coast, which resulted in their being driven back to the coast itself and in his becoming master of the whole Rif. He thereupon proclaimed this region an independent republic with himself as its President, thus creating the latest, and perhaps the last, all-Berber State in history, and sought international recognition; and for the next four years he carried on guerrilla warfare against the Spanish forces, losing some ground in the east but in the west reoccupying Chaouen and capturing Raisuli, who had by now become enfeebled and of little account. But in 1925, intoxicated with success, he declared a *jihad* or Holy War against the Christians and extended his operations southwards into the French Zone, where he threatened Ouezzane and Taza and sent bands almost to the gates of Fez. His ambition to have himself proclaimed Sultan of all Morocco in Fez itself was not, however, to be realized, for the imminent peril drove French and Spaniards into belated co-operation, with the result that his forces were gradually driven back; and in 1926 he surrendered to the French, who exiled him to the Island of Réunion.

His subsequent history, incidentally, is sad: for in 1947 the French tried to bring him back to Morocco in the hopes of using him to rally opposition to the Sultan, who was already becoming too independent-minded for their taste, but he jumped ship in the Suez Canal and took refuge in Egypt; here he became President of the 'North African Defence League', which was organizing opposition to the French in the Maghrib, but found himself out of sympathy with the younger Nationalists, who had other gods than his traditionalism, and faded into an obscurity in which he died in 1964. He was shrewd and brave, but like the Glawi an anachronism.

By 1927 the pacification of the Spanish Zone was complete, and from then onwards the Spaniards could begin to administer it and to fill some of the yawning gaps in its medical, educational, and public works services. From the first, perhaps not surprisingly in view of the intimate relationship which had existed between Spain and Morocco in the past, they showed themselves better disposed towards the Nationalist movement in their Zone than the French to theirs; and after the outbreak of the Spanish Civil war in 1936, when the Spanish Republicans, anxious to secure the sympathy of the French, rebuffed a Moroccan Nationalist delegation which went to Madrid to plead their cause, the Spanish Nationalists were lavish in promises of future support for the Moroccans and, even though the Rif War was only ten years back, received open support from them. Some divergence resulted between the Moroccan Nationalists in the two Zones, as those in the French Zone were close to the French Left, which was of course supporting the Spanish Republicans; but the French action in deposing and exiling the Sultan in 1953, which was violently opposed by the population of both Zones, not only healed the breach but increased the prestige of the Spanish Protectorate régime, which openly disapproved of the French action. Spaniards can indeed claim with pride that, once the Rif War was over, there was never any violence against individual Spaniards in their Zone, such as the French had to endure in theirs.

From Tetuan I drove the forty miles into the foothills of the Rif to Chaouen, which until the Spaniards first occupied it in 1920 had been almost as remote as Lhasa, but is now a tourist attraction. That overworked adjective 'picturesque' alone describes this little gem of a place, perched in a fold of a steep hill, with a market-place in its centre under the walls of a ruined Qasba, and behind it the most complicated labyrinth of courts and passages that I saw anywhere in the Maghrib. Here the women, dressed always in white, seemed more heavily veiled than anywhere else; the walls and houses were white too, and the colours of the men's *jellabas* and of the piles of mandarins in the market looked all the brighter against them. On the other hand tourism seems to have spoilt the children, who were worse behaved than anywhere that I had been; though I was disarmed by one small boy whom I had occasion to rebuke for pestering me and who made the surprising retort of 'Heil Hitler' before he ducked out of reach.

My drive next day was the most beautiful of my whole journey – which is high praise. It led due east from Chaouen along a road not long since reconstructed for motor-traffic, which follows the backbone of the Rif range for a hundred miles, at an average height of between 4,500 and 6,000 feet, before plunging down to the coast. Along the hundred miles it swings from one side of the crest to the other, the north side giving a view of a very blue Mediterranean beyond line upon line of foothills, while from the south, which is flanked by a precipice dropping thousands of feet into a deep valley, the great central plain of Morocco shows beyond more lines of hills. Sometimes the road runs through forest, of cedar, evergreen oak, or juniper; sometimes across heather-moors; sometimes over bareness; but always the colours, near and far, are magnificent. When at last it abandons the heights and, in a series of sweeping curves, runs down to the coastal plain, it gives on the way more glorious views of receding planes of misty headlands thrusting out into the blueness beyond.

I came in the evening to Al Hoceimas, a small fishing-port which is also a bathing resort, and found a good hotel on the edge of a cliff, with a horseshoe bay below. Round the point was the port, a little marred by oil-storage tanks, but filled with barques, each with its acetylene lamp for night spearing, just putting to sea with all the accompanying bustle and shouting; and on the quays red nets were drying. The place seems to have been a port for many centuries, for in 917 we hear of its being occupied by the Fatimid Obaidullah and then recaptured by a local Amir with the aid of the Arabs from Cordova; and in 1661 English merchants were permitted by the paramount Sheikh of the Rif to open a trading post here, only to have it swept away by Moulay Rashid when he conquered the Sheikh in question and opened his own post. Over the years it has had close trading relations with Spain, which since 1679 has owned a tiny island off the coast.

This coast, above which I had been travelling all day, is almost inaccessible at present owing to lack of approach roads, but from what I could see of it in the distance it looks enchanting and eminently suitable for development for the benefit of modern sun-worshippers, provided that the local Berbers, who must be amongst the most isolated in the country, can be conditioned to the sight of the undraped female form, as they have been in Jerba and elsewhere. Along this stretch is at least one point of interest: this is Badis, which in the Middle Ages was a thriving port, connected with Fez by a main road, but was ruined when the Spaniards in the course of their eighteenth century 'crusade' made their own port at Peñon de Velez, just offshore; incidentally, having lost this island to the Turks in 1564 they recaptured it a few years later and still hold it. There must be other remains of the same sort along this coast, situated as it is over against the coast of Andalusia.

Beyond Al Hoceimas the road continues rather more inland, and then forks, one branch going southwards to Oujda, the other northwards to Melilla, one of the two Spanish enclaves. I took the latter and with surprisingly little difficulty was able to cross the international frontier into Melilla.

This town began as a Phoenician station called Rusaddir, which unlike most of their stations was apparently designed primarily for trade with the interior. In the first century A.D. it was occupied by the Romans, who retained its name, and formed the Western end of their *limes* until in the third century these were extended farther to the south. In A.D. 927 it was garrisoned by Abdurrahman III of Cordova, who took the title of Caliph two years later, and it depended from Cordova until the fall of the Caliphate in 1031. What happened to it there-after is obscure, but in 1492 Boabdil, the last King of the Mus-lim State of Granada, landed there after his State had been captured by the Spaniards. In 1496 it was captured in a sort of privateering raid by a Spaniard, who turned it over to the Spanish Crown ten years later, and it has remained a Spanish possession ever since, despite repeated attempts by a succession of Berber tribes and dynasties to get possession of it.

Its main importance lies in its export of well over a million tons a year of iron-ore from the mines at Nador, just inland, which are exploited by three Spanish companies. In 1909 an attack on Spanish miners at these mines, which at that time were covered by a concession given by the pretender Bou Hamara, resulted in the landing of a Spanish expeditionary force and the enlarging of the boundaries of the enclave of

Melilla to their present limits; it was a link in the chain of events which led, three years later, to the establishment of the Protectorate. Today it consists of two separate towns, one Berber, dominated by the old Qasba overlooking the port, the other modern Spanish. As the natural outlet for the iron ore, it serves a useful purpose in the economy of Morocco, and looks reasonably prosperous for a small town of no great distinction.

Returning through the frontier to the fork, I went on eastwards almost to the Algerian frontier, where at Saidia is the finest plage in North Africa and one which, if exploited in Palm Beach fashion, could achieve fame. At this point I turned back and retraced my way along that glorious mountain road – which was no hardship – to Chaouen, and thence due north through Tetuan until I again traversed a frontier into the other Spanish enclave of Ceuta.

This has a longer history than Melilla. It is built on an isthmus jutting out from the land to Mount Hacho, which legend identifies with Abyla, one of the Pillars of Hercules; and it owes its name to the Arabic 'sebta', meaning seven, from the seven points on the summit ridge of Mount Moussa, directly behind it. So obvious a point of vantage was naturally occupied by the Phoenicians and then the Romans, and it was probably here that the Vandals landed in the fifth century, to begin their occupation of the Maghrib coast. About A.D. 681, when the Arab leader Oqba ibn Nafi made his second raid into the Maghrib and reached the sea, it was probably here that he met a somewhat shadowy figure called Count Julien, described by one of the Arab historians as 'Lord of Algeciras and Ceuta', who seems to have been the ruler of the last piece of Maghrib territory controlled by the Byzantines and who, when questioned by Oqba about conditions in the territory, seems to have adroitly steered him to the south by convincing him that plunder could be more easily obtained in the Sous. When, however, in 711 or thereabouts the Arabs returned to the north and expressed interest in Spain, at that time occupied by the Visigoths, Julien accompanied the host which, under Tariq, embarked at Ceuta to seek their fortunes there. In 931 Ceuta, like Melilla, was garrisoned by Abdurrahman III of Cordova, and later fell successively into the hands of the Almoravids (whose greatest ruler, Yusuf ibn Tashfin, embarked from it for Spain), the Almohads, and the Merinids, but in 1415 it was captured by King John I of Portugal and in 1580 became Spanish when the crowns of Portugal and Spain were temporarily united. In 1649, when they separated again, the people of Ceuta asked that the town should remain with Spain, which it has done ever since, even though, like Melilla, it has had to survive numerous attacks and sieges by different Moroccan leaders. In 1860 a squabble over its boundaries served as a pretext for the Spanish Government, which was in internal difficulties and needed a foreign distraction, to declare war on Morocco, and this brief and rather unnecessary contest ended in its territory being enlarged, in addition to which the defeated Moroccans had to pay the Spaniards a stiff indemnity and also to hand over to them the enclave of Ifni, in the extreme south. Since then it has existed peacefully and with no special distinction; and I found no cause to linger in this survival of the past.

CHAPTER 16

The End of the Journey

I came then to Tangier, probably the oldest continuously inhabited town in the Maghrib; for its site, where Africa is
closest to Europe and where the Mediterranean meets the
Atlantic, must have been colonized since man first began
to trade. Its original Pyoenician settlement certainly antedates Carthage. The Romans occupied it in 82 B.C., and in
38 B.C. Octavius gave it the privileges of a Roman city for
having taken his side in the civil war; in A.D. 42 it became the
capital of Mauretania Tingitana and remained the main commercial centre of this province even when the capital was transferred to Volubilis. There was a hiatus after the Roman
withdrawal, but the Byzantines reoccupied it in the sixth
century and held on until well after the arrival of the Arabs in
the eighth.

The first Arab leader to occupy it was Musa ibn Nasir, in
about 705, and shortly afterwards came the combined Arab
and Berber expedition into Spain, which smashed the Visigoths
and swept on until beaten back by Charles Martel at Poitiers
in 732; out of this developed the Arab Empire in Spain which
lasted until 1492. About 742 there began in Tangier the revolt
of the Kharijites, which was destined to spread through the
Maghrib and in the long run to end by substituting Berber for
Arab rule; and it was from Tangier that Idris I in 788 initiated
the movement which resulted in the establishment of the Idrisid
Kingdom of Fez, the last survivors from which, after it had
been destroyed by the Fatimids two centuries later, held out
in the mountains near Tangier until the Cordovan Caliphate
made an end of them. During the next five centuries Tangier
was held in succession by the Cordovan Caliphate, the Fatimids, the Zirids, the Hafsids, the Merinids, and the Wattasids,
but in 1471 it was captured by the Portuguese and for nearly

two hundred years was held by them, or nominally by Spain during the period when it engulfed Portugal.

In 1661 Tangier passed to England as part of the dowry of Catherine of Braganza when she married Charles II. The English built a jetty and fortifications, and held it against a strong attack by Moulay Ismail; but the latter's hostility destroyed its trade with the interior and in 1684 the English Parliament came to the conclusion that it had become an economic liability and ordered its evacuation on the grounds that its garrison 'might be exposed to the taint of Popery', whereupon the troops were withdrawn after destroying what they had built, thus presenting Moulay Ismail with a cheap victory.

Since then Tangier has remained in at least nominal Moroccan possession; but during the nineteenth century it became the diplomatic capital and acquired a large foreign community and important foreign investments, so that when the Franco-Moroccan Treaty of Fez was concluded in 1912 it included a provision, which was reproduced in the Franco-Spanish Agreement of the same year, that Tangier should 'retain the special character which it has been recognized to possess'. The outbreak of the First World War delayed the execution of this provision until 1923, but in that year an Anglo-Franco-Spanish Agreement was signed setting up a 'Statute of Tangier'. This instituted a Committee of Control composed of the Consuls of all the Powers (excluding the beaten enemies Germany and Austria) which had signed the Act of Algeciras in 1906, but recognized the ultimate authority of the Sultan, who was to be represented in the territory by a 'Mendoub' or agent; neutralized the territory, and guaranteed economic equality for all nations in it; and set up Mixed Courts with European judges to replace the former Consular Courts. In 1928 Italy and Portugal were admitted to participation in the Committee of Control, which continued to function until, in 1940, the Spaniards used the Second World War as a pretext for occupying the territory.

In 1945 Great Britain, the United States, and France decided on the restoration of the international régime, to which both the

o

United States and Soviet Russia became parties, though the latter, through dislike of the Franco régime in Spain, never directly participated in it. The position remained unchanged for the next ten years, despite much pocket diplomacy and jockeying for position in the Committee; but when in 1956 France, having restored the exiled Sultan, announced her intention of also restoring full Moroccan independence, the Powers concerned could only agree to the abolition of the Statute and the incorporation of Tangier in Morocco, which was done by means of a declaration signed the same year. Some of the fiscal and commercial privileges which the Territory had enjoyed by virtue of its international status remained in force until, in 1960, they were abolished and Tangier became a normal part of Morocco and the capital of a province.

It must always have been a colourful place. The last three chapters of George Borrow's *The Bible in Spain* give a lively picture of what it was like in about 1839, when it was almost entirely Moorish and Spanish. When I myself first knew it, almost a century later, and not long after the First World War, it had an exotic and variegated foreign community, living for the most part in bougainvillaea-clad villas on the so-called 'Mountain', a hill behind the port whence they could look out through their cypresses and pines on to the Straits; and its younger members maintained a Tent Club (the only one outside India), which periodically met to stick wild boar on what are now built-up areas on the outskirts of the city. On these occasions, a fine old Moorish notable, Al Menebhi, who had been the Sultan's Minister of War and in that capacity had been given an honorary Knighthood by King Edward VII, used to erect an immense black and white marquee on the edge of the hunting area and reward the pig-stickers for their exertions with gargantuan Moorish luncheons.

But the climate was too good and the place altogether too attractive to remain quiet and small. An influx of immigrants and a building boom destroyed both these qualities, and in the hectic years which followed the liberation of North Africa and preceded the restoration of Moroccan independence, the international régime provided favourable conditions for every kind

of financial and commercial speculator, legitimate and otherwise, so that the population swelled fast and not always desir-
ably. The abolition of the international régime in 1960 resulted
in a flight of capital and of many foreigners and foreign con-
cerns, and the city fell into a state of depression which was
worsened by a flood of penurious tribesmen from the Rif seeking non-existent work. But this could only be a temporary
phase; for Tangier had far too much to offer in the matter
of tourist amenities not to prosper in the long run. The
possibilities of smuggling across the Straits and the traffic in
'kif', as marijuana is known in North Africa where it has
always been easy to obtain, would attract doubtful characters;
but I know of few places where I would sooner pass my
winters, and few that I would sooner visit at any time of the
year.

I had come to the end of my journey through the Maghrib.
The ferry carrying me, and my car, to Gibraltar was already
half-way across the Straits, where a fresh wind from the Atlantic was blowing the crests off the short waves.

All through the history of the Maghrib this waterway recurs.
Across it Hannibal, and a thousand years later the Arabs,
brought largely Berber armies, both bent on conquest in Europe.
Between these two the Vandals brought over an army in the
reverse direction, bent on conquest in the Maghrib. Between
the eighth and the fifteenth centuries the Straits became a
link rather than a barrier between the Muslim States to the
north and south of them; but when the former was destroyed
they once again became a military highway, first for the
Spaniards and Portuguese following the Muslims back into the
Maghrib, and later for the French and Spaniards when they
established their Protectorates over Morocco. In 1942 the Anglo-
American armada came through to make what could be the
last foreign invasion of the Maghrib; and since then the Straits
have become a highway for the newly established tourist industry, while retaining the commercial importance which they
have never lost.

.   .   .   .   .

To the south, as I sat on deck, the coast of the Maghrib was withdrawing behind a veil of brown mist. As I watched it disappear, I was thinking of the country which I had just left, of its three neighbours, and of the land, or Island, which they composed.

Scenically, Morocco was the best of the four. It had no ruins to compare with those which are strewn about the other three, and by the end of summer the green and the flowers of the countryside would have been burnt as brown as a pall of sacking. But none of the others could show as rich and varied a store of beauty as the Atlas snows, the Fez *medersas*, the Portuguese battlements, the Jama'a Fna at Marrakesh, and the red Berber castles beyond the Atlas.

Tourism should, in fact, bring Morocco an increasing income, to add to that of its phosphates, its minerals, and its agriculture. Lacking oil, the country could not hope to be rich, but it should be able to manage, provided always that it could remain politically stable and thus be able to attract the capital and the foreign aid which it would long continue to need.

It had an asset in its young King, whose shrewdness had already been demonstrated and who could provide leadership, and moderation, and decision, when needed. On the other hand support for the Throne derived largely from the more conservative elements, the tribal leaders and the commercial community, against whom was liable to be ranged the modernism of those younger political elements who admired the ideas of 'Arab Socialism' launched by Nasser. Much statesmanship would be needed if the basic conflict between these opposing forces was to be resolved; so that, while Morocco's prospects appeared to me to be more promising than those of any of the other States except perhaps Tunisia, an element of doubt must remain.

All four countries of the Maghrib were in fact having to contend with different forms of the same problems, not only how to develop their economies and remedy the shortcomings in their administrations and social services, but also how to readjust themselves to new conditions and the impact of new ideas: in

Libya, the possession of great wealth; in Algeria, the painful reconstruction of the whole structure by new leaders working under – or out – a new philosophy; in Morocco, and in a lesser sense Tunisia, the application of increased State control and uniformity on social structures which had hitherto been traditionalist and largely uncontrolled. Libya, Tunisia, and Morocco would also be obliged, sooner or later, to deal with the jolt which must inevitably be caused by the eventual disappearance from the scene of the strong personalities at present guiding them, and Algeria, in all probability, to a series of such jolts.

Could they come together, to the point of becoming one nation? In logic, there seemed every reason why they should, for they were one people in one land. But the political divisions which the Turks had made had crystallized, and the long years of foreign domination had developed them differently; and a more fundamental obstacle to any form of union was that the two main racial components of all four peoples, Berbers and Arabs, were both fierce individualists who had never, at any time in either of their histories, given proof of any ability to co-operate with anyone else. Self-interest might bring about some form of economic link, but politically I believed that they would continue to go their own ways.

Whatever men did, the land would remain. New pipelines might scar its deserts and new terminals rise on its coasts, here and there a new factory or mine might disfigure the landscape or new systems of agriculture or land-tenure change the appearance of the plateaux, the plains or the valleys. But this was veneer. The Mountains – the Atlas, and the Rif, and the Kabylies, and the Aures – would always be there, and the Tell and the Sahil and the great salty depressions, and the Saharan sand lapping like a sea round the edges of the sown; and each night the sun would go down over the Island of the sunset, as it was going down now over the hills behind Tangier.

Note on Berber Tribal Divisions

Arab historians, and certain French writers like E. F. Gautier, have devoted considerable attention to the question of the original tribal diversions of the Berbers, from which their great dynasties came. The subject is an abstruse one, and the information available insufficient for firm conclusions, but the following is a summary of what is known or has been propounded.

Ibn Khaldun, whose *History of the Berbers* is the most comprehensive work extant on the Middle Ages in the Maghrib, holds that the perpetual inter-dynastic conflicts which strew his pages reflect and result from a basic division of the Berber people into two sections, the Botr and the Beranes, names which he derives from those of mythical ancestors; though one French writer (W. Marçais) has ingeniously suggested that the words really come from the distinctive dress of the two sections, the Beranes being the wearers of the *burnous*, the striped and hooded cloak which is the traditional wear of the sedentary Algerians and Tunisians, while the Botr wore the short garment of that name which is commonly used by camel-riders. In a different context Ibn Khaldun divides the people into 'Zenata' and 'Berbers' and calls the principal subdivision of the latter 'Sanhaja'; probably these names, Zenata and Sanhaja, gradually replaced Botr and Beranes as these subdivisions became paramount.

Some writers have attempted to identify these divisions with 'sedentaries' and 'nomads', because the conflict between these two ways of life must always have been alive in the Maghrib; but the information which we have about their location does not entirely square with such an identification. It is hard to see how it could: for both nomads and sedentaries are capable of changing their ways of life. Some of the sedentaries who cultivated the Tell in Roman times must have been forced to become nomads once the protection of the *limes* was withdrawn and their lands exposed to marauding Bedouin; while nomads are always liable to become sedentaries when changed conditions make grazing unprofitable. Probably the nearest we shall get to a definition is to suggest that most Beranes, or Sanhaja, were sedentaries, and most Zenata nomads.

The Sanhaja seem in fact to have consisted of two main groups: one was the sedentary inhabitants of the Kabylie and the Atlas, the other a number of nomad tribes inhabiting the Sahara south of the Atlas. The Zenata, apart from one or two semi-sedentary tribes inhabiting the Aures, seem to have been all nomads and all located within a belt of territory which runs from the Jebel Nafusa of Tripolitania through the Shott el Jerid in southern Tunisia and the Zab plain of southern Algeria, then slants across the Hodna and follows the 'Rocade Sud', skirting the Ouarsenis, through Tiaret and south of Tlemsen, until it passes through the 'Taza Gap' into the plains of central Morocco. This belt, the line of which was also followed by the Roman *limes*, is the most clearly defined geographical feature of the central Maghrib, and is a natural route of approach for nomads: part of it is indeed used today by nomads who winter in the Zab and summer on the Ouarsenis. North of it lies the cultivated, or at least cultivable, regions of the Tell and Sahil, south of it the desert.

Gautier, whose theories are always arresting even when unproven, suggests that the Zenata migrated into this belt some time after the introduction of the camel into the Maghrib made such migration feasible, and that as they did so they infiltrated between the two main blocks of sedentary Sanhaja in the northeast and south-west. From Ibn Khaldun's statement that some of the tribes in the belt, e.g. the Jerawa who followed Al-Kohina, were Jewish, he makes the further suggestion that the migration may have been a consequence of the Jewish revolt which took place in Cyrenaica in the second century A.D.

It has been objected that the tribes inhabiting the belt are today Arabic-speaking and claim Arab descent. To this Gautier returns the convincing answer that the two Arab invasions were too few in numbers to have fathered all these tribes; but that, as the Arabs, being nomads, almost certainly followed the belt as they came in, it was with the Zenata already there that they must first have come into contact, and conflict, and later fused, leaving the Sanhaja sedentaries relatively unmolested in their mountains and coastal areas. In other words he maintains that the Zenata, whatever their claims of ancestry, were in fact Arabized Berbers; and in support of his contention he cites the names of the tribes generally regarded as Zenata – and so listed by Ibn Khaldun – and their areas, all of which lie within the belt.

Gautier further asserts that the Kharijite movement was mainly Zenata, and adduces as proof the fact that the regions which it mainly affected – from central Morocco to Tiaret, Kairouan, and Mahdiya and into Tripolitania – all lie within the Zenata belt; if he is right, then the two dynasties resulting from it, the Idrisids of Fez and the Rostemids of Tiaret, would also be Zenata; though this is disputed by other writers. However this may be, it seems clear that all the earlier Berber dynasties, the Fatimids, Zirids, Hammadids, and Hafsids, were based on the Sanhaja tribes of the north, and the later Moroccan dynasties, the Almoravids and Almohads, on the Sanhaja tribes of the south; but that this Sanhaja domination, which lasted from the tenth to the thirteenth century, was then destroyed by the advent of the Beni Hilal, who seem to have made common cause with the Zenata and enabled them to establish dynasties of their own, the Merinids and Abdul Wadids and later the Wattasids. The latter were the last of the Berber dynasties, for those which succeeded them, the Sa'adians and the Alawis, were – or at least claim to be – of direct Arab descent.

Chronology

(Most dates prior to 250 B.C. and between about A.D. 650 and 1100 must be taken as approximate)

B.C.

1101	Phoenicians founded Utica.
814	Phoenicians founded Carthage.
631	Battus I landed in Cyrenaica.
623	Battus I founded Cyrene.
574	Phoenicia conquered by Assyria; Carthage became *de facto* independent.
520	Carthaginians repelled Dorieus and his Spartans.
515	Cambyses' expedition into Cyrenaica.
440	Republic established in Cyrenaica.
322	Ophellas installed as Governor of Cyrenaica by Ptolemy I.
310	Agathocles' expedition against Carthage. Ophellas' host destroyed in 'gap' trying to join him.
283	Magas, Ptolemaic Governor of Cyrenaica, proclaimed himself independent.
262–241	First Punic War.
246	Cyrenaica reverted to Ptolemaic rule.
241–237	Revolt of mercenaries against Carthage.
218–201	Second Punic War, ending with Roman victory at Zama.
150	Massinissa's victory over Carthage.
147–146	Third Punic War, ending with destruction of Carthage. Creation of Province of Africa.
107–104	Roman campaign against Jugurtha.
96	Rome inherited Pentapolis.
82	Romans occupied Tingi (Tangier).
74	Romans made Cyrenaica into a province.
46	Caesar's victory over Pompey and Juba I at Thapsus. Roman occupation of Numidia.
45	Roman occupation of the Emporia.
30	Numidia reconstituted under Juba II.
25	Juba II transferred to become King of Mauretania and Numidia re-incorporated into enlarged province of Africa. Legio III Augusta stationed at Ammadaea.

A.D.

14–21   Tacfarinas' revolt.
37   Caligula cut off Numidia from 'Africa'.
42   Rome annexed Mauretania after death of Juba II's son Ptolemy.
68   Festus repelled invasion of Garamantes.
75   Legio III Augusta transferred to Theveste.
82   Legio III Augusta transferred to Lambaesis; Thamugadi and Mascula developed.
115   Jewish revolt in Cyrenaica.
200*   Septimius Severus constructed *limes*.
238   Legio III Augusta disbanded.
297*   Diocletian's administrative reorganization.
395   Augustine became Bishop of Hippo Regius.
410   Ecclesiastical Council in Carthage pronounced against Donatists.
429   Vandals under Genseric landed in Magrib as Rome withdrew.
439   Genseric captured Carthage and made it his capital.
477   Genseric died.
484   Ecclesiastical Council in Carthage pronounced for Arians.
534   Byzantines captured Carthage and expelled Vandals.
642   Arab advance from Egypt into Maghrib began.
647   Byzantine General Gregory defeated by Arabs. End of Byzantine rule.
670   Oqba ibn Nafi founded Kairouan.
681   Oqba ibn Nafi met Count Julien at (?) Ceuta.
682/3   Oqba ibn Nafi killed by Kusaila. Berbers took Kairouan.
686   Kusaila killed by Arab leader Zuhair.
697   Arabs defeated by Berbers under Al-Kohina, thrown back into Tripolitania.
698   Arabs returned, took Carthage and destroyed it. Tunis founded.
702   Arabs defeated and killed Al-Kohina.
705   Arabs occupied Tangier.
711   Arab/Berber army under Tariq crossed into Spain.
742   Kharijite revolt began in Tangier.
757   Kharijites founded Sijilmassa.
758   Kharijites (Ibadites) captured Tripoli.
    Kharijites (Sufrites) captured Kairouan, but expelled from it by Ibadites.
761   Arabs recaptured Kairouan.
    Abdurrahman ibn Rostem established capital at Tiaret and instituted ROSTEMID dynasty.
787   Abdurrahman ibn Rostem made peace with Arabs in Kairouan.
788   Idris I (Moulay Idris) established himself at Walila.
789   Idris I founded Fez, instituted Idrisid dynasty.

* And following years.

A.D.

800   AGHLABID dynasty instituted in Kairouan by Abbasid Caliphate.

809   Idris II refounded Fez.

893   Abu Abdullah raised Kutama against Aghlabids.

910   FATIMID dynasty founded at Raqqada by Obaidullah.

911   Fatimids conquered Rostemids and drove Kharijites to Ouergla, later Ghardaia.

912   Fatimid Caliph founded capital at Mahdiya.

929   Revolt of Abu Yazid ('The Man with the Donkey') began.

947   Abu Yazid failed to capture Mahdiya, died in Hodna.

969   Fatimids conquered Egypt and founded Cairo.

973   Fatimid Caliph El-Moizz transferred his capital to Cairo, appointed Bolouggin ibn Ziri his Governor of the Maghrib.

974   ZIRID dynasty instituted by Bolouggin ibn Ziri at Ashir. Algiers founded by him.

975–978 Bolouggin ibn Ziri captured Tiaret, Tlemsen, and Tripolitania.

1007   Hammad, brother of Bolouggin, founded Qala'at Beni Hammad.

1014   HAMMADID dynasty instituted there.

1048   Zirid leader El-Moizz transferred allegiance from Fatimids to Abbasids.

1051   Beni Hilal and Beni Sulaim began Second Arab invasion.

1056   ALMORAVIDS took Taroudant and began their advance.

1057   Zirids took refuge from Beni Hilal in Mahdiya.
       Beni Hilal sacked Kairouan.

1060   Marrakesh founded by Yusuf ibn Tashfin the Almoravid.

1083   Yusuf ibn Tashfin invaded Spain.

1106   Yusuf ibn Tashfin died, at zenith of Almoravid power.

1122   ALMOHAD dynasty instituted by Abdul Mumin, who proclaimed himself Caliph.

1134   Roger II of Sicily captured Jerba.

1140   Roger II of Sicily captured Tripoli.

1146   Roger II of Sicily captured Mahdiya, ended Zirid dynasty.

1148   Almohads expelled Almoravids from Morocco and Tlemsen.

1151   Almohads captured Bougie and Qala'at Beni Hammad, ending Hammadid dynasty.

1152   Almohads defeated Beni Hilal at Sétif.

1159   Almohads captured Mahdiya and expelled Roger II of Sicily from Maghrib.

1163   Abdul Mumin died.

1184–1204 Almoravid tribe from Balearic Islands occupied central Maghrib.

1196   Almohad leader Al Mansur routed Spaniards at Alarcos.

1204   Al Mansur's successor An Nasir smashed Almoravids, so that Almohads ruled the entire Maghrib.

A.D.

1207   HAFSID dynasty instituted in Tunis by Almohads.
1235   ABDUL WADID dynasty instituted in Tlemsen) ⎱ as Almohads
1248   MERINID dynasty instituted in Fez   ⎰ crumbled.
1270   French 'crusade' in Maghrib ended with death of St. Louis at
          Carthage.
1284   Roger de Loria took Jerba.
1306   Merinids founded Tetuan.
1331   Raymond Montaner took Jerba.
1335   Merinids retook Jerba.
1337   Merinids took Tlemsen from Abdul Wadids.
1359   Abdul Wadids retook Tlemsen.
1399   Henri III of Castille destroyed Tetuan.
1420   WATTASID dynasty instituted in Fez, ending Merinids.
1471   Portuguese occupied Tangier.
1492   Fall of Granada and end of Muslim power in Spain.
1509–1510 Spanish 'crusade' in Maghrib: Oran, Algiers, Bougie, Tripoli
          and other ports occupied.
1514   Barbarossas established themselves at Djidjelli.
1516   Algerians appealed to Barbarossas, who captured Algiers.
1502–1518 Portuguese occupied Moroccan Atlantic ports.
1530   Tripoli given to Knights of Malta by Charles V.
1541   Barbarossas destroyed Charles V's expedition under Andrea
          Doria.
        Sa'adians expelled Portuguese from Agadir and other Moroc-
          can ports.
1545   Sa'adians occupied Fez.
1551   Dragut expelled Knights of Malta from Tripoli, which became
          Turkish.
1554   Sa'adians occupied all Morocco and ended Abdul Wadid dy-
          nasty.
1560   Dragut destroyed Papal fleet off Jerba and massacred Spanish
          garrison of Jerba.
1574   Turks completed occupation of Tunisia and ended Hafsid
          dynasty.
1578   Portuguese Army destroyed at 'Battle of the Three Kings' in
          Morocco.
1587   Turks instituted 'Regencies' in Tripolitania, Tunisia, and
          Algeria.
1609   Spanish decree of expulsion of Muslims and Jews.
1610   Spaniards occupied Larache.
1640   Turks occupied Cyrenaica.
1659   End of Sa'adian dynasty in Morocco.
1660   ALAWI dynasty instituted in Morocco.
1661   England acquired Tangier from Portugal.
1671   MOURADID dynasty of semi-independent Beys instituted in
          Tunisia.

A.D.

1672–1727 Reign of Moulay Ismail in Morocco. Spanish-occupied ports recovered.
1684   English evacuated Tangier.
1705   HUSAINID dynasty instituted in Tunisia.
1708   Spaniards expelled from Oran.
1732   Spaniards reoccupied Oran.
1769   Portuguese expelled from Mazagan, their last Moroccan foothold.
1792   Spaniards finally evacuated Oran.
1801–1805 Turko-American war over Tripoli.
1830   French invasion of Algeria.
1834   Sanusi order founded in Cyrenaica.
1835   Karamanli family replaced as Governors of Tripoli by Porte nominees.
1848   French occupation of Algeria completed.
1880   Convention of Madrid to regularize foreign protection in Morocco concluded.
1881   French Protectorate declared over Tunisia.
1904   Anglo-French 'Entente Cordiale' gave France a free hand in Morocco.
1906   Conference of Algeciras over Morocco.
1911   Kaiser sent warship to Agadir.
           Italy invaded and annexed Libya.
1912   French Protectorate declared over Morocco.
           Franco-Spanish agreement instituted Spanish Protectorate.
1921–1926 Rif War.
1922   Seyyid Idris expelled from Libya by Italians.
1923   Statute of Tangier promulgated.
1942   Anglo-American invasion of North Africa.
1943   Expulsion of German and Italian forces from North Africa.
1944   Massacre of Muslims in Algeria.
1947   Seyyid Idris returned to Libya.
1951   Libya became independent.
1953   Sultan of Morocco deposed and exiled by French.
1954   Outbreak of revolt in Algeria.
1955   Sultan of Morocco restored, took title of King.
1956   Morocco and Tunisia became independent.
1957   Tunisia became a Republic.
1958   Provisional Algerian Republican Government proclaimed in Cairo.
1961   King Muhammad V of Morocco died, succeeded by King Hassan II.
1962   Algeria became independent.

Short Bibliography

AFRICANUS, Leo, *History and Description of Africa* (3 vols.), Hakluyt Society, London, 1896.

ARON, Raymond, *La Tragédie Algérienne*, Paris, 1957.

BARADEZ, J., *Organisation Romaine dans le Sud Algérian*, Art et Métiers, Paris, 1949.

BARBOUR, Nevill, *A Survey of North-West Africa*, Royal Institute of International Affairs, 2nd ed. 1962.

BATES, Oric, *The Eastern Libyans*, Macmillan, 1914.

BATTUTA, Ibn, *Travels in Asia and Africa*, (tr. H. A. R. Gibb), G. Routledge, 1929

BEHIR, EDWARD, *The Algerian Problem*, Hodder & Stoughton, 1961.

BERNARD, Augustin, *L'Algérie*, F. Alcan, Pais, 1931.

BERNARD, Augustin, *Le Maroc*, Larousse, Paris, 1931.

BOUSQUET, G., *Les Berbères*, Vendôme, Paris, 1951.

BOVILL, W. B. *The Golden Trade of the Moors*, Oxford U.P., 1958.

BRIGGS, Lloyd C., *Tribes of the Sahara*, Harvard U.P., 1960.

BROMBERGER, Serge, *Les Rebelles Algériens*, Paris, 1958.

BUONAIUTI, E., *Il Christianismo nell'Africa Romana*, Bari, 1928.

CARCOPINO, J., *Le Maroc Antique*, Paris, 1943.

CASTRIES, Colonel H. de, *Sources Inédites de l'Histoire du Maroc*, E. Leroux, 1918–25.

CHARLES-PICARD, G. and C., *La Vie Quotidienne à Carthage au Temps d'Hannibal*. Allen & Unwin, 1961 (translation).

CHARLES-PICHARD, C. and G., *Civilisation de l'Afrique Romaine*.

CHARLES-ROUX, F., *France et l'Afrique du Nord avant 1830*, Paris, 1932.

CHURCHILL, Winston, *History of World War II*, Vol. IV, Cassell, 1951.

COURTOIS, C., *Les Vandales et l'Afrique*, Paris, 1955.

CHOURAQUI, André, *Les Juifs de l'Afrique du Nord*, Paris, 1952.

DESPOIS, J., *L'Afrique du Nord*, Presses Universitaires de France, 1949–50.

DESPOIS, J., *Le Hodna*, Presses Universitaires de France, 1953.

DESPOIS, J., *La Tunisie*, Colin, Paris, 1961.

DONALDSON, A. S. *The Church in North Africa*, A.D. 200, Cambridge U.P., 1909.

ERSKINE, Mrs. Stuart, *Vanished Cities of North Africa*, Hutchinson, 1927.

EVANS-PRITCHARD, E. E., *The Sanusi of Cyrenaica*, Oxford U.P., 1949.

FISHER, Godfrey, *Barbary Legend*, Oxford U.P., 1957.

FISHER, H. A. L., *A History of Europe*, Arnold, 1938.

FORBES, Rosita, *El Raisuni*, Th. Butterworth, 1924.

GAUTIER, E. F., *L'Afrique Blanche*, Fayard, Paris, 1939.

GAUTIER, E. F., *Le Passé de l'Afrique du Nord*, Payot, Paris, 1932.

GONZALEZ, Palencia, *Historia de la España musulmana*, Barcelona, 1925.

GRAMMONT, H. de, *Histoire de l'Afrique sous la domination turque, 1515–1830*, Paris, 1887.

GSELL, Stephane, *La Tripolitaine et le Sahara au IIIme Siècle.*

GSELL, Stephane, *Histoire Ancienne de l'Afrique du Nord* (8 vols), Hachette, 1913–28.

HARRIS, W. B., *The Morocco That Was*, Blackwood, 1921.

HAYNES, D. E. L., *The Antiquities of Tripolitania*, E. Baylis, 1959.

HOLMBOE, Knud (tr. H. Halbek), *Desert Encounter*, Harrap, 1936.

HOUDES, O., *Le Maroc de 1631 à 1812.*

ISNARD, H., *Algérie*, Arthand, Paris, 1952.

JULIEN, C.–A., *Histoire de l'Afrique du Nord* (2 vols.), Payot, Paris, 1931.

JULIEN C. A., *L'Afrique du Nord en Marche*, Jalleaud, 1953.

KHADDOURI, Majid, *Modern Libya*, John Hopkins Press, 1961.

KHALDUN, Ibn (tr. by Slane), *Histoire des Berbéres*, Algiers, 1852–6.

KHALIDI, Ismail Raguib, *Constitutional Development in Libya*, Beirut, 1956.

LANDAU, Rom, *Moroccan Drama, 1950–55*, R. Hale, 1956.

LEONE, Enrico de, *La Colonizzazione dell' Africa del Nord*, (2 vols.), Padua, 1957.

McBURNEY, C. B. M., *The Stone Age of North Africa*, Penguin, 1960.

MARÇAIS, Georges, *Les Arabes en Berberie du 11me–14me Siècle*, Constantine, 1913.

MARÇAIS, Georges, *La Berberie Musulmane et l'Orient au Moyen Age*, Paris, 1946.

MAUROIS, André (tr. by Hamish Miles), *Marshal Lyautey*, John Lane, The Bodley Head, 1931.

MICKLEM, P. A., *Church and Empire in Roman Africa*, Budd & Gilliwill, 1964.

MILLET, René, *Les Almohades*, Paris, 1923.

MORTON, H. V., *A Stranger in Spain*, Methuen, 1955.

NICHOLSON, Harold, *Lord Carnock*, Constable, 1930.

S. MARTIN, Vivien de, *Le Nord de l'Afrique dans l'Antiquité*, Imprimerie Impériale, Paris, 1863.

SCHMIEDLER, Dr. O. and WILHELMY, Dr. V., *Die Faschistiche Kolonisation in Nord Afrika*, Leipzig, 1939.

SCOTT O'CONNOR, *A Vision of Morocco*, Th. Butterworth, 1923.

STUART, G. H., *The International City of Tangier*, Stamford, California, 1955.

TERRASSE, H., *Histoire du Maroc, des Origines à l'Etablissement du Protectorat Francais*, Casablanca, 1949–50

VOLPI DI MISURATA, Count Giuseppi, *La Renascità della Tripolitania*, Milan, 1926.

WARMINGTON, B. H., *Carthage*, Hale, 1960.

CLASSICAL AUTHORS (in standard translations)
 Vergil (Aeneid).
 Homer (Odyssey).
 Herodotus.
 Pliny.
 Polybius.
 Ptolemy.
 Sallust.
 Strabo.

GUIDE BOOKS
 Guide Bleu de l'Algérie et de la Tunisie, Hachette, 1955.
 Guide Nagel du Maroc, Geneva, 1963.
 Your Guide to Morocco, H. Dennis-Jones, Alvin Redman, 1965.

Index

NOTE. Place-names are followed by (L.), (T.,) (A.), or (M.), to indicate Libya, Tunisia, Algeria or Morocco.

Abbasid Caliphate of Baghdad, 19, 39, 60, 62, 148
Abdul Kader, **109**, 138, 140, 143, 176
Abdul Krim el Khattabi, 191–2
Abdul Malik ibn Muhammad (Sa'adian), 162–3
Abdul Mumin (Almohad), 98, **160–1**, 182
Abdul Wadid dynasty, 101, **142**, 150, 162, 207
Abdullah bin Yasin, 158
Abdurrahman III of Cordova, 195–6
Abu Abdullah, 62–3
Abu Bakr (Almoravid), 158–9
Abul Hassan, al Somlali, 173–4
Abul Khattab (Kharijite Imam), 128
Abu Muhammad ibn Abu Hafs (Hafsid), 77
Abu Qubais, *zawiya*, 22
Abu Thabit (Merinid), 190
Abu Yaqub al Mansur (Merinid), 142
Abu Yaqub (Almohad), 161
Abu Yazid ('The Man with the Donkey'), 64, 99, **128–9**
Abu Yusuf (Merinid), 149
Abyla, *see* Mount Hacho
Adjim (T.), 54
Affreville (A.), 136
Africa, Province of, 45, 74, 93; meaning of word, 73
Agadir (A.), 142
Agadir (M.), 162, **167–8**, 176–7
Agathocles, 33, 71, 75
Aga Khan, 62
Aghas, 78, 106
Aghlabid dynasty, **60–3**, 128
Aghmat (M.), 158, 166
Agysimba, 46
Ahmad al-Mansur, *see* al-Mansur
Ahmed ash-Sharif, 22–3
Air, 46

Aissaoua, 178–9
Ajdir (M.), 191
Ajedabia (L.), 23
Alamein, battle of, 9; cemetery at, 10
Alarcos, 161
Alawi dynasty, 145, 164, **173–7**, 207
Alexander the Great, 16, 33
Alexander of Tunis, Field-Marshal Earl, 9, 75
Alexandria, 11, 13, 19
Algeciras, 159, 199; Conference of, 168; Act of, 176
Algeria, 2, 3, 5, 6, 12, 21, 59, 65; dispute with Morocco, 146; future of, 143, 203
Algerians, 3; revolt of against French, 95, 98–9, **115–7**; working in France, 112
Algiers (Icosium) (A.), 12, 96, 159; description and history, **103–8**
Ali bin Yusuf (Almoravid), 160
Almohad dynasty, 6, 40, 61, 77; suppress Christianity, 87; history of, **160–2**; 100, 145, 149, 166–7, 189, 197, 207
Almoravid dynasty, 138, 145, 149, 153; history of, **157–60**; 161, 166–7, 197, 207
Alphonse VI, King of Castille, 159
America, United States of, war with Turks, 12–13; rôle of on Libya, 24–5; forces in Tunisia, 56; aid to Tunisia, 81; policy in Morocco, 187; rôle of in Tangier, 199–200
Ammadaea, *see* Haidra
Andalusian-Arab art, 141, 148, 150, 165
Antioch, 18
Antiquities Department, of Libya, 39; of Tunisia, 65
Antonines, 18
Antoninus Pius, (Emperor), 134